MY DIARY
NORTH AND SOUTH

William Howard Russell, a contemporary engraving

MY DIARY

NORTH AND SOUTH

by

William Howard Russell

Edited and Introduced by

FLETCHER PRATT

Illustrated

Harper & Brothers   Publishers   New York

Illustrations

Preface

When news of what was going on in America at the close of 1860 and the beginning of 1861 reached London, it occurred to the editors of the *Times* that there was a very fine row brewing on the opposite side of the Atlantic, and that they had better get someone who knew the military business on the job. Their choice fell on William Howard Russell, who had been their correspondent during the Crimean War, and who had shown no little ability to see things and to set down what he saw in language that could be comprehended by anyone. Also—and public demand seems to make this inseparable from military experting—he was a reasonably good man with a crystal ball; could look into a situation and describe its military result with a high degree of probability.

Russell reached New York in March, after Lincoln's inauguration, and went to Washington almost immediately, thus arriving in that strange twilight hour when the new administration had been installed but Sumter had not been fired on, and nobody knew quite what was going to happen. His introductions were impeccable and his activity immense; he saw everybody of any importance at the time and a number of persons whose importance only developed later, then put into his diary what he thought of them and what they said. After about a month, he concluded that he had squeezed the Washington orange dry for the time being, and set out for the South, via steamer to Norfolk.

Virginia was still a part of the Union when the journey began, but Russell was hardly aboard the train for Charleston when word came of the attack on and fall of Sumter. At Charleston he visited the forts, of course, and made his usual comprehensive roundup of interesting or important personalities, saw something of life on Carolina plantations, then pushed on to Savannah for more visiting and sampling of public opinion. From Savannah he went to Montgomery, where he talked with and made a shrewd estimate of Jefferson Davis and saw some of the men around him, but he did not investigate the Confederate government quite as thoroughly as he had that at Washington, probably because the surrounding physical environment was so uncomfortable.

From Montgomery he went to Mobile, where he persuaded a schooner to take him along the coast to Fort Pickens, still in Union hands, and examined the preparations both for attack and defense. The next stop was New Orleans, where he spent some time and saw a good deal of another type of plantation and of Negro life. News of the blockade had now arrived; Russell feared being unable to get his dispatches out, which is the most fatal of all events for a war correspondent, so he made his way northward to Chicago, finding the beginnings of military movement in western Kentucky on the way. It is rather a pity he skipped St. Louis, where things were really happening, but he did; and his investigation of the Middle West was cut short by advices which seemed to indicate that there would soon be fighting between Washington and Richmond. He was back in the capital in time to look over the campus and accompany the army that was marching out to be beaten at Bull Run, and he was an eyewitness to the retreat in which the battle ended.

The day after the battle, he filed the celebrated long dispatch which caused him to be known ever after as "Bull Run" Russell. The raw material of that dispatch will be found in these pages; it is a description of a disgraceful panic on the part of unwilling and utterly green troops under officers who know nothing of their business. The dispatch earned Russell an unpopularity which was cordial and universal, but he stayed on, mostly in Washington, filing regularly to his paper until the spring of 1862. At that point McClellan made his move to the Peninsula of the James for an advance on Richmond, and Russell applied for a pass to accompany him.

It was refused—"because I told the truth about Bull Run," insists Russell on various occasions. Without laboring the point, it can be indicated that the truth he told was a partial truth (for he saw none of the fighting, only the rear areas and the rout), and this partial truth was accompanied by editorial opinion indicating Russell's judgment that the South was going to win. This made him at least a not very desirable correspondent in a Federal camp. The case was carried to Lincoln, who refused to interfere, so Russell went home to London, built out his diary from notes (there were gaps in it) and published it. The American edition appeared at about the time of Gettysburg. It made no sensation; people had other things than Bull Run on their minds at that time.

This new edition will be welcomed by everyone who shares the waxing interest in the great conflict, both because the original (and only) other one has become excessively hard to obtain and was printed in almost microscopic type. Considerable cuts have been made, both because the republication of the full original text would have made the book intolerably costly, and because it contained much material of no possible interest to the modern reader. When Russell reaches Niagara Falls, for instance, he stops to give a long conventional picture of the falls themselves, and another of the War of 1812 on the Niagara frontier; there is a very long description of the sail to Fort Pickens, which is no different from any other ride in a sailboat, and there are various reflections on the life of a planter, which chiefly demonstrate that Russell has been reading Adam Smith. You will have to take the present editor's word for it that no essential fact or opinion, or above all, no important personal contact has been omitted. These were the men who made the war, caught in arrested motion as it is about to begin; no one else has seen them through so objective an eye.

For the most important fact about *My Diary North and South* is its objectivity at a time when almost nobody was being objective; that is, unless the fact that Russell wrote very well be considered important. He had a low opinion of Germans and a not much higher one of the Irish, but it is pretty hard to catch him in any other prejudices. In other documents of that period before the fighting became serious, Lincoln appears as an ignorant buffoon, or a timid politician, or a cracker-barrel philosopher engaged in a task that was probably too big for him, but Russell had some concept that he was dealing with a great man and was certain he was talking to a very able one. Unlike so many during that twilight hour, the correspondent was never for a moment fooled into thinking Seward was the real force of the administration, and his long portrait of Seward is as perceptive and stands up as well in historical perspective as that of Lincoln.

Russell was a good deal with McDowell before Bull Run and paints a curious picture of the difficulties of that commander of the Army of the Potomac by showing him in a railroad station trying to trace the whereabouts of a single errant battery because he has no staff that can do it for him. John C. Frémont he saw, and made a very just estimate of him before Frémont began his fantastic military career in the West; he sizes up Ben Butler with accuracy, and long before anyone else in Washington was aware of it, Russell had determined that McClellan was a great man for drill and parade, but a poor one to lead an offensive campaign.

On the Confederate side Russell early came to the conclusion that Beauregard was not an officer of first-rate ability; decided that Jefferson Davis was less impressive than Lincoln, and made sharp estimates of Slidell and Judah P. Benjamin. But these were all leading personalities of the time and natural game for a reporter. Much of the peculiar quality of the book, its singular interest for us today, lies in the number and extent of the portraits of persons who were nobodies when Russell met them, but developed into determining figures. Here is Kate Chase, newly arrived in Washington, and finding her way about. Here are General William Nelson, Hardee, Braxton Bragg and Vallandigham, all caught on the rise, and there are a couple of remarkable bits about an officer Russell rated highly at the time, and others came to later—William Tecumseh Sherman.

The correspondent dines with a group of naval officers, including David Porter and Dahlgren, and though he finds almost nothing to praise in the American military establishment at the time, is moved to remark: "It will run hard against the Confederates when they get such men at work on the rivers and coasts"—a piece of very good military experting indeed. The country between Washington and Manassas and the lack of scouting on the Union side gave him the perfectly correct idea that any clash between McDowell's and Beauregard's armies would be a blind and formless struggle, and he was quite right in believing the North would shake off the effects of Bull Run.

That is, he was a war correspondent of the first order. Was he never wrong? Of course he was. He lived much with the diplomatic corps in Washington, and quite agreed with their general opinion that the Union was broken forever, that nothing either Lincoln or his soldiers could do would restore it. Moreover, Russell erred by the character of his contacts, which were with the upper levels of government on the Northern side, and with the middle levels of society on the Southern. In the South he saw the plantations and the homes, was in the cities, visited slave pens, but never reached the degree of intimacy with the leading figures that he did in the North. In the North, he became quite familiar with the top numbers of the Washington scene, but never got out among the farmers of the Middle West, and never visited New England at all. There is a curious mis-estimate of what New England was and stood for underlying the text—Russell seems to be convinced that a New Englander is a kind of fanatic and slightly tetched. He met Senator Sumner several times, but does not seem to have been impressed; the usual portrait is lacking.

Another mis-estimate, this time of the spirit and technical skills of the contestants, arose from the circumstances of Russell's travels. He left the North during the period of doubt and uncertainty when many were willing to "let the erring sisters go" and reached the South just after the firing on Sumter had produced the explosion of flag-waving, cheering, enlistments and enthusiasm; that is, left an indecisive and divided North for a positive and decided South. His last days in the South were insulated from any expression of popular feeling, and he returned to the North just in time to catch the reaction wave that culminated at Bull Run. Thus the North he saw was at first shaken and then prematurely war-weary, the South he visited a coherent unit, and it is not surprising that he drew the conclusion that the Confederates would win. He knew absolutely nothing of what happened in Chicago or Boston or Indianapolis or Milwaukee at the news from Sumter, or of the grim determination that took hold of the Western country after Bull Run. He used the evidence he had, but it was incomplete.

Similarly, he comments on the good horse stocks and riding skill of the Southerners; thinks they will make good cavalry—as indeed they did. But he is fairly caustic about the wild variation of gun calibers in McClellan's army and the moderate competence of artillery officers. This was what he saw; he did not see the factories of Pittsburgh, painting the clouds night and day to turn out the most powerful artillery the world had seen, nor the race of mechanics who could handle them in the field almost without supervision.

This was not Russell's fault. It is perhaps a little more surprising that he makes no mention of Grant. The first great blow had been struck in the West long before Russell left for Europe and the papers had a good deal to say about the stocky brigadier, but all Russell knows about it is that "Forts Donaldson [sic] and Henry have been taken by some gunboats."

All right, score one against him for that. The total score is so much on his side that he can be forgiven a few errors. He has caught nuances missed by everyone else, and has seen things that no one else set down. He called on Captain Adams of the Union Navy when that officer learned that his two sons had enlisted in the Confederate Army. He was ill; a "big Virginia doctor" prescribed mint juleps every two hours, with "powders." One wonders what those powders contained, but Russell apparently only had to undergo a couple of days of this heroic regime. Before McClellan came east, Russell looked over the territory of the Peninsula and thought of a campaign up it as a logical alternative to the overland movement via Manassas. In fact, he may have suggested the idea to McClellan; he saw the general fairly frequently, and the general respected his opinion, as one Crimean veteran to another. There is also a picture of the Peedee country, with its endless long trestles over the marshes and slow streams, and the Southerner who said: "This is the kind of country we'll catch the Yankees in." Prophetic; for they did catch the Yankees in that country, but the Yankees they caught were Sherman's invincible Army of the West, whom neither snow nor cold nor heat nor gloom of night could stay in the swift completion of their appointed round of destroying the Confederacy that Russell thought would last. There are fascinating long passages on Southern duels, pictures of the streets of New York, and an account of a steamboat ride by night down the Alabama River, and something about the difficulties of travel when you had to change cars across town in most cities.

It is a book of pictures in movement; a picture book of what the war looked at as it was about to begin. No one else has left anything comparable.

FLETCHER PRATT

[xiii]

MY DIARY
NORTH AND SOUTH

Chapter I

————⋆◄►◄————

ON THE evening of 3rd March, 1861, I was transferred
from the little steam-tender, which plies between Cork
and the anchorage of the Cunard steamers at the entrance of the
harbour, to the deck of the good steamship *Arabia,* Captain
Stone; and at nightfall we were breasting the long rolling waves
of the Atlantic.

The Americans on board were, of course, the most interesting
passengers to one like myself, who was going out to visit the great
Republic under very peculiar circumstances. There was, first,
Major Garnett, a Virginian, who was going back to his State to
follow her fortunes. He was an officer of the regular Army of the
United States, who had served with distinction in Mexico; an
accomplished, well-read man; reserved, and rather gloomy; full
of the doctrine of States' Rights, and animated with a considerable feeling of contempt for the New Englanders, and with the
strongest prejudices in favour of the institution of slavery. He
laughed to scorn the doctrine that all men are born equal in the
sense of all men having equal rights. Some were born to be
slaves—some to be labourers in the lower strata above the slaves
—others to follow useful mechanical arts—the rest were born to
rule and to own their fellow-men. There was next a young Carolinian, who had left his post as attaché at St. Petersburg to return

[1]

to his State: thus, in all probability, avoiding the inevitable supercession which awaited him at the hands of the new Government at Washington. He represented, in an intensified form, all the Virginian's opinions, and held that Mr. Calhoun's interpretation of the Constitution was incontrovertibly right. There were difficulties in the way of State sovereignty, he confessed; but they were only in detail—the principle was unassailable.

To Mr. Mitchell, South Carolina represented a power quite sufficient to meet all the Northern States in arms. "The North will attempt to blockade our coast," said he; "and in that case, the South must march to the attack by land, and will probably act in Virginia." "But if the North attempts to do more than institute a blockade?—for instance, if their fleet attack your seaport towns and land men to occupy them?" "Oh, in that case, we are quite certain of beating them." Mr. Julian Mitchell was indignant at the idea of submitting to the rule of a "rail-splitter," and of such men as Seward and Cameron. "No gentleman could tolerate such a Government."

An American family from Nashville, consisting of a lady and her son and daughter, were warm advocates of a "gentlemanly" government, and derided the Yankees with great bitterness. But they were by no means as ready to encounter the evils of war, or to break up the Union, as the South Carolinian or the Virginian; and in that respect they represented, I was told, the negative feelings of the Border States, which are disposed to a temporising, moderate course of action, most distasteful to the passionate Seceders.

There were also two Louisiana sugar-planters on board—one owning five hundred slaves, the other rich in some thousands of acres; they seemed to care very little for the political aspects of the question of Secession, and regarded it merely in reference to its bearing on the sugar crop, and the security of slave property. Secession was regarded by them as a very extreme and violent measure, to which the State had resorted with reluctance; but it

[2]

was obvious, at the same time, that, in event of a general Secession of the Slave States from the North, Louisiana could neither have maintained her connection with the North, nor have stood in isolation from her sister States.

Now take the other side. First there was an exceedingly intelligent, well-informed young merchant of New York—nephew of an English county Member, known for his wealth, liberality, and munificence. Educated at a university in the Northern States, he had lived a good deal in England, and was returning to his father from a course of bookkeeping in the house of his uncle's firm in Liverpool. In the war of 1812, the brothers were about sailing in a privateer fitted out to prey against the British, when accident fixed one of them in Liverpool, where he founded the house which has grown so greatly with the development of trade between New York and Lancashire, whilst the other settled in the States. Without being violent in tone, the young Northerner was very resolute in temper, and determined to do all which lay in his power to prevent the "glorious Union" being broken up.

But did Mr. Brown, or the other Americans who shared his views, unreservedly approve of American institutions, and consider them faultless? By no means. The New Yorkers especially were eloquent on the evils of the suffrage, and of the licence of the Press in their own city; and displayed much irritation on the subject of naturalisation.

Thus the agriculturist and the trader—the grower of raw produce and the merchant who dealt in it—were at the opposite sides of the question—wide apart as the Northern and Southern Poles. They sat apart, ate apart, talked apart—two distinct nations, with intense antipathies on the part of the South, which was active and aggressive in all its demonstrations.

The most vehement Northerners in the steamer are Germans, who are going to the States for the first time, or returning there. They have become satisfied, no doubt, by long process of reasoning, that there is some anomaly in the condition of a country

[3]

which calls itself the land of liberty, and is at the same time the potent palladium of serfdom and human chattelry. When they are not sea-sick, which is seldom, the Teutons rise up in all the might of their misery and dirt, and, making spasmodic efforts to smoke, blurt out between the puffs, sundry remarks on American politics. "These are the swine," quoth Garnett, "who are swept out of German gutters as too foul for them, and who come over to the States and presume to control the fate and the wishes of our people. In their own country they proved they were incapable of either earning a living, or exercising the duties of citizenship; and they seek in our country a licence denied them in their own, and the means of living which they could not acquire anywhere else."

It was on the morning of the fourteenth day that the shores of New York loomed through the drift of a cold wintry sea, laden-grey and comfortless, and in a little time more the coast, covered with snow, rose in sight. Towards the afternoon the sun came out and brightened the waters and the sails of the pretty trim schooners and coasters which were dancing around us. How different the graceful, tautly-rigged, clean white-sailed vessels from the round-sterned, lumpish billyboys and nondescripts of the eastern coast of our isle! Presently there came bowling down towards us a lively little schooner-yacht, very like the once famed *America*, brightly painted in green, sails dazzling white, lofty ponderous masts, no tops. As she came nearer, we saw she was crowded with men in chimney-pot black hats, and coats, and the like—perhaps a party of citizens on pleasure, cold as the day was. Nothing of the kind. The craft was our pilot-boat and the hats and coats belonged to the hardy mariners who act as guides to the port of New York. Their boat was lowered, and was soon under our mainchains; and a chimney-pot hat having duly come over the side, delivered a mass of newspapers to the captain, which were distributed among the eager passengers, when each at once became the centre of a spell-bound circle.

[4]

Chapter II

It was dark as the steamer hauled up alongside the wharf on the New Jersey side of the river; but ere the sun set I could form some idea of the activity and industry of the people from the enormous ferry-boats moving backwards and forwards like arks on the water, impelled by the great walking-beam engines, the crowded stream full of merchantmen, steamers, and small craft, the smoke of the factories, the tall chimneys—the network of boats and rafts—all the evidences of commercial life in full development. What a swarming, eager crowd on the quay-wall! What a wonderful ragged regiment of labourers and porters, hailing us in broken or Hibernianized English! "These are all Irish and Germans," anxiously explained a New Yorker. "I'll bet fifty dollars there's not a native-born American among them."

With Anglo-Saxon disregard of official insignia, American Custom House officers dress very much like their British brethren, without any sign of authority as faint as even the brass button and crown, so that the stranger is somewhat uneasy when he sees unauthorised-looking people taking liberties with his plunder, especially after the admonition he has received on board ship to look sharp about his things as soon as he lands. I was provided with an introduction to one of the principal officers, and he facilitated my egress, and at last I was bundled out through a gate into a dark alley, ankle deep in melted snow and mud, where I was at once engaged in a brisk encounter with my Irish porterhood, and, after a long struggle, succeeded in stowing my effects in and about a remarkable specimen of the hackney-coach of the last century, very high in the axle, and weak in the springs, which plashed down towards the river through a crowd of men shouting out, "You haven't paid me yet, your honour. You haven't given anything to your own man that's been waiting here the last six months for your honour!" "*I'm* the man that put the luggage up, sir," &c., &c. The coach darted on board a great steam ferry-boat, which had on board a number of similar vehicles, and omnibuses, and the gliding, shifting lights, and the deep, strong breathing of the engine, told me I was moving and afloat before I was otherwise aware of it. A few minutes brought us over to the lights on the New York side—a jerk or two up a steep incline—and we were rattling over a most abominable pavement, plunging into mudholes, squashing through snow-heaps in ill-lighted, narrow streets of low, mean-looking, wooden houses, of which an unusual proportion appeared to be larger-beer salons, whiskey-shops, oyster-houses, and billiard and smoking establishments.

Whilst I was crossing the sea, the President's Inaugural Message, the composition of which is generally attributed to Mr. Seward, had been delivered, and had reached Europe, and the causes which were at work in destroying the cohesion of the Union, had acquired greater strength and violence.

But the moving force of revolution is neither reason nor justice—it is most frequently passion—it is often interest. According to the deeds and words of Americans, it is difficult to see why South Carolina should not use the rights claimed for each of the thirteen colonies, "to alter and abolish a form of government when it becomes destructive of the ends for which it is established, and to institute a new one." At present I find public attention is concentrated on the two Federal forts, Pickens and Sumter, called after two officers of the Revolutionary Armies in the old war. As Alabama and South Carolina have gone out, they now demand the possession of these forts, as of the soil of their several states and attached to their sovereignty. On the other hand, the Gov-

[6]

ernment of Mr. Lincoln considers it has no right to give up any thing belonging to the Federal Government, but evidently desires to temporise and evade any decision which might precipitate an attack on the forts by the batteries and forces prepared to act against them. There is not sufficient garrison in either for an adequate defence, and the difficulty of procuring supplies is very great. Under the circumstances every one is asking what the Government is going to do? The Southern people have declared they will resist any attempt to supply or reinforce the garrisons, and in Charleston, at least, have shown they mean to keep their word. It is a strange situation.

Sunday, 17th March. In the afternoon I called on Mr. Bancroft, formerly minister to England, whose work on America must be rather rudely interrupted by this crisis. Any thing with an "ex" to it in America is of little weight—ex-presidents are nobodies, though they have had the advantage, during their four years' tenure of office, of being prayed for as long as they live. So it is of ex-ministers, whom nobody prays for at all. Mr. Bancroft conversed for some time on the aspect of affairs, but he appeared to be unable to arrive at any settled conclusion, except that the Republic, though in danger, was the most stable and beneficial form of government in the world, and that as a Government it had no power to coerce the people of the South or to save itself from the danger.

I dined with a New York banker, who gave such a dinner as bankers generally give all over the world. He is a man still young, very kindly, hospitable, well-informed, with a most charming household—an American by theory, an Englishman in instincts and tastes—educated in Europe and sprung from British stock. Considering the enormous interests he has at stake, I was astonished to perceive how calmly he spoke of the impending troubles. His friends, all men of position in New York society, had the same dilettante tone, and were as little anxious for the future, or excited by the present, as a party of *savants* chronicling the movements of a "magnetic storm."

[7]

Chapter III

March 19. In the afternoon a number of gentlemen called, and made the kindest offers of service; letters of introduction to all parts of the States; facilities of every description—all tendered with frankness.

I was astonished to find little sympathy and no respect for the newly installed Government. They were regarded as obscure or undistinguished men. I alluded to the circumstance that one of the journals continued to speak of "The President" in the most contemptuous manner, and to designate him as the great "Rail-Splitter." "Oh yes," said the gentleman with whom I was conversing, "that must strike you as a strange way of mentioning the Chief Magistrate of our great Republic, but the fact is, no one minds what the man writes of anyone, his game is to abuse every respectable man in the country in order to take his revenge on them for his social exclusion, and at the same time to please the ignorant masses who delight in vituperation and scandal."

In the evening, dining again with my friend the banker, I had a favourable opportunity of hearing more of the special pleading which is brought to bear on the solution of the gravest political questions. It would seem as if a council of physicians were wrangling with each other over abstract dogmas respecting life and health, whilst their patient was struggling in the agonies of death before them! In the comfortable and well-appointed house wherein I met several men of position, acquirements, and natural sagacity, there was not the smallest evidence of uneasi-

[8]

ness on account of circumstances which, to the eye of a stranger, betokened an awful crisis, if not the impending dissolution of society itself.

Among the guests were the Hon. Horatio Seymour, a former Governor of the State of New York; Mr. Tylden, an acute lawyer; and Mr. Bancroft; the result left on my mind by their conversations and arguments was that, according to the Constitution, the Government could not employ force to prevent secession, or to compel States which had seceded by the will of the people to acknowledge the Federal power. In fact, according to them, the Federal Government was the mere machine put forward by a Society of Sovereign States, as a common instrument for certain ministerial acts, more particularly those which affected the external relations of the Confederation. I do not think that any of the guests sought to turn the channel of talk upon politics, but the occasion offered itself to Mr. Horatio Seymour to give me his views of the Constitution of the United States, and by degrees the theme spread over the table. I had bought the "Constitution" for three cents in Broadway in the forenoon, and had read it carefully, but I could not find that it was self-expounding; it referred itself to the Supreme Court, but what was to support the Supreme Court in a contest with armed power, either of Government or people? There was not a man who maintained the Government had any power to coerce the people of a State, or to force a State to remain in the Union, or under the action of the Federal Government; in other words, the symbol of power at Washington is not at all analogous to that which represents an established Government in other countries. Although they admitted the Southern leaders had meditated "the treason against the Union" years ago, they could not bring themselves to allow their old opponents, the Republicans now in power, to dispose of the armed force of the Union against their brother Democrats in the Southern States.

Mr. Seymour is a man of compromise, but his views go farther than those which were entertained by his party ten years

[9]

ago. Although Secession would produce revolution, it was, nevertheless, "a right," founded on abstract principles, which could scarcely be abrogated consistently with due regard to the original compact. One of the company made a remark which was true enough, I dare say. We were talking of the difficulty of relieving Fort Sumter—an infallible topic just now. "If the British or any foreign power were threatening the fort," said he, "our Government would find means of relieving it fast enough." In fact, the Federal Government is groping in the dark; and whilst its friends are telling it to advance boldly, there are myriad voices shrieking out in its ears, "If you put out a foot you are lost." There is neither army nor navy available, and the ministers have no machinery of rewards, and means of intrigue, or modes of gaining adherents known to European administrations. The Democrats behold with silent satisfaction the troubles into which the Republican triumph has plunged the country, and are not at all disposed to extricate them. The most notable way of impeding their efforts is to knock them down with the "Constitution" every time they rise to the surface and begin to swim out.

Chapter IV

————◄◆►————

March 20th. New York has certainly all the air of a "nouveau riche." There is about it an utter absence of any appearance of a grandfather—one does not see even such evidences of eccentric taste as are afforded in Paris and London, by the existence of shops where the old families of a country cast off their "exuviae" which are sought by the new, that they may persuade the world they are old; there is no curiosity shop, not to speak of a Wardour Street, and such efforts as are made to supply the deficiency reveal an enormous amount of ignorance or of bad taste. The new arts, however, flourish; the plague of photography has spread through all the corners of the city, and the shop-windows glare with flagrant displays of the most tawdry art. In some of the large booksellers' shops—Appleton's for example—are striking proofs of the activity of the American press, if not of the vigour and originality of the American intellect. I passed down long rows of shelves laden with the works of European authors, for the most part, oh shame! stolen and translated into American type without the smallest compunction or scruple, and without the least intention of ever yielding the most pitiful deodand to the authors. Mr. Appleton sells no less than one million and a half of Webster's spelling books a year; his tables are covered with a flood of pamphlets, some for, others against coercion; some for, others opposed to slavery,—but when I asked for a single solid, substantial work on the present difficulty, I was told there was not one published worth a cent. With such men as Audubon and Wilson in natural history, Prescott and Motley in history, Washington Irving and Cooper in fiction, Longfellow and Edgar Poe in poetry, even Bryant and the respectabilities in rhyme, and Emerson as essayist, there is no reason why New York should be a paltry imitation of Leipzig, without the good faith of Tauchnitz.

I dined with a litterateur well known in England to many people a year or two ago—sprightly, loquacious, and well informed, if neither witty nor profound—now a Southern man with Southern proclivities, as Americans say; once a Southern man with such strong anti-slavery convictions that his expression of them in an English quarterly had secured him the hostility of his own people—one of the emanations of American literary life for which their own country finds no fitting receiver. As the best proof of his sincerity, he has just now abandoned his connection with one of the New York papers on the Republican side, because he believed that the course of the journal was dictated by anti-Southern fanaticism. He is, in fact, persuaded that there will be a civil war, and that the South will have much of the right on its side in the contest.

March 22nd. A snow-storm worthy of Moscow or Riga flew through New York all day, depositing more food for the mud. I paid a visit to Mr. Horace Greeley, and had a long conversation with him. He expressed great pleasure at the intelligence that I was going to visit the Southern States. "Be sure you examine the slave-pens. *They* will be afraid to refuse you, and you can tell the truth." As the capital and the South form the chief attractions at present, I am preparing to escape from "the divine calm" and snows of New York.

March 23rd. It is announced positively that the authorities in Pensacola and Charleston have refused to allow any further supplies to be sent to Fort Pickens, the United States fleet in the Gulf, and to Fort Sumter. Everywhere the Southern leaders are forcing on a solution with decision and enegry, whilst the Government appears to be helplessly drifting with the current of events, having neither bow nor stern, neither keel nor deck, neither rudder, compass, sails, nor steam. Mr. Seward has declined to receive or hold any intercourse with the three gentlemen called Southern Commissioners, who repaired to Washington accredited by the Government and Congress of the Seceding States now sitting at Montgomery, so that there is no channel of mediation or means of adjustment left open. I hear, indeed, that Government is secretly preparing what force it can to strengthen the garrison at Pickens, and to reinforce Sumter at any hazard; but that its want of men, ships, and money compels it to temporise, lest the Southern authorities should forestall their designs by a vigorous attack on the enfeebled forts.

There is, in reality, very little done by New York to support or encourage the Government in any decided policy, and the journals are more engaged now in abusing each other, and in small party aggressive warfare, than in the performance of the duties of a patriotic press, whose mission at such a time is beyond all question the resignation of little differences for the sake of the whole country, and an entire devotion to its safety, honour and integrity. But the New York people must have their intellectual drams every morning, and it matters little what the course of Government may be, so long as the aristocratic Democrat can be amused by ridicule of the Great Rail-Splitter, or a vivid portraiture of Mr. Horace Greeley's old coat, hat, breeches, and umbrella. "Slang" in its worst Americanised form is freely used in sensational headings and leaders, and a class of advertisements which are not allowed to appear in respectable English papers, have possession of columns of the principal newspapers, few, indeed, excluding them. It is strange, too, to see in journals which profess to represent the civilisation and intelligence of the most enlightened and highly educated people on the face of the earth, advertisements of sorcerers, wizards, and fortune tellers by the score—"wonderful clairvoyants," "the seventh child of a seventh child," "mesmeristic necromancers," and the like, who can tell your thoughts as soon as you enter the room, can secure the affections you prize, give lucky numbers in lotteries, and make everybody's fortunes but their own. Then there are the most impudent quack programmes—very doubtful "personals" addressed to "the young lady with black hair and blue eyes who got out of the omnibus at the corner of 7th Street"—appeals by "a lady about to be confined" to any respectable person who is desirous of adopting a child: all rather curious reading for a stranger, or for a family.

March 25th. I had an invitation to meet several members of the New York press association at breakfast. Among the company were—Mr. Bayard Taylor, with whose extensive notes of travel his countrymen are familiar—a kind of enlarged Inglis, full of the genial spirit which makes travelling in company so agreeable, but he has come back as travellers generally do, satisfied there is

[13]

no country like his own; Mr. Raymond of the *New York Times* (formerly Lieutenant-Governor of the State); Mr. Olmsted, the indefatigable, able, and earnest writer, whom to describe simply as an Abolitionist would be to confound with ignorant if zealous, unphilosophical, and impracticable men; Mr. Dana, of the *Tribune;* Mr. Hurlbert, of the *Times;* the Editor of the *Courier des États Unis;* Mr. Young of the *Albion,* which is the only English journal published in the States; and others. There was a good deal of pleasant conversation, though every one differed with his neighbour, as a matter of course, as soon as he touched on politics. There was talk *de omnibus rebus et quibus-dam aliis,* such as Heenan and Sayers, Secession and Sumter, the press, politicians, New York life, and so on. The first topic occupied a larger place than it was entitled to, because in all likelihood the sporting editor of one of the papers who was present expressed, perhaps, some justifiable feeling in reference to the refusal of the belt to the American.

One of the gentlemen present said that England might dispute the right of the United States Government to blockade the ports of her own States, to which she was entitled to access under treaty, and might urge that such a blockade was not justifiable; but then, it was argued, that the President could open and shut ports as he pleased; and that he might close the Southern ports by a proclamation in the nature of an Order of Council. It was taken for granted that Great Britain would only act on sordid motives, but that the well-known affection of France for the United States is to check the selfishness of her rival, and prevent a speedy recognition.

Chapter V

———◄•••►———

At six o'clock P.M. I left the Clarendon, and was conveyed over
the roughest and most execrable pavements through several miles
of unsympathetic, gloomy, dirty streets, and crowded thoroughfares, over jaw-wrenching street-railway tracks, to a large wooden
shed covered with inscriptions respecting routes and destinations
on the bank of the river, which as far as the eye could see, was
bordered by similar establishments, where my baggage was
deposited in the mud. There were no porters, none of the recognised and established aides to locomotion to which we are accustomed in Europe, but a number of amateurs divided the spoil,
and carried it into the offices, whilst I was directed to struggle for
my ticket in another little wooden box, from which I presently
received the necessary document, full of the dreadful warnings
and conditions, which railway companies inflict on the public in
all free countries.

The whole of my luggage, except a large bag, was taken charge
of by a man at the New York side of the ferry, who "checked it
through" to the capital—giving me a slip of brass with a number
corresponding with a brass ticket for each piece. When the boat
arrived at the stage at the other side of the Hudson, in my inno-
cence I called for a porter to take my bag. The passengers were
moving out of the capacious ferry-boat in a steady stream, and
the steam throat and bell of the engine were going whilst I was
looking for my porter; but at last a gentleman passing said, "I
guess y'ill remain here a considerable time before y'ill get any one

to come for that bag of yours," and taking the hint, I just got off in time to stumble into a long box on wheels, with a double row of most uncomfortable seats, and a passage down the middle, where I found a place beside Mr. Sanford, the newly-appointed United States Minister to Belgium, who was kind enough to take me under his charge to Washington.

The night was closing in very fast as the train started, but such glimpses as I had of the continuous line of pretty-looking villages of wooden houses, two stories high, painted white, each with its Corinthian portico, gave a most favourable impression of the comfort and prosperity of the people. The rail passed through the main street of most of these hamlets and villages, and the bell of the engine was toll'd to warn the inhabitants, who drew up on the sidewalks and let us go by. The passengers were crowded as close as they could pack, and as there was an immense iron stove in the centre of the car, the heat and stuffiness became most trying, although I had been undergoing the ordeal of the stove-heated New York houses for nearly a week. Once a minute, at least, the door at either end of the carriage was opened, and then closed with a sharp crashing noise, that jarred the nerves, and effectually prevented sleep. It generally was done by a man whose sole object seemed to be to walk up the centre of the carriage in order to go out of the opposite door—occasionally it was the work of the newspaper boy, with a sheaf of journals and trashy illustrated papers under his arm. Now and then it was the conductor; but the periodical visitor was a young gentleman with a chain and rings, who bore a tray before him, and solicited orders for "gum drops," and "lemon drops," which, with tobacco, apples, and cakes, were consumed in great quantities by the passengers.

At ten o'clock P.M., we crossed the river by a ferry-boat to Philadelphia, and drove through the streets, stopping for supper for a few moments at the La Pierre Hotel. To judge from the vast extent of the streets, of small, low, yet snug-looking houses, through which we passed, Philadelphia must contain in comfort

[16]

the largest number of small householders of any city in the world. At the other terminus of the rail, to which we drove in a carriage, we procured for a small sum, a dollar I think, berths in a sleeping car, an American institution of considerable merit. Unfortunately a party of prize-fighters had mind to make themselves comfortable, and the result was anything but conducive to sleep. They had plenty of whiskey, and were full of song and fight, nor was it possible to escape their urgent solicitations "to take a drink," by feigning the soundest sleep. One of these, a big man, with a broken nose, a mellow eye, and a very large display of rings, jewels, chains and pins, was in very high spirits, and informed us he was "Going to Washington to get a foreign mission from Bill Seward. He wouldn't take Paris, as he didn't care much about French or Frenchmen; but he'd just like to show John Bull how to do it; or he'd take Japan if they were very pressing." Another told us he was "Going to the bosom of Uncle Abe" (meaning the President)—"that he knew him well in Kentucky years ago, and a high-toned gentleman he was." Any attempts to persuade them to retire to rest made by the conductors were treated with the sovereign contempt, but at last whiskey asserted its supremacy, and having established the point that they "would not sleep unless they —— pleased," they slept and snored.

At 6:00 A.M., we were roused up by the arrival of the train at Washington, having crossed great rivers and traversed cities without knowing it during the night. I looked out and saw a vast mass of white marble towering above us on the left, stretching out in colonnaded porticoes, and long flanks of windowed masonry, and surmounted by an unfinished cupola, from which scaffold and cranes raised their black arms. This was the Capitol. To the right was a cleared space of mud, sand, and fields studded with wooden sheds and huts, beyond which, again, could be seen rudimentary streets of small red brick houses, and some church-spires above them.

Emerging from the station, we found a vociferous crowd of

blacks, who were the hackney-coachmen of the place; but Mr. Sanford had his carriage in waiting, and drove me straight to Willard's Hotel, where he consigned me to the landlord at the bar. Our route lay through Pennsylvania Avenue—a street of much breadth and length, lined with ailanthus trees, each in a whitewashed wooden sentry box, and by most irregularly-built houses in all kinds of material, from deal plank to marble—of all heights, and every sort of trade. Few shop-windows were open, and the principal population consisted of blacks, who were moving about on domestic affairs. At one end of the long vista there is the Capitol; and at the other, the Treasury buildings—a fine block in marble, with the usual American classical colonnades.

Close to these rises the great pile of Willard's Hotel, now occupied by applicants for office, and by the members of the newly-assembled Congress. It is a quadrangular mass of rooms, six stories high, and some hundred yards square; and it probably contains at this moment more scheming, plotting, planning heads than any building of the same size ever held in the world. I was ushered into a bedroom which had just been vacated by some candidate—whether he succeeded or not I cannot tell, but if his testimonials spoke truth, he ought to have been selected at once for the highest office. The room was littered with printed copies of letters testifying that J. Smith, of Hartford, Conn., was about the ablest, honestest, cleverest, and best man the writers ever knew. Up and down the long passages doors were opening and shutting for men with papers bulgings out of their pockets, who hurried as if for their life in and out, and the building almost shook with the tread of the candidature.

At present not less than twenty-five hundred people dine in the public room every day. On the kitchen floor there is a vast apartment, a hall without carpets or any furniture but plain chairs and tables, which are ranged in close rows, at which flocks of people are feeding, or discoursing, or from which they are flying away. The servants never cease shoving the chairs to

[18]

and fro with a harsh screeching noise over the floor, so that one can scarce hear his neighbour speak. If he did, he would probably hear, as I did, at this very hotel, a man order breakfast, "Black tea and toast, scrambled eggs, fresh spring shad, wild pigeon, pigs' feet, two robins on toast, oysters," and a quantity of breads and cakes of various denominations. The tumult, the miscellaneous nature of the company—my friends the prize-fighters are already in possession of the doorway—the heated, muggy rooms, not to speak of the great abominableness of the passages and halls, despite a most liberal provision of spittoons, conduce to render these institutions by no means agreeable to a European.

I dined at Mr. Sanford's, where I was introduced to Mr. Seward, Secretary of State; Mr. Truman Smith, an ex-senator, much respected among the Republican party; Mr. Antony, a senator of the United States, a journalist, a very intelligent-looking man, with an Israelitish cast of face; Colonel Foster of the Illinois railway, of reputation in the States as a geologist; and one or two more gentlemen. Mr. Seward is a slight, middle-sized man, of feeble build, with the stoop contracted from sedentary habits and application to the desk, and has a peculiar attitude when seated, which immediately attracts attention. A well-formed and large head is placed on a long, slender neck, and projects over the chest in an argumentative kind of way, as if the keen eyes were seeking for an adversary; the mouth is re-markably flexible, large but well-formed, the nose prominent and aquiline, the eyes secret, but penetrating, and lively with humour of some kind twinkling about them; the brow bold and broad, but not remarkably elevated; the white hair silvery and fine—a subtle, quick man, rejoicing in power, given to perorate and to oracular utterances, fond of badinage, bursting with the im-portance of state mysteries, and with the dignity of directing the foreign policy of the greatest country—as all Americans think—in the world. After dinner he told some stories of the pressure on the President for place, which very much amused the guests who knew the men, and talked freely and pleasantly of many things— stating, however, few facts positively. In reference to an assertion in a New York paper, that orders had been given to evacuate Sumter, "That," he said, "is a plain lie—no such orders have been given. We will give up nothing we have—abandon nothing that has been entrusted to us. If people would only read these statements by the light of the President's inaugural, they would not be deceived." He wanted no extra session of Congress. "History tells us that kings who call extra parliaments lose their heads," and he informed the company he had impressed the President with his historical parallels.

All through this conversation his tone was that of a man very sanguine, and with a supreme contempt for those who thought there was anything serious in Secession. "Why," said he, "I myself, my brothers, and sisters, have been all Secessionists—we seceded from home when we were young, but we all went back to it sooner or later. These States will all come back in the same way." I doubt if he was ever in the South; but he affirmed that the state of living and of society there was something like that in the State of New York sixty or seventy years ago. In the North all was life, enterprise, industry, mechanical skill. In the South there was dependence on black labour, and an idle extravagance which was mistaken for elegant luxury—tumble-down old hackney-coaches, such as had not been seen north of the Potomac for half a century, harness never cleaned, undergroomed horses, worked at the mill one day and sent to town the next, bady furnished houses, bad cookery, imperfect education. No parallel could be drawn between them and the Northern States at all.

The company addressed him as "Governor," which led to Mr. Seward's mentioning that when he was in England he was induced to put his name down with that prefix in a hotel book, and caused a discussion among the waiters as to whether he was the "Governor" of a prison or of a public company. I hope the great people of England treated Mr. Seward with the attention due to his position, as he would assuredly feel and resent very much any slight on the part of those in high places.

March 27th. This morning, after breakfast, Mr. Sanford called, according to his promise, and took me to the State Department. It is a very humble—in fact, dingy—mansion, two stories high, and situated at the end of the magnificent line of colonnade in white marble, called the Treasury, which is hereafter to do duty as the headquarters of nearly all the public departments.

In a moderately sized, but very comfortable, apartment, surrounded with bookshelves, and ornamented with a few engravings, we found the Secretary of State seated at his table, and enjoying a cigar; he received me with great courtesy and kindness, and after a time said he would take occasion to present me to the President, who was to give audience that day to the minister of the new kingdom of Italy, who had hitherto represented the kingdom of Sardinia.

I have already described Mr. Seward's personal appearance; his son, to whom he introduced me, is the Assistant Secretary of State, and is editor or proprietor of a journal in the State of New York, which has a reputation for ability and fairness. Mr. Frederick Seward is a slight delicate-looking man, with a high forehead, thoughtful brow, dark eyes, and amiable expression; his manner is very placid and modest, and, if not reserved, he is by no means loquacious. As we were speaking, a carriage drove up to the door, and Mr. Seward exclaimed to his father, with something like dismay in his voice, "Here comes the Chevalier in full uniform!"—and in a few seconds in effect the Chevalier Bertinatti made his appearance, in cocked hat, white gloves, diplomatic suit of blue and silver lace, sword, sash, and riband of the Cross of Savoy. I thought there was a quiet smile on Mr. Seward's face as he saw his brilliant companion, who contrasted so strongly with the more than republican simplicity of his own attire. "Fred, do you take Mr. Russell round to the President's, whilst I go with the Chevalier. We will meet at the White House." We accordingly set out through a private door leading to the grounds, and within a few seconds entered the hall of the moderate mansion, White House, which has very much the air of a portion of a bank or public office, being provided with glass doors and plain heavy chairs and forms. The domestic who was in attendance was dressed like any ordinary citizen, and seemed perfectly indifferent to the high position of the great personage with whom he conversed, when Mr. Seward asked him, "Where is the President?" Passing through one of the doors on the left, we entered a handsome spacious room, richly and rather gorgeously furnished, and rejoicing in a kind of *demi-jour,* which gave increased effect to the gilt chairs and ormolu ornaments.

Soon afterward there entered, with a shambling, loose, irregular, almost unsteady gait, a tall, lank, lean man, considerably over six feet in height, with stooping shoulders, long pendulous arms, terminating in hands of extraordinary dimensions, which, however, were far exceeded in proportion by his feet. He was dressed in an ill-fitting, wrinkled suit of black, which put one in mind of an undertaker's uniform at a funeral; round his neck a rope of black silk was knotted in a large bulb, with flying ends projecting beyond the collar of his coat; his turned-down shirt-collar disclosed a sinewy muscular yellow neck, and above that, nestling in a great black mass of hair, bristling and compact like a riff of mourning pins, rose the strange quaint face and head, covered with its thatch of wild republican hair, of President Lincoln. The impression produced by the size of his extremities, and by his flapping and wide projecting ears, may be removed by the appearance of kindliness, sagacity, and the awkward bonhommie of his face; the mouth is absolutely prodigious; the lips, straggling and extending almost from one line of black beard to the other, are only kept in order by two deep furrows from the nostril to the chin; the nose itself—a prominent organ—stands

[22]

out from the face with an inquiring, anxious air, as though it were sniffing for some good thing in the wind; the eyes dark, full, and deeply set, are penetrating, but full of an expression which almost amounts to tenderness; and above them projects the shaggy brow, running into the small hard frontal space, the development of which can scarcely be estimated accurately, owing to the irregular flocks of thick hair carelessly brushed across it. One would say that, although the mouth was made to enjoy a joke, it could also utter the severest sentence which the head could dictate, but that Mr. Lincoln would be ever more willing to temper justice with mercy, and to enjoy what he considers the amenities of life, than to take a harsh view of men's nature and of the world, and to estimate things in an ascetic or puritan spirit. A person who met Mr. Lincoln in the street would not take him to be what—according to the usages of European society—is called a "gentleman"; and, indeed, since I came to the United States, I have heard more disparaging allusions made by Americans to him on that account than I could have expected among simple republicans, where all should be equals; but at the same time, it would not be possible for the most indifferent observer to pass him in the street without notice.

As he advanced through the room, he evidently controlled a desire to shake hands all round with everybody, and smiled good-humouredly till he was suddenly brought up by the staid deportment of Mr. Seward, and by the profound diplomatic bows of the Chevalier Bertinatti. Then, indeed, he suddenly jerked himself back, and stood in front of the two ministers, with his body slightly drooped forward, and his hands behind his back, his knees touching, and his feet apart. Mr. Seward formally presented the minister, whereupon the President made a prodigiously violent demonstration of his body in a bow which had almost the effect of a smack in its rapidity and abruptness, and, recovering himself, proceeded to give his utmost attention, whilst the Chevalier, with another bow, read from a paper a long address in presenting the royal letter accrediting him as "minister resident"; and when he said that "the king desired to give, under your enlightened administration, all possible strength and extent to those sentiments of frank sympathy which do not cease to be exhibited every moment between the two peoples, and whose origin dates back as far as the exertions which have presided over their common destiny as self-governing and free nations," the President gave another bow still more violent, as much as to accept the allusion.

The minister forthwith handed his letter to the President, who gave it into the custody of Mr. Seward, and then, dipping his hand into his coat pocket, Mr. Lincoln drew out a sheet of paper, from which he read his reply, the most remarkable part of which was his doctrine "that the United States were bound by duty not to interfere with the differences of foreign governments and countries." After some words of compliment, the President shook hands with the minister, who soon afterwards retired. Mr. Seward then took me by the hand and said—"Mr. President, allow me to present to you Mr. Russell of the London *Times*." On which Mr. Lincoln put out his hand in a very friendly manner, and said, "Mr. Russell, I am very glad to make your acquaintance, and to see you in this country. The London *Times* is one of the greatest powers in the world—in fact, I don't know anything which has much more power,—except perhaps the Mississippi. I am glad to know you as its minister." Conversation ensued for some minutes, which the President enlivened by two or three peculiar little sallies, and I left agreeably impressed with his shrewdness, humour, and natural sagacity.

In the evening I dined with Mr. Seward, in company with his son, Mr. Seward, junior, Mr. Sanford, and a quaint, natural specimen of an American rustic lawyer, who was going to Brussels as Secretary of Legation. His chief, Mr. Sanford, did not appear altogether happy when introduced to his secretary, for he found that he had a very limited knowledge (if any) of French, and of other things which it is generally considered desirable that secretaries should know.

Very naturally, conversation turned on politics. Although no man can foresee the nature of the crisis which is coming, nor the mode in which it is to be encountered, the faith of men like Mr. Sanford and Mr. Seward in the ultimate success of their principles, and in the integrity of the Republic, is very remarkable. Mr. Seward asserted that the Ministers of England or of France had no right to make any allusion to the civil war which appeared imminent; and that the Southern Commissioners who had been sent abroad could not be received by the Government of any foreign power, officially or otherwise, even to hand in a document or to make a representation, without incurring the risk of breaking off relations with the Government of the United States. As regards the great object of public curiosity, the relief of Fort Sumter, Mr. Seward maintains a profound silence, beyond the mere declaration, made with a pleasant twinkle of the eye, that "the whole policy of the Government, on that and other questions, is put forth in the President's inaugural, from which there will be no deviation."

On returning to my hotel, I found a card from the President, inviting me to dinner the following day.

Chapter VI

March 28th. I was honoured today by visits from a great number of Members of Congress, journalists, and others. Judging from the expressions of most of the Washington people, they would gladly see a Southern Cabinet installed in their city. The cold shoulder is given to Mr. Lincoln, and all kinds of stories and jokes are circulated at his expense. People take particular pleasure in telling how he came towards the seat of his Government disguised in a Scotch cap and cloak, whatever that may mean.

In the evening I repaired to the White House. From the unpretending antechamber, a walk across the lofty hall led us to the reception room, which was the same as that in which the President held his interview yesterday.

Mrs. Lincoln was already seated to receive her guests. She is of the middle age and height, of a plumpness degenerating to the *embonpoint* natural to her years; her features are plain, her nose and mouth of an ordinary type, and her manners and appearance homely, stiffened, however, by the consciousness that her position requires her to be something more than plain Mrs. Lincoln, the wife of the Illinois lawyer; she is profuse in the introduction of the word "sir" in every sentence, which is now almost an Americanism confined to certain classes, although it was once as common in England. Her dress I shall not attempt to describe, though it was very gorgeous and highly coloured. She handled a fan with much energy, displaying a round, well-proportioned arm, and was adorned with some simple jewellery.

Mrs. Lincoln struck me as being desirous of making herself agreeable; and I own I was agreeably disappointed, as the Secessionist ladies at Washington had been amusing themselves by anecdotes which could scarcely have been founded on fact.

Several of the Ministers had already arrived; by-and-by all had come, and the party only waited for General Scott, who seemed to be the representative man in Washington of the monarchical idea. Whilst we were waiting, Mr. Seward took me round, and introduced me to the Ministers, and to their wives and daughters, among the latter, Miss Chase, who is very attractive, agreeable, and sprightly. Her father, the Finance Minister, struck me as one of the most intelligent and distinguished persons in the whole assemblage; tall, of a good presence, with a well-formed head, fine forehead, and a face indicating energy and power. There is a peculiar droop and motion of the lid of one eye, which seems to have suffered from some injury, that detracts from the agreeable effect of his face; but, on the whole, he is one who would not pass quite unnoticed in a European crowd of the same description.

Mr. Cameron, the Secretary for War, a slight man, above the middle height, with grey hair, deep-set keen grey eyes, and a thin mouth, gave me the idea of a person of ability and adroitness. His colleague, the Secretary of the Navy, a small man, with a great long grey beard and spectacles, did not look like one of much originality or ability; but people who know Mr. Welles declare that he is possessed of administrative power, although they admit that he does not know the stem from the stern of a ship, and are in doubt whether he ever saw the sea in his life. Mr. Smith, the Minister of the Interior, is a bright-eyed, smart (I use the word in the English sense) gentleman, with the reputation of being one of the most conservative members of the cabinet. Mr. Blair, the Postmaster-General, is a person of much greater influence than his position would indicate. He has the reputation of being one of the most determined Republicans in the Ministry; but he held peculiar notions with reference to the black and the white races, which, if carried out, would not by any means conduce to the comfort or happiness of free Negroes in the United States. He is a tall, lean man, with a hard, Scotch, practical-looking head—an anvil for ideas to be hammered on. His eyes are small and deeply set, and have a rat-like expression; and he speaks with caution, as though he weighed every word before he uttered it. The last of the Ministers is Mr. Bates, a stout, thick-set, common-looking man, with a large beard, who fills the office of Attorney-General. Some of the gentlemen were in evening dress; others wore black frock coats, which it seems, as in Turkey, are considered to be *en règle* at a Republican Ministerial dinner.

In the conversation which occurred before dinner, I was amused to observe the manner in which Mr. Lincoln used the anecdotes for which he is famous. Where men bred in courts, accustomed to the world, or versed in diplomacy, would use some subterfuge, or would make a polite speech, or give a shrug of the shoulders as the means of getting out of an embarrassing position, Mr. Lincoln raises a laugh by some bold west-country anecdote, and moves off in the cloud of merriment produced by his joke. Thus, when Mr. Bates was remonstrating apparently against the appointment of some indifferent lawyer to a place of judicial importance, the President interposed with, "Come, now, Bates, he's not half as bad as you think. Besides that, I must tell you, he did me a good turn long ago. When I took to the law, I was going to court one morning, with some ten or twelve miles of bad road before me, and I had no horse. The judge overtook me in his wagon. 'Hollo, Lincoln! Are you not going to the court-house? Come in and I'll give you a seat.' Well, I got in, and the judge went on reading his papers. Presently the wagon struck a stump on one side of the road; then it hopped off to the other. I looked out, and I saw the driver was jerking from side to side in his seat; so says I, 'Judge, I think your coachman has been taking a little drop too much this morning.' 'Well I declare, Lincoln,' said he, 'I should not much wonder if you are right, for he has nearly upset me half-a-dozen times since starting.' So, putting his head out of the window, he shouted, 'Why, you infernal scoundrel, you are drunk!' Upon which, pulling up his horses, and turning round with great gravity, the coachman said, 'By gorra! that's the first rightful decision you have given for the last twelve-month.' " Whilst the company were laughing, the President beat a quiet retreat from the neighborhood of the Attorney-General.

It was at last announced that General Scott was unable to be present, and that, although actually in the house, he had been compelled to retire from indisposition, and we moved in to the banqueting-hall. The first "state dinner," as it is called, of the President was not remarkable for ostentation. No liveried servants, no Persic splendour of ancient plate, or *chefs d'oeuvre* of art glittered round the board. Vases of flowers decorated the table, combined with dishes in what may be called the "Gallo-American" style, with wines which owed their parentage to France, and their rearing and education to the United States, which abound in cunning nurses for such productions. The conversation was suited to the state dinner of a cabinet at which women and strangers were present. I was seated next Mr. Bates and the very agreeable and lively Secretary of the President, Mr. Hay, and except when there was an attentive silence caused by one of the President's stories, there was a Babel of small talk round the table, in which I was surprised to find a diversity of accent almost as great as if a number of foreigners had been speaking English.

After dinner the ladies and gentlemen retired to the drawing room, and the circle was increased by the addition of several politicians. I had an opportunity of conversing with some of the Ministers, if not with all, from time to time, and I was struck by the uniform tendency of their remarks in reference to the policy

[29]

of Great Britain. They seemed to think that England was bound by her anti-slavery antecedents to discourage to the utmost any attempts of the South to establish its independence on a basis of slavery, and to assume that they were the representatives of an active war of emancipation.

March 29th, Good Friday. At dinner there was the very largest naval officer I have seen in company, although I must own that our own service is not destitute of some good specimens, and I have seen an Austrian admiral at Pola, and the superintendent of the Arsenal at Tophaneh, who were not unfit to be marshals of France. This Lieutenant, named Nelson, was certainly greater in one sense than his British namesake, for he weighed 260 pounds.

The Lieutenant was a strong Union man, and he inveighed fiercely, and even coarsely, against the members of his profession who had thrown up their commissions. The superintendent of the Washington Navy Yard is supposed to be very little disposed in favour of this present Government; in fact, Captain Buchanan may be called a Secessionist, nevertheless, I am invited to the wedding of his daughter, in order to see the President give away the bride. Mr. Nelson says, Sumter and Pickens are to be reinforced. Charleston is to be reduced to order, and all traitors hanged, or he will know the reason why; and, says he, "I have some weight in the country." In the evening, as we were going home, notwithstanding the cold, we saw a number of ladies sitting out on the doorsteps, in white dresses. The streets were remarkably quiet and deserted; all the coloured population had been sent to bed long ago. The fire-bell, as usual, made an alarm or two about midnight.

Chapter VII

———◆———

March 30th. The great employment of four-fifths of the people at Willard's at present seems to be to hunt senators and congressmen through the lobbies. Every man is heavy with documents—those which he cannot carry in his pockets and hat, occupy his hands, or are thrust under his arms. The whole city is placarded with announcements of facilities for assaulting the powers that be, among which must not be forgotten the claims of the "excelsior card-writer," at Willard's, who prepares names, addresses, styles, and titles in superior penmanship. There are men at Willard's who have come literally thousands of miles to seek for places which can only be theirs for four years, and who with true American facility have abandoned the calling and pursuits of a lifetime for this doubtful canvas; and I was told of one gentleman, who having been informed that he could not get a judgeship, condescended to seek a place in the Post Office, and finally applied to Mr. Chase to be appointed keeper of a "lighthouse," he was not particular where. In the forenoon I drove to the Washington Navy Yard, in company with Lieutenant Nelson and two friends. It is about two miles outside the city, situated on a fork of land projecting between a creek and the Potomac River, which is here three-quarters of a mile broad.

The Navy Yard is surrounded by high brick walls; in the gateway stood two sentries in dark blue tunics, yellow facings, with eagle buttons, brightly polished arms, and white Berlin gloves, very clean and creditable. Inside are some few trophies of guns taken from us at York Town, and from the Mexicans in the land of Cortez. Close to the river are the workshops: of course there is smoke and noise of steam and machinery. In a modest office, surrounded by books, papers, drawings, and models, as well as by shell and shot and racks of arms of different descriptions, we found Capt. Dahlgren, the acting superintendent of the yard, and the inventor of the famous gun which bears his name, and is the favourite armament of the American Navy. By our own sailors they are irreverently termed "soda-water bottles," owing to their shape. Capt. Dahlgren contends that guns capable of throwing the heaviest shot may be constructed of cast iron, carefully prepared and moulded so that the greatest thickness of metal may be placed at the points of resistance, at the base of the gun, the muzzle and forward portions being of very moderate thickness.

On returning to the hotel, I found a magnificent bouquet of flowers, with a card attached to them, with Mrs. Lincoln's compliments, and another card announcing that she had a "reception" at 3 o'clock. It was rather late before I could get to the White House, and there were only two or three ladies in the drawing-room when I arrived. I was informed afterwards that the attendance was very scanty. The Washington ladies have not yet made up their minds that Mrs. Lincoln is the fashion. They miss their Southern friends, and constantly draw comparisons between them and the vulgar Yankee women and men who are now in power. I do not know enough to say whether the affectation of superiority be justified; but assuredly if New York be Yankee, there is nothing in which it does not far surpass this preposterous capital. The impression of homeliness produced by Mrs. Lincoln on first sight is not diminished by closer acquaintance. Few women not to the manner born there are whose heads would not be disordered, and circulation disturbed, by a rapid transition, almost instantaneous, from a condition of obscurity in a country town to be mistress of the White House. Her smiles and her frowns become a matter of consequence to the whole American world.

March 31st, Easter Sunday. I dined with Lord Lyons and the members of the Legation; the only stranger present being Senator Sumner. Politics were of course eschewed, for Mr. Sumner is Chairman of the Committee on Foreign Relations of the Senate, and Lord Lyons is a very discreet Minister, but still there crept in a word of Pickens and Sumter, and that was all. Mr. Fox, formerly of the United States Navy, and since that a master of a steamer in the commercial marine, who is related to Mr. Blair, has been sent on some mission to Fort Sumter, and has been allowed to visit Major Anderson by the authorities at Charleston; but it is not known what was the object of his mission. Everywhere there is Secession resignation, in a military sense of the word. The Southern Commissioners declare they will soon retire to Montgomery, and that any attempt to reinforce or supply the forts will be a *casus belli.* There is the utmost anxiety to know what Virginia will do. General Scott belongs to the State, and it is feared he may be shaken if the State goes out. Already the authorities of Richmond have intimated they will not allow the foundry to furnish guns to the seaboard forts, such as Monroe and Norfolk in Virginia. This concession of an autonomy is really a recognition of States' Rights. For if a State can vote itself in or out of the Union, why can it not make war or peace, and accept or refuse the Federal Government? In fact, the Federal system is radically defective against internal convulsion, however excellent it is or may be for purposes of external polity. I walked home with Mr. Sumner to his rooms, and heard some of his views, which were not so sanguine as those of Mr. Seward, and I thought I detected a desire to let the Southern States go out with their slavery if they so desired it. Mr. Chase, by the way, expressed sentiments of the same kind more decidedly the other day.

April 1st. On Easter Monday, after breakfast with Mr. Olm-

[33]

sted, I drove over to visit Senator Douglas. Originally engaged in some mechanical avocation, by his ability and eloquence he has raised himself to the highest position in the State short of the Presidency, which might have been his but for the extraordinary success of his opponent in a fortuitous suffrage scramble. He is called the Little Giant, being *modo bipedali statura,* but his head entitles him to some recognition of intellectual height. His sketch of the causes which had led to the present disruption of parties, and the hazard of civil war, was most vivid and able; and for more than an hour he spoke with a vigour of thought and terseness of phrase which, even on such dreary and uninviting themes as squatter sovereignty and the Kansas-Nebraska question, interested a foreigner in the man and the subject. Although his sympathies seemed to go with the South on the question of slavery and territorial extension, he condemned altogether the attempt to destroy the Union.

April 3rd. I had an interview with the Southern Commissioners today, at their hotel. For more than an hour I heard, from men of position and of different sections in the South, expressions which satisfied me the Union could never be restored, if they truly represented the feelings and opinions of their fellow-citizens. They have the idea they are ministers of a foreign power treating with Yankeedom, and their indignation is moved by the refusal of Government to negotiate with them, armed as they are with full authority to arrange all questions arising out of an amicable separation—such as the adjustment of Federal claims for property, forts, stores, public works, debt, land purchases, and the like. One of the Judges of the Supreme Court of the United States, Mr. Campbell, is their intermediary, and of course it is not known what hopes Mr. Seward has held out to him; but there is some imputation of Punic faith against the Government on account of recent acts, and there is no doubt the Commissioners hear, as I do, that there are preparations at the Navy Yard and at New York to relieve Sumter, at any rate, with provision, and that Pickens has actually been reinforced by sea. In the evening I dined at the British Legation, and went over to the house of the Russian minister, M. de Stoeckl, in the evening. The diplomatic body in Washington constitute a small and very agreeable society of their own, in which few Americans mingle except at the receptions and large evening assemblies. As the people now in power are *novi homines,* the wives and daughters of ministers and attachés are deprived of their friends who belonged to the old society in Washington, and who have either gone off to Secession, or sympathise so deeply with the Southern States that it is scarcely becoming to hold very intimate relations with them in the face of Government. From the house of M. de Stoeckl I went to a party at the residence of M. Tassara, the Spanish Minister, where there was a crowd of diplomats, young and old. Diplomatists seldom or never talk politics, and so Pickens and Sumter were unheard of; but it is stated nevertheless that Virginia is on the eve of secession, and will certainly go if the President attempts to use force in relieving and strengthening the Federal forts.

April 4th. I had a long interview with Mr. Seward today at the State Department. He set forth at great length the helpless condition in which the President and the Cabinet found themselves when they began the conduct of public affairs at Washington. The last Cabinet had tampered with treason, and had contained traitors; a miserable imbecility had encouraged the leaders of the South to mature their plans, and had furnished them with the means of carrying out their design. One Minister had purposely sent away the Navy of the United States to distant and scattered stations; another had purposely placed the arms, ordnance, and munitions of war in undue proportions in the Southern States, and had weakened the Federal Government so that they might easily fall into the hands of the traitors and enable them to secure the war *matériel* of the Union; a Minister had stolen the public funds for traitorous purposes—in every port, in every department of the State, at home and abroad, on sea and by land, men were placed who were engaged in this deep conspiracy—and when the voice of the people declared Mr. Lincoln President of the United States, they set to work as one man to destroy the Union under the most flimsy pretexts. The President's duty was clearly defined by the Constitution. He had to guard what he had, and to regain, if possible, what he had lost. He would not consent to any dismemberment of the Union nor to the abandonment of one iota of Federal property—nor could he do so if he desired.

These and many more topics were presented to me to show that the Cabinet were not accountable for the temporising policy of inaction, which was forced upon them by circumstances, and that they would deal vigorously with the Secession movement— as vigorously as Jackson did with nullification in South Carolina, if they had the means. But what could they do when such men as Twiggs surrendered his trust and sacrificed his troops to a crowd of Texans; or when naval and military officers resigned *en masse,* that they might accept service in the rebel forces? All this excitement would come right in a very short time—it was a brief madness, which would pass away when the people had opportunity for reflection. Meantime the danger was that foreign powers would be led to imagine the Federal Government was too weak to defend its rights, and that the attempt to destroy the Union and to set up a Southern Confederacy was successful. In other words, again, Mr. Seward fears that, in this transition state between their forced inaction and the *coup* by which they intend to strike down Secession, Great Britain may recognize the Government established at Montgomery, and he is ready, if needs be, to threaten Great Britain with war as the consequence of such recognition. But he certainly assumed the existence of strong Union sentiments in many of the seceded States, as a basis for his remarks, and admitted that it would not become the spirit of the American Government, or of the Federal system, to use

[36]

armed force in subjugating the Southern States against the will of the majority of the people. Therefore if the majority desire Secession, Mr. Seward would let them have it—but he cannot believe in anything so monstrous, for to him the Federal Government and Constitution, as interpreted by his party, are divine, heaven-born.

But I had seen that day an assemblage of men doing a goose-step march forth dressed in blue tunics and grey trousers, shakoes and cross-belts, armed with musket and bayonet, cheering and hurrahing in the square before the War Department, who were, I am told, the District of Columbia volunteers and militia. They had indeed been visible in various forms parading, marching, and trumpeting about the town with a poor imitation of French *pas* and *élan,* but they did not, to the eye of a soldier, give any appearance of military efficiency, or to the eye of the anxious statesman any indication of the *animus pugnandi.* Starved, washed-out creatures most of them, interpolated with Irish and flat-footed, stumpy Germans. It was a matter for wonderment that the Foreign Minister of a nation which was in such imminent danger in its very capital, and which, with its chief and his cabinet, was almost at the mercy of the enemy, should hold to the language I was aware he had transmitted to the most powerful nations of Europe.

April 5th. Dined with the Southern Commissioners and a small party at Gautier's, a French restaurateur in Pennsylvania Avenue. The gentlemen present were, I need not say, all of one way of thinking; but as these leaves will see the light before the civil war is at an end, it is advisable not to give their names, for it would expose persons resident in Washington, who may not be suspected by the Government, to those marks of attention which they have not yet ceased to pay to their political enemies. Although I confess that in my judgment too much stress has been laid in England on the severity with which the Federal authorities have acted towards their political enemies, who were seeking their destruction, it may be candidly admitted, that they have forfeited all claim to the lofty position they once occupied as a Government existing by moral force, and by the consent of the governed.

As Col. Pickett and Mr. Banks are notorious Secessionists, and Mr. Phillips has since gone South, after the arrest of his wife on account of her anti-Federal tendencies, it may be permitted to mention that they were among the guests. I had pleasure in making the acquaintance of Governor Roman. Mr. Crawford, his brother commissioner, is a much younger man, of considerably greater energy and determination, but probably of less judgment. The third commissioner, Mr. Forsyth, is fanatical in his opposition to any suggestions of compromise or reconstruction; but, indeed, upon that point, there is little difference of opinion amongst any of the real adherents of the South. Mr. Lincoln they spoke of with contempt; Mr. Seward they evidently regarded as the ablest and most unscrupulous of their enemies; but the tone in which they alluded to the whole of the Northern people indicated the clear conviction that trade, commerce, the pursuit of gain, manufacture, and the base mechanical arts, had so degraded the whole race, they would never attempt to strike a blow in fair fight for what they prized so highly in theory and in words. Whether it be in consequence of some secret influence which slavery has upon the minds of men, or that the aggression of the North upon their institutions has been of a nature to excite the deepest animosity and most vindictive hate, certain it is there is a degree of something like ferocity in the Southern mind towards New England which exceeds belief. I am persuaded that these feelings of contempt are extended towards England. They believe that we, too, have had the canker of peace upon us. One evidence of this, according to Southern men, is the abolition of duelling. This practice, according to them, is highly wholesome and meritorious; and, indeed, it may be admitted that in the state of society which is reported to exist in the Southern States,

[38]

it is a useful check on such men as it restrained in our own islands in the last century. In the course of conversation, one gentleman remarked, that he considered it disgraceful for any man to take money for the dishonour of his wife or his daughter. "With us," he said, "there is but one mode of dealing known. The man who dares tamper with the honour of a white woman, knows what he has to expect. We shoot him down like a dog, and no jury in the South will ever find any man guilty of murder for punishing such a scoundrel." An argument which can scarcely be alluded to was used by them, to show that these offences in slave States had not the excuse which might be adduced to diminish their gravity when they occurred in States where all the population were white. Indeed, in this, as in some other matters of similar character, slavery is their *summum bonum* of morality, physical excellence, and social purity. I was inclined to question the correctness of the standard which they had set up, and to inquire whether the virtue which needed this murderous use of the pistol and the dagger to defend it, was not open to some doubt; but I found there was very little sympathy with my views among the company.

The gentlemen at the table asserted that the white men in the slave States are physically superior to the men of the free States; and indulged in curious theories in morals and physics to which I was a stranger. Disbelief of anything a Northern man—that is, a Republican—can say, is a fixed principle in their minds. I could not help remarking when the conversation turned on the duplicity of Mr. Seward, and the wickedness of the Federal Government in refusing to give the assurance Sumter would not be relieved by force of arms, that it must be of very little consequence what promises Mr. Seward made, as, according to them, not the least reliance was to be placed on his word. The notion that the Northern men are cowards is justified by instances in which Congressmen have been insulted by Southern men without calling them out, and Mr. Sumner's case was quoted as the type of the affairs of the kind between the two sides.

The acts of Mr. Floyd and Mr. Howell Cobb, which must be esteemed of doubtful morality, are here justified by the States' Rights doctrine. If the States had a right to go out, they were quite right in obtaining their quota of the national property which would not have been given to them by the Lincolnites. Therefore, their friends were not to be censured because they had sent arms and money to the South.

April 6th. Today I paid a visit to General Scott, who received me very kindly, and made many inquiries respecting the events in the Crimea and the Indian mutiny and rebellion. He professed to have no apprehension for the safety of the capital; but in reality there are only some seven or eight hundred regulars to protect it and the Navy Yard, and two field batteries, commanded by an officer of very doubtful attachment to the Union. The head of the Navy Yard is openly accused of treasonable sympathies.

Mr. Seward has definitely refused to hold any intercourse whatever with the Southern Commissioners, and they will retire almost immediately from the capital. As matters look very threatening, I must go South and see with my own eyes how affairs stand there, before the two sections come to open rupture. Mr. Seward, the other day, in talking of the South, described them as being in every respect behind the age, with fashions, habits, level of thought, and modes of life, belonging to the worst part of the last century. But still he never has been there himself! The Southern men come up to the Northern cities and springs, but the Northerner rarely travels southwards. Indeed, I am informed, that if he were a well-known Abolitionist, it would not be safe for him to appear in a Southern City.

Chapter VIII

April 8th. How it does rain! Last night there were torrents of water in the streets literally a foot deep. It still runs in muddy whirling streams through the channels, and the rain is falling incessantly from a dull leaden sky. The air is warm and clammy. There are all kind of rumors abroad, and the barbers' shops shook with "shaves" this morning. Sumter, of course, was the main topic. Some reported that the President had promised the Southern Commissioners, through their friend Mr. Campbell, Judge of the Supreme Court, not to use force in respect to Pickens or Sumter. I wrote to Mr. Seward, to ask him if he could enable me to make any definite statement on these important matters. The Southerners are alarmed at the accounts they have received of great activity and preparations in the Brooklyn and Boston Navy Yards, and declare that "treachery" is meant. I find myself quite incapable of comprehending their position. How can the United States Government be guilty of "treachery" towards subjects of States which are preparing to assert their independence, unless that Government has been guilty of false-hood or admitted the justice of the decision to which the States had arrived?

On returning to my hotel, I found a note from Mr. Seward, asking me to visit him at nine o'clock. On going to his house, I was shown to the drawing room, and found there only the Secretary of State, his son, and Mrs. Seward. I made a *parti carré* for a friendly rubber of whist, and Mr. Seward, who was my partner, talked as he played, so that the score of the game was not favourable. But his talk was very interesting. "All the preparations of which you hear mean this only. The Government, finding the property of the State and Federal forts neglected and left without protection, are determined to take steps to relieve them from that neglect, and to protect them. But we are determined in doing so to make no aggression. The President's inaugural clearly shadows out our policy. We will not go beyond it—we have no intention of doing so—nor will we withdraw from it." After a time Mr. Seward put down his cards, and told his son to go for a portfolio which he would find in a drawer of his table. Mrs. Seward lighted the drop light of the gas, and on her husband's return with the paper left the room. The Secretary then lit his cigar, gave one to me, and proceeded to read slowly and with marked emphasis a very long, strong, and able dispatch, which he told me was to be read by Mr. Adams, the American minister in London, to Lord John Russell. It struck me that the tone of the paper was hostile, that there was an undercurrent of menace through it, and that it contained insinuations that Great Britain would interfere to split up the Republic, if she could, and was pleased at the prospect of the dangers which threatened it.

At all the stronger passages Mr. Seward raised his voice, and made a pause at their conclusion as if to challenge remark or approval. At length I could not help saying, that the dispatch would, no doubt, have an excellent effect when it came to light in Congress, and that the Americans would think highly of the writer; but I ventured to express an opinion that it would not be quite so acceptable to the Government and people of Great Britain. This Mr. Seward, as an American statesman, had a right to make but a secondary consideration. By affecting to regard Secession as a mere political heresy which can be easily confuted, and by forbidding foreign countries alluding to it, Mr. Seward thinks he can establish the supremacy of his own Government, and at the same time gratify the vanity of the people. Even war with us may not be out of the list of those means which would be available for re-fusing the broken Union into a mass once more. However, the Secretary is quite confident in what he calls "re-action." "When the Southern States," he says, "see that we mean them no wrong—that we intend no violence to persons, rights, or things—that the Federal Government seeks only to fulfill obligations imposed on it in respect to the national property, they will see their mistake, and one after another they will come back into the Union." Mr. Seward anticipates this process will at once begin, and that Secession will all be done and over in three months—at least, so he says. It was after midnight ere our conversation was over.

Chapter IX

————◄◆►————

April 10th. Today I received a characteristic note from General Scott, asking me to dine with him tomorrow, and apologising for the shortness of his invitation, which arose from his only having just heard that I was about to leave so soon for the South. The General is much admired by his countrymen, though they do not spare some "amiable weaknesses"; but, in my mind, he can only be accused of a little vanity, which is often found in characters of the highest standard. He likes to display his reading, and is troubled with a desire to indulge in fine writing. Some time ago he wrote a long letter to the *National Intelligencer,* in which he quoted Shakespeare and Paley to prove that President Buchanan ought to have garrisoned the forts at Charleston and Pensacola, as he advised him to do; and he has been the victim of poetic aspirations. The General's dinner hour was early; and when I arrived at his modest lodgings, which, however, were in the house of a famous French cook, I found a troop of mounted volunteers of the District parading up and down the street. They were not bad of their class, and the horses, though light, were active, hardy and spirited; but the men put on their uniforms badly, wore long hair, their coats and buttons and boots were unbrushed, and the horses' coats and accoutrements bore evidence of neglect. The General, who wore an undress blue frock coat, with eagle-covered brass buttons, and velvet collar and cuffs, was with Mr. Seward and Mr. Bates, the Attorney-General, and received me very courteously. He was interrupted by cheering from the soldiers in the street, and by clamours for "General Scott." He moves with difficulty, owing to a fall from his horse, and from the pressure of increasing years; and he evidently would not have gone out if he could have avoided it. But there is not privacy for public men in America.

Out the General went to them, and addressed a few words to his audience in the usual style about "rallying round," and "dying gloriously," and "old flag of our country," and all that kind of thing; after which, the band struck up "Yankee Doodle." Mr. Seward called out "General, make them play the 'Star-Spangled Banner,' and 'Hail Columbia.'" And so I was treated to the strains of the old bacchanalian chant, "When Bibo," &c., which the Americans have impressed to do duty as a national air. Then came an attempt to play "God Save the Queen," which I duly appreciated as a compliment; and then followed dinner, which did credit to the cook, and wine, which was most excellent, from France, Spain, and Madeira. The only addition to our party was Major Cullum, aide-de-camp to General Scott, a United States engineer, educated at West Point. The general underwent a little badinage about the phrase "a hasty plate of soup," which he used in one of his dispatches during the Mexican War, and he appealed to me to decide whether it was so erroneous or ridiculous as Mr. Seward insisted. I said I was not a judge, but certainly similar liberal usage of a well-known figure of prosody might be found to justify the phrase. The only attendants at table were the General's English valet and a coloured servant; and the table apparatus which bore such good things was simple and unpretending. Of course the conversation was of a general character, and the General, evidently picking out his words with great precision, took the lead in it, telling anecdotes of great length, graced now and then with episodes, and fortified by such episodes as—"Bear with me, dear sir, for a while, that I may here diverge from the main current of my story, and proceed to mention a curious—" &c., and so on.

Chapter X

April 12th. This morning I received an intimation that the Government had resolved on taking decisive steps which would lead to a development of events in the South and test the sincerity of Secession. The Confederate general at Charleston, Beauregard, has sent to the Federal officer in command at Sumter, Major Anderson, to say, that all communication between his garrison and the city must cease; and, at the same time, or probably before it, the Government at Washington informed the Confederate authorities that they intended to forward supplies to Major Anderson, peaceably if permitted, but at all hazards to send them. The Charleston people are manning the batteries they have erected against Sumter, have fired on a vessel under the United States flag, endeavoring to communicate with the fort, and have called out and organised a large force in the islands opposite the place and in the city of Charleston.

I resolved therefore to start for the Southern States today, proceeding by Baltimore to Norfolk instead of going by Richmond, which was cut off by the floods. Before leaving, I visited Lord Lyons, Mr. Seward, the French and Russian Ministers; left cards on the President, Mrs. Lincoln, General Scott, Mr. Douglas, Mr. Sumner, and others. There was no appearance of any excitement in Washington, but Lord Lyons mentioned as an unusual circumstance, that he had received no telegraphic communication from Mr. Bunch, the British Consul at Charleston. Some ladies said to me that when I came back I would find some nice people at Washington, and that the rail-splitter, his wife, the Sewards, and all the rest of them, would be driven to the place where they ought to be: "Varina Davis is a lady, at all events, not like the other. We can't put up with such people as these!" A naval officer whom I met, told me, "If the Government are really going to try force at Charleston, you'll see they'll be beaten, and we'll have a war between the gentlemen and the Yankee rowdies; if they attempt violence, you know how that will end." The Government are so uneasy that they have put soldiers into the Capitol, and are preparing it for defence.

At 6:00 P.M. I drove to the Baltimore station in a storm of rain, accompanied by Mr. Warre, of the British Legation. In the train there was a crowd of people, many of them disappointed place-hunters, and much discussion took place respecting the propriety of giving supplies to Sumter by force, the weight of opinion being against the propriety of such a step. The tone in which the President and his Cabinet were spoken of was very disrespectful. One big man in a fur coat, who was sitting near me, said, "Well, darn me if I wouldn't draw a bead on Old Abe, Seward—aye, or General Scott himself, though I've got a pretty good thing out of them, if they do try to use their soldiers and sailors to beat down States' Rights. If they want to go they've a right to go." To which many said, "That's so! That's true!"

When we arrived at Baltimore, at 8:00 P.M., the streets were deep in water. A coachman, seeing I was a stranger, asked me two dollars, or 8s. 4d., to drive to the Eutaw House, a quarter of a mile distant; but I was not surprised, as I had paid three-and-a-half and four dollars to go to dinner and return to the hotel in Washington. On my arrival, the landlord, no less a person than a major or colonel, took me aside, and asked me if I had heard the news. "No, what is it?" "The President of the Telegraph Company tells me he has received a message from his clerk at Charleston that the batteries have opened fire on Sumter because the Government has sent down a fleet to force in supplies." The news had, however, spread. The hall and bar of the hotel were full, and I was asked by many people whom I had never seen in my life, what my opinions were as to the authenticity of the rumour. There was nothing surprising in the fact that the Charleston people had resented any attempt to reinforce the forts, as I was aware, from the language of the Southern Commissioners, that they would resist any such attempt to the last, and make it a *casus* and *causa belli*.

April 13. At dark I started for Norfolk, in the steamer *Georgianna*.

Chapter XI

———————◆◆◆◆◁———————

Sunday, April 14. A night of disturbed sleep, owing to the ponderous thumping of the walking beam close to my head, the whizzing of steam, and the roaring of the steam-trumpet to warn vessels out of the way—mosquitoes, too, had a good deal to say to me in spite of my dirty gauze curtains. Soon after dawn the vessel ran alongside the jetty at Fortress Monroe, and I saw indistinctly the water face of the work which is in some danger of being attacked, it is said, by the Virginians. There was no flag on the staff above the walls, and the place looked dreary and desolate. A few soldiers were lounging on the jetty, and after we had discharged a tipsy old officer, a few Negroes, and some parcels, the steam-pipe brayed—it does not whistle—again, and we proceeded across the mouth of the channel and James River towards Elizabeth River, on which stand Portsmouth and Gosport.

The steamer in a few minutes came alongside a dirty, broken-down, wooden quay, lined with open booths, on which a small crowd, mostly of Negroes, had gathered. Behind the shed there rose tiled and shingled roofs of mean dingy houses, and we could catch glimpses of the line of poor streets, narrow, crooked, ill-paved, surmounted by a few church steeples, and the large sprawling advertisement-boards of the tobacco stores and oyster-sellers, which was all we could see of Portsmouth or Gosport. Our vessel was in a narrow creek; at one side was the town—in the centre of the stream the old *Pennsylvania,* intended to be of 120 guns, but never commissioned, and used as receiving ship, was anchored—alongside the wall of the Navy Yard below us, lay the *Merrimac,* apparently in ordinary. The only man-of-war fit for sea was a curiosity—a stumpy bluff-bowed, Dutch-built-looking sloop, called the *Cumberland.* Two or three smaller vessels, dismasted, were below the *Merrimac,* and we could just see the building-sheds in which were one or two others, I believe, on the stocks. A fleet of oyster-boats anchored, or in sail-less observance of the Sunday, dotted the waters. There was an ancient and fishlike smell about the town worthy of its appearance and of its functions as a seaport. As the vessel came close alongside, there was the usual greeting between friends, and many a cry, "Well, you've heard the news? The Yankees out of Sumter! Isn't it fine?" There were few who did not participate in that sentiment, but there were some who looked black as night and said nothing.

An execrable, tooth-cracking drive ended at last in front of the Atlantic Hotel, where I was doomed to take up my quarters. It is a dilapidated, uncleanly place, with tobacco-stained floor, full of flies and strong odours. The waiters were all slaves: untidy, slip-shod, and careless creatures. I was shut up in a small room, with the usual notice on the door, that the proprietor would not be responsible for anything, and that you were to lock your doors for fear of robbers, and that you must take your meals at certain hours, and other matters of the kind. After a poor meal, in a long room filled with "citizens," all of them discussing Sumter, I went out into the street.

The people, I observe, are of a new and marked type, very tall, loosely yet powerfully made, with dark complexions, strongly-marked features, prominent noses, large angular mouths in square jaws, deep-seated bright eyes, low, narrow foreheads,—and are all of them much given to ruminate tobacco. The bells of the churches were tolling, and I turned into one; but the heat, great enough outside, soon became nearly intolerable; nor was it rendered more bearable by my proximity to some blacks, who were, I presume, servants or slaves of the great people in the forward pews. The clergyman or minister had got to the Psalms, when a bustle arose near the door which attracted his attention, and caused all to turn around. Several persons were standing up and whispering, whilst others were stealing on tiptoe out of the church. The influence extended itself gradually, and all the men near the doors were leaving rapidly. The minister, obviously interested, continued to read, raising his eyes towards the door. At last the persons near him rose up and walked boldly forth, and I at length followed the example, and getting into the street saw men running towards the hotel. "What is it?" exclaimed I to one. "Come along, the telegraph's in at the Day Book. The Yankees are whipped!" and so continued. I came at last to a crowd of men, struggling, with their faces toward the wall of a shabby house, increased by fresh arrivals, and diminished by those who, having satisfied their curiosity, came elbowing forth in a state of much excitement, exultation, and perspiration. "It's all right enough!" "Didn't I tell you so?" "Bully for Beauregard and the Palmetto State!" I shoved on, and read at last the programme of the cannonade and bombardment, and of the effects upon the forts, on a dirty piece of yellowish paper on the wall. It was a terrible writing. At all the street corners men were discussing the news with every symptom of joy and gratification.

Sunday is a very dull day in Norfolk—no mails, no post, no steamers; and, at the best, Norfolk must be dull exceedingly. The superintendent of the Seaboard and Roanoke Railway, having heard that I was about proceeding to Charleston, called upon me to offer every facility in his power. Sent Moses with letters to post office. At night the mosquitoes were very aggressive and successful.

Chapter XII

Monday, April 15. Up at dawn. Crossed by ferry to Portsmouth, and arrived at railway station, which was at no place in particular, in a street down which the rails were laid. Mr. Robinson, the superintendent, gave me permission to take a seat in the engine car, to which I mounted accordingly, was duly introduced to, and shook hands with the engineer and the stoker, and took my seat next the boiler.

Mr. Robinson, a young man some twenty-seven years of age, was an excellent representative of the young American—full of intelligence, well-read, a little romantic in spite of his practical habits and dealings with matters of fact, much attached to the literature, if not to the people, of the old country; and so far satisfied that English engineers knew something of their business, as to be anxious to show that American engineers were not behind them. He asked me about Washington politics with as much interest as if he had never read a newspaper. I made a remark to that effect. "Oh, sir, we can't believe," exclaimed he, "a word we read in our papers. They tell a story one day, to contradict it the next. We never know when to trust them and that's one reason, I believe, you find us all so anxious to ask questions and get information from gentlemen we meet travelling." Of the future he spoke with apprehension; "But," said he, "I am here representing the interests of a large number of Northern shareholders, and I will do my best for them. If it comes to blows after this, they will lose all, and I must stand by my own friends down South, though I don't belong to it."

By degrees we got beyond the swamps, and came upon patches of cleared land—that is, the forest had been cut down, and the only traces left of it were the stumps, some four or five feet high, "snagging" up above the ground; or the trees had been girdled round, so as to kill them, and the black trunks and stiff arms gave an air of meagre melancholy and desertion to the place, which was quite opposite to their real condition. Presently we came in sight of a flag fluttering from a lofty pine, which had been stripped of its branches, throwing broad bars of red and white to the air, with a blue square in the upper quarter containing seven stars. "That's our flag," said the engineer, who was a quiet man, much given to turning steam cocks, examining gauges, wiping his hands in fluffy impromptu handkerchiefs, and smoking tobacco—"That's our flag! And long may it wave—o'er the land of the free and the home of the ber-rave!" As we passed, a small crowd of men, women, and children, of all colours, in front of a group of poor broken-down shanties or log huts, cheered—to speak more correctly—whooped and yelled vehemently. The cry was returned by the passengers in the train. "We're all right sort hereabouts," said the engineer. "Hurrah for Jeff Davis!" The right sort were not particularly flourishing in outward aspect, at all events. The women, pale-faced, were tawdry and ragged; the men, yellow, seedy-looking. For the first time in the States, I noticed barefooted people.

At Goldsborough, which is the first place of importance on the line, the wave of the Secession tide struck us in full career. The station, the hotels, the street through which the rail ran was filled with an excited mob, all carrying arms, with signs here and there of a desire to get up some kind of uniform—flushed faces, wild eyes, screaming mouths, hurrahing for "Jeff Davis" and "the Southern Confederacy," so that the yells overpowered the discordant bands which were busy with "Dixie's Land." Here was the true revolutionary furor in full sway. The men hectored, swore, cheered, and slapped each other on the backs; the women in their best, waved handkerchiefs and flung down garlands from the windows. All was noise, dust, and patriotism.

It was a strange sight and a wonderful event at which we were assisting. These men were a levy of the people of North Carolina called out by the Governor of the State for the purpose of seizing upon Forts Caswell and Macon, belonging to the Federal Government, and left unprotected and undefended. The enthusiasm of the "citizens" was unbounded, nor was it quite free from a taint of alcohol. Many of the volunteers had flint firelocks, only a few had rifles. All kinds of head-dress were visible, and caps, belts and pouches of infinite variety. A man in a large wide-awake, with a cock's feather in it, a blue frock coat, with a red sash and a pair of cotton trousers thrust into his boots, came out of Griswold's hotel with a sword under his arm, and an article, which might have been a napkin of long service, in one hand.

He waved the article enthusiastically, swaying to and fro on his legs, and ejaculating, "H'ra for Jeff Dav's—H'ra for S'thern E'r'rights!" and tottered over to the carriage through the crowd amid the violent vibration of all the ladies' handkerchiefs in the balcony. Just as he got into the train, a man in uniform dashed after him, and caught him by the elbow, exclaiming, "Them's not the cars, General! The cars this way, General!" The military dignitary, however, felt that if he permitted such liberties in the hour of victory he was degraded forever, so, screwing up his lips and looking grave and grand, he proceeded as follows: "Sergeant, you go be——. I say these are my cars! They're *all* my cars! I'll send them where I please—to —— if I like, sir. They shall go where I please—to New York, sir, or New Orleans, sir! And —— sir, I'll arrest you." This famous idea distracted the General's attention from his project of entering the train, and muttering, "I'll arrest you," he tacked backwards and forwards to the hotel again.

As the train started on its journey, there was renewed yelling, which split the ear—a savage cry many notes higher than the most ringing cheer. At the wayside inn, where we dined—*pièce de résistance* being pig—the attendants, comely, well-dressed, clean Negresses, were slaves—"worth a thousand dollars each." I am not favourably impressed by either the food or the mode of living, or the manners of the company. One man made very coarse jokes about "Abe Lincoln" and "Negro wenches," which nothing but extreme party passion and bad taste could tolerate. Several of the passengers had been clerks in Government offices at Washington, and had been dismissed because they would not take the oath of allegiance. They were hurrying off full of zeal and patriotism to tender their services to the Montgomery Government.

Chapter XIII

———————•◆‣‣◄———————

Early next morning, soon after dawn, I crossed the Cape Fear
River, on which Wilmington is situated, by a steam ferryboat.
On the quay lay quantities of shot and shell. "How came these
here?" I inquired. "They're anti-abolition pills," said my neighbour; "They've been waiting here for two months back, but now
that Sumter's taken, I guess they won't be wanted." From the
small glance I had of Wilmington, with its fleet of schooners and
brigs crowding the broad and rapid river, I should think it was
a thriving place. Confederate flags waved over the public buildings, and I was informed that the Forts had been seized without
opposition or difficulty. I can see no sign here of the "affection
to the Union," which, according to Mr. Seward, underlies all
"Secession proclivities."

As we traversed the flat and uninteresting country, through
which the rail passes, Confederate flags and sentiments greeted
us everywhere; men and women repeated the national cry; at
every station militia men and volunteers were waiting for the
train, and the everlasting word "Sumter" ran through all the
conversation in the cars.

The Carolinians are capable of turning out a fair force of
cavalry. At each stopping-place I observed saddle-horses tethered
under the trees, and light driving vehicles, drawn by wiry muscular animals, not remarkable for size, but strong-looking and
active. Some farmers in blue jackets, and yellow braid and facings, handed round their swords to be admired by the company.

[54]

A few blades had flashed in obscure Mexican skirmishes—one, however, had been borne against "the Britishers." I inquired of a fine, tall, fair-haired young fellow whom they expected to fight. "That's more than I can tell," quoth he. "The Yankees ain't such cussed fools as to think they can come here and whip us, let alone the British." "Why, what have the British got to do with it?" "They are bound to take our part: if they don't we'll just give them a hint about cotton, and that will set matters right." This was said very much with the air of a man who knows what he is talking about, and who was quite satisfied "he had you there." I found it was still displeasing to most people, particularly one or two of the fair sex, that more Yankees were not killed at Sumter. All the people who addressed me prefixed my name, which they soon found out, by "Major" or "Colonel"—"Captain" is very low, almost indicative of contempt. The conductor who took our tickets was called "Captain."

At the Peedee River the rail is carried over marsh and stream on trestle work for two miles. "This is the kind of country we'll catch the Yankees in, if they come to invade us. They'll have some pretty tall swimming, and get knocked on the head, if ever they gets to land. I wish there was ten thousand of the cusses in it this minute." At Nichol's station on the frontiers of South Carolina, our baggage was regularly examined at the Custom House, but I did not see any one pay duties. As the train approached the level and marshy land near Charleston, the square block of Fort Sumter was seen rising above the water with the "Stars and Bars" flying over it, and the spectacle created great enthusiasm among the passengers. The smoke was still rising from an angle of the walls. Outside the village-like suburbs of the city a regiment was marching for old Virginny amid the cheers of the people—cavalry were picketed in the fields and gardens—tents and men were visible in the byways.

It was nearly dark when we reached the station. I was recommended to go to the Mills House, and on arriving there found

Mr. Ward, whom I had already met in New York and Washington, and who gave me an account of the bombardment and surrender of the fort. The hotel was full of notabilities. I was introduced to ex-Governor Manning, Senator Chesnut, Hon. Porcher Miles, on the staff of General Beauregard, and to Colonel Lucas, aide-de-camp to Governor Pickens. I was taken after dinner and introduced to General Beauregard, who was engaged, late as it was, in his room at the Headquarters writing dispatches. The General is a small, compact man, about thirty-six years of age, with a quick and intelligent eye and action, and a good deal of the Frenchman in his manner and look. He received me in the most cordial manner, and introduced me to his engineer officer, Major Whiting, whom he assigned to lead me over the works next day.

After some general conversation I took my leave; but before I went, the General said, "You shall go everywhere and see everything; we rely on your discretion, and knowledge of what is fair in dealing with what you see. Of course you don't expect to find regular soldiers in our camps or very scientific works." I answered the General, that he might rely on my making no improper use of what I saw in this country, but, "unless you tell me to the contrary, I shall write an account of all I see to the other side of the water, and if, when it comes back, there are things you would rather not have known, you must not blame me." He smiled and said, "I dare say we'll have great changes by that time."

About 8:30 P.M., a deep bell began to toll. "What is that?" "It's for all the coloured people to clear out of the streets and go home. The guards will arrest any who are found out without passes in half an hour." There was much noise in the streets, drums beating, men cheering, and marching, and the hotel is crammed full with soldiers.

April 17th. After breakfast I went down to the quay, with a party of the General's staff, to visit Fort Sumter. The senators and governors turned soldiers wore blue military caps, with palmetto trees embroidered thereon; blue frock coats, with upright collars, and shoulder-straps edged with lace, and marked with two silver bars, to designate their rank of captain; gilt buttons, with the palmetto in relief; blue trousers, with a gold lace cord, and brass spurs—no straps. The day was sweltering, but a strong breeze blew in the harbour, and puffed the dust of Charleston, coating our clothes, and filling our eyes with powder. The streets were crowded with lanky lads, clanking spurs, and sabres, with awkward squads marching to and fro, with drummers beating calls, and ruffles, and points of war, around them groups of grinning Negroes delighted with the glare and glitter, a holiday, and a new idea for them—Secession flags waving out of all the windows—little Irish boys shouting out, "Battle of Fort Sumter! New edishun!" As we walked towards the quay, where the steamer was lying, numerous traces of the unsettled state of men's minds broke out in the hurried conversations of the various friends who stopped to speak for a few moments. "Well, governor, the old Union is gone at last!" "Have you heard what Abe is going to do?" "I don't think Beauregard will have much more fighting for it. What do you think?" And so on. Our little Creole friend, by the bye, is popular beyond description. There are all kinds of doggerel rhymes in his honour—one with a refrain—

"With cannon and musket, with shell and petard,

We salute the North with our Beau-regard"—

is much in favour.

Chapter XIV

There was a large crowd around the pier staring at the men in uniform on the boat, which was filled with bales of goods, commissariat stores, trusses of hay, and hampers, supplies for the volunteer army on Morris' Island. I was amused by the names of the various corps, "Tigers," "Lions," "Scorpions," "Palmetto Eagles," "Guards," of Pickens, Sumter, Marion and of various other denominations, painted on the boxes. The original formation of these volunteers is in companies, and they know nothing of battalions or regiments. The tendency in volunteer outbursts is sometimes to gratify the greatest vanity of the greatest number. These companies do not muster more than fifty or sixty strong. Some were "dandies," and "swells," and affected to look down on their neighbours and comrades. Major Whiting told me there was difficulty in getting them to obey orders at first, as each man had an idea that he was as good an engineer as anybody else, "and a good deal better, if it came to that." It was easy to perceive it was the old story of volunteer and regular in this little army.

As we got on deck, the major saw a number of rough, long-haired-looking fellows in coarse gray tunics, with pewter buttons and worsted braid lying on the hay-bales smoking their cigars. "Gentlemen," quoth he, very courteously, "you'll oblige me by not smoking over the hay. There's powder below." "I don't believe we're going to burn the hay this time, kernel," was the reply, "and anyway, we'll put it out afore it reaches the 'bustibles," and they went on smoking. The major grumbled, and worse, and drew off.

I was presented to many judges, colonels, and others of the mass of society on board, and, "after compliments," as the Orientals say, I was generally asked, in the first place, what I thought of the capture of Sumter, and in the second, what England would do when the news reached the other side. Already the Carolinians regard the Northern States as an alien and detested enemy, and entertain, or profess, an immense affection for Great Britain.

The shore opposite Charleston is more than a mile distant, and is low and sandy, covered here and there with brilliant patches of vegetation, and long lines of trees. It is cut up with creeks, which divide it into islands, so that passages out to sea exist between some of them for light craft, though the navigation is perplexed and difficult. The city lies on a spur or promontory between the Ashley and the Cooper rivers, and the land behind it is divided in the same manner by similar creeks, and is sandy and light, bearing, nevertheless, very fine crops, and trees of magnificent vegetation. The steeples, the domes of public buildings, the rows of massive warehouses and cotton stores on the wharves, and the bright colours of the houses, render the appearance of Charleston, as seen from the river front, rather imposing. From the mastheads of the few large vessels in harbour floated the Confederate flag. Looking to our right, the same standard was visible, waving on the low, white parapets of the earth-works which had been engaged in reducing Sumter.

That much-talked-of fortress lay some two miles ahead of us now, rising up out of the water near the middle of the passage out to sea between James' Island and Sullivan's Island. It struck me at first as being like one of the smaller forts off Cronstadt, but a closer inspection very much diminished its importance; the material is brick, not stone, and the size of the place is exaggerated by the low background, and by contrast with the sea-

[59]

line. The land contracts on both sides opposite the fort, a projection of Morris' Island, called "Cumming's Point," running out on the left. There is a similar promontory from Sullivan's Island, on which is erected Fort Moultrie, on the right from the sea entrance. Castle Pinckney, which stands on a small island at the exit of the Cooper River, is a place of no importance, and it was too far from Sumter to take any share in the bombardment. The same remarks apply to Fort Johnson on James' Island, on the right bank of the Ashley River below Charleston. The works which did the mischief were the batteries of sand on Morris' Island, at Cumming's Point, and Fort Moultrie. The floating battery, covered with railroad-iron, lay a long way off, and could not have contributed much to the result.

As we approached Morris' Island, which is an accumulation of sand covered with mounds of the same material, on which there is a scanty vegetation alternating with salt water marshes, we could perceive a few tents in the distance among the sandhills. The sandbag batteries, and an ugly black parapet, with guns peering through portholes as if from a ship's side, lay before us. Around them men were swarming like ants, and a crowd in uniform were gathered on the beach to receive us as we landed from the boat of the steamer, all eager for news, and provisions, and newspapers, of which an immense flight immediately fell upon them. A guard with bayonets crossed in a very odd sort of manner prevented any unathorized persons from landing. They wore the universal coarse gray jacket and trousers, with worsted braid and yellow facings, uncouth caps, lead buttons stamped with the palmetto tree. Their unbronzed firelocks were covered with rust. The soldiers lounging about were mostly tall, well-grown men, young and old, some with the air of gentlemen; others coarse, long-haired fellows, without any semblance of military bearing, but full of fight, and burning with enthusiasm, not unaided, is some instances, by coarser stimulus.

The whole of the island was full of life and excitement.

Officers were galloping about as if on a field day or in action. Commissariat carts were toiling to and fro between the beach and the camps, and sounds of laughter and revelling came from the tents. These were pitched without order, and were of all shapes, hues, and sizes, many being disfigured by rude charcoal drawings outside, and inscriptions such as "The Live Tigers," "Rattlesnake's-hole," "Yankee Smashers," &c. The vicinity of the camps was in an intolerable state, and on calling the attention of the medical officer who was with me, to the danger arising from such a condition of things, he said with a sigh, "I know it all. But we can do nothing. Remember they're all volunteers, and do just as they please."

In every tent was hospitality, and a hearty welcome to all comers. Cases of champagne and claret, French *pâtés,* and the like, were piled outside the canvas walls, when there was no room for them inside. In the middle of these excited gatherings I felt like a man in the full possession of his senses coming in late to a wine party. "Won't you drink with me, sir, to the—(something awful)—of Lincoln and all Yankees?" "No! if you'll be good enough to excuse me." "Well, I think you're the only Englishman who won't." Our Carolinians are very fine fellows, but a little given to the Boabdil style—hectoring after a cavalier fashion, which they fondly believe to be theirs by hereditary right. They assume that the British crown rests on a cotton bale, as the Lord Chancellor sits on a pack of wool.

After a long and tiresome promenade in the dust, heat, and fine sand, through the tents, our party returned to the beach, where we took boat, and pushed off for Fort Sumter. The Confederate flag rose above the walls. On near approach the marks of the shot against the *pain coupé,* and the embrasures near the salient were visible enough; but the damage done to the hard brickwork was trifling, except at the angles: the edges of the parapets were ragged and pock-marked, and the quay wall was rifted here and there by shot; but no injury of a kind to render

[61]

the work untenable could be made out. The greatest damage inflicted was, no doubt, the burning of the barracks, which were culpably erected inside the fort, close to the flank wall facing Cumming's Point.

As the boat touched the quay of the fort, a tall, powerful-looking man came through the shattered gateway, and with uneven steps strode over the rubbish towards a skiff which was waiting to receive him, and into which he jumped and rowed off. Recognising one of my companions as he passed our boat, he suddenly stood up, and with a leap and a scramble tumbled in among us, to the imminent danger of upsetting the party. Our new friend was dressed in the blue frock coat of a civilian, round which he had tied a red silk sash—his waistbelt supported a straight sword, something like those worn with Court dress. His muscular neck was surrounded with a loosely-fastened silk hand-kerchief; and wild masses of black hair, tinged with grey, fell from under a civilian's hat over his collar; his unstrapped trousers were gathered up high on his legs, displaying ample boots, garnished with formidable brass spurs. But his face was not one to be forgotten—a straight, broad brow, from which the hair rose up like the vegetation on a riverbank, beetling black eyebrows—a mouth coarse and grim, yet full of power, a square jaw—a thick argumentative nose—a new growth of scrubby beard and moustache—these were relieved by eyes of wonderful depth and light, such as I never saw before but in the head of a wild beast. If you look some day when the sun is not too bright into the eye of the Bengal tiger, in the Regent's Park, as the keeper is coming round, you will form some notion of the expression I mean. It was flashing, fierce, yet calm—with a well of fire burning behind and spouting through it, an eye pitiless in anger, which now and then sought to conceal its expression beneath half-closed lids, and then burst out with an angry glare, as if disdaining concealment.

This was none other than Louis T. Wigfall, Colonel (then

of his own creation) in the Confederate Army, and Senator from Texas in the United States—a good type of the men whom the institutions of the country produce or throw off—a remarkable man, noted for his ready, natural eloquence; his exceeding ability as a quick, bitter debater; the acerbity of his taunts; and his readiness for personal encounter. To the last he stood in his place in the Senate at Washington, when nearly every other Southern man had seceded, lashing with a venomous and instant tongue, and covering with insults, ridicule, and abuse such men as Mr. Chandler, of Michigan, and other Republicans: never missing a sitting of the House, and seeking out adversaries in the bar rooms or the gambling tables. The other day, when the fire against Sumter was at its height, and the fort, in flames, was reduced almost to silence, a small boat put off from the shore, and steered through the shot and the splashing waters right for the walls. It bore the Colonel and a Negro oarsman. Holding up a white handkerchief on the end of his sword, Wigfall landed on the quay, clambered through an embrasure, and presented himself before the astonished Federals with a proposal to surrender, quite unauthorised, and "on his own hook," which led to the final capitulation of Major Anderson.

I am sorry to say, our distinguished friend had just been paying his respects *sans bornes* to Bacchus or Bourbon, for he was decidedly unsteady in his gait and thick in speech; but his head was quite clear, and he was determined I should know all about his exploit. Major Whiting desired to show me round the works, but he had no chance. "Here is where I got in," quoth Colonel Wigfall. "I found a Yankee standing here by the traverse, out of the way of our shot. He was pretty well scared when he saw me, but I told him not to be alarmed, but to take me to the officers. There they were, huddled up in that corner behind the brick-work, for our shells were tumbling into the yard, and bursting like—" &c. (The Colonel used strong illustrations and strange expletives in narrative.) Major Whiting shook his military head,

[63]

and said something uncivil to me, in private, in reference to volunteer colonels and the like, which give him relief; whilst the martial Senator—I forgot to say that he has the name, particularly in the North, of having killed more than half a dozen men in duels—(I had an escape of being another)—conducted me through the casemates with uneven steps, stopping at every traverse to expatiate on some phase of his personal experiences, with his sword dangling between his legs, and spurs involved in rubbish and soldiers' blankets.

Chapter XV

April 18th. Second and third editions and extras! News of Secession meetings and of Union meetings! Every one is filled with indignation against the city of New York, on account of the way in which the news of the reduction of Fort Sumter has been received there. New England has acted just as was expected, but better things were anticipated on the part of the Empire city. There is no sign of shrinking from a contest: on the contrary, the Carolinians are full of eagerness to test their force in the field. "Let them come!" is their boastful *mot d'ordre*.

The anger which is reported to exist in the North only adds to the fury and animosity of the Carolinians. They are determined now to act on their sovereign rights as a state, cost what it may, and uphold the Ordinance of Secession. The answers of several State Governors to President Lincoln's demand for troops have delighted our friends. Beriah Magoffin, of Kentucky, declares he won't give any men for such a wicked purpose; and another gubernatorial dignitary laconically replied to the demand for so many thousand soldiers, "Nary one." Letcher, Governor of Virginia, has also sent a refusal. From the North comes news of mass meetings, of hauling down Secession colours, mobbing Secession papers, of military bodies turning out, banks subscribing and lending.

Jefferson Davis has met President Lincoln's proclamation by a counter manifesto, issuing letters of marque and reprisal—on all sides preparations for war. The Southern agents are buying steamers, but they fear the Northern states will use their Navy to enforce a blockade, which is much dreaded, as it will cut off supplies and injure the commerce on which they so much depend. Assuredly Mr. Seward cannot know anything of the feeling of the South, or he would not be so confident as he was that all would blow over, and that the States, deprived of the care and fostering influences of the general Government, would get tired of their Secession ordinances, and of their experiment to maintain a national life, so that the United States will be re-established before long.

I went over and saw General Beauregard at his quarters. He was busy with papers, orderlies, and dispatches, and the outer room was crowded with officers. His present task, he told me, was to put Sumter in a state of defence, and to disarm the works bearing on it, so as to get their fire directed on the harbour approaches as "the North in its madness" might attempt a naval attack on Charleston. His manner of transacting business is clear and rapid. Two vases filled with flowers on his table, flanking his maps and plans; and a little hand bouquet of roses, geraniums, and scented flowers lay on a letter which he was writing as I came in, by way of paper weight. He offered me every assistance and facility, relying, of course, on my strict observance of a neutral's duty. I reminded him once more, that as the representative of an English journal, it would be my duty to write freely to England respecting what I saw; and that I must not be held accountable if, on the return of my letters to America, a month after they were written, it was found they contained information to which circumstances might attach an objectionable character. The General said, "I quite understand you. We must take our chance of that, and leave you to exercise your discretion."

In the evening I dined with our excellent Consul, Mr. Bunch, who had a small and very agreeable party to meet me. One very venerable old gentleman named Huger (pronounced as Hugeē), was particularly interesting in appearance and conversation. He formerly held some official appointment under the Federal Government, but had gone out with his state, and had been confirmed in his appointment by the Confederate Government. Still he was not happy at the prospect before him or his country. "I have lived too long," he exclaimed; "I should have died ere these evil days arrived." What thoughts, indeed, must have troubled his mind when he reflected that his country was but little older than himself; for he was one who had shaken hands with the framers of the Declaration of Independence. But though the tears rolled down his cheeks when he spoke of the prospect of civil war, there was no symptom of apprehension for the result, or indeed of any regret for the contest, which he regarded as the natural consequence of the insults, injustice, and aggression of the North against Southern rights.

Chapter XVI

———————•◦•◦•———————

April 19th. I again called on General Beauregard, and had a few moments' conversation with him. He told me that an immense deal depended on Virginia, and that as yet the action of the people in that State had not been as prompt as might have been hoped, for the President's proclamation was a declaration of war against the South, in which all would be ultimately involved. He is going to Montgomery to confer with Mr. Jefferson Davis. I have no doubt there is to be some movement made in Virginia. Whiting is under orders to repair there, and he hinted that he had a task of no common nicety and difficulty to perform. He is to visit the forts which had been seized on the coast of North Carolina, and probably will have a look at Portsmouth. It is incredible that the Federal authorities should have neglected to secure this place.

Later I visited the Governor of the State, Mr. Pickens, to whom I was conducted by Colonel Lucas, his aide-de-camp. His palace was a very humble shed-like edifice with large rooms, on the doors of which were pasted pieces of paper with sundry high-reading inscriptions, such as "Adjutant General's Dept.," "Quartermaster-General's Dept.," "Attorney-General of State," &c., and through the doorways could be seen men in uniform, and grave, earnest people busy at their desks with pen, ink, paper, tobacco, and spittoons. The governor, a stout man, of a big head, and a large important-looking face, with watery eyes and flabby features, was seated in a barrack-like room, furnished in the

[67]

plainest way and decorated by the inevitable portrait of George Washington, close to which was the "Ordinance of Secession of the State of South Carolina" of last year.

Governor Pickens is considerably laughed at by his subjects, and I was amused by a little middy, who described with much unction the Governor's alarm on his visit to Fort Pickens, when he was told that there were a number of live shells and a quantity of powder still in the place. He is said to have commenced one of his speeches with "Born insensible to fear," &c. To me the governor was very courteous, but I confess the heat of the day did not dispose me to listen with due attention to a lecture on political economy with which he favoured me. I was told, however, that he had practised with success on the late Czar when he was the United States Minister to St. Petersburg, and that he does not suffer his immediate staff to escape from having their minds improved on the relations of capital to labour, and on the vicious condition of capital and labour in the North.

"In the North, then, you will perceive, Mr. Russell, they have maximised the hostile condition of opposed interests in the accumulation of capital and in the employment of labour, whilst we in the South, by the peculiar excellence of our domestic institution, have minimised their opposition and maximised the identity of interest by the investment of capital in the labourer himself," and so on, or something like it. I could not help remarking it struck me there was "another difference betwixt the North and South which he had overlooked—the capital of the North is represented by gold, silver, notes, and other exponents, which are good all the world over and are recognised as such; your capital has no power of locomotion and ceases to exist the moment it crosses a geographical line." "That remark, sir," said the Governor, "requires that I should call your attention to the fundamental principles on which the abstract idea of capital should be formed. In order to clear the ground, let us first inquire into the soundness of the ideas put forward by your Adam Smith"—I

[68]

had to look at my watch and to promise I would come back to be illuminated on some other occasion, and hurried off to keep an engagement with myself to write letters by the next mail.

April 20th. I visited the editors of the *Charleston Mercury* and the *Charleston Courier* today at their offices. The Rhett family have been active agitators for Secession, and it is said they are not over-well pleased with Jefferson Davis for neglecting their claims to office. The elder, a pompous, hard, ambitious man, possesses ability. He is fond of alluding to his English connections and predilections, and is intolerant of New England to the last degree. I received from him, ere I left, a pamphlet on his life, career, and services.

I called on several of the leading merchants and bankers, such as Mr. Rose, Mr. Muir, Mr. Trenholm, and others. With all it was the same story. Their young men were off to the wars—no business doing. In one office I saw an announcement of a company for a direct communication by steamers between a southern port and Europe. "When do you expect that line to be opened?" I asked. "The United States' cruisers will surely interfere with it." "Why, I expect, sir," replied the merchant, "that if those miserable Yankees try to blockade us, and keep you from our cotton, you'll just send their ships to the bottom and acknowledge us. That will be before autumn, I think." It was in vain I assured him he would be disappointed. "Look out there," he said, pointing to the wharf, on which were piled some cotton bales; "there's the key will open all our ports, and put us into John Bull's strong box as well."

Chapter XVII

April 22nd. Today was fixed for the visit to Mr. Pringle's plantation, which lies above Georgetown near the Peedee River. Our party, which consisted of Mr. Mitchell, an eminent lawyer of Charleston, Colonel Reed, a neighbouring planter, Mr. Ward of New York, our host, and myself, were on board the Georgetown steamer at seven o'clock, A.M., and started with a quantity of commissariat stores, ammunition, and the like, for the use of the troops quartered along the coast. At that early hour invitations to the "bar" were not uncommon, where the news was discussed by long-legged, grave, sallow men. There was a good deal of joking about "old Abe Lincoln's paper blockade," and the report that the Government had ordered their cruisers to treat the crew of Confederate privateers as "pirates" provoked derisive and menacing comments.

A civil war and persecution have already commenced. "Suspected Abolitionists" are ill-treated in the South and "suspected Secessionists" are mobbed and beaten in the North. The news of the attack on the 6th Massachusetts, and the Pennsylvania regiment, by the mob in Baltimore, has been received with great delight; but some long-headed people say that it will only expose Baltimore and Maryland to the full force of the Northern States.

It was five o'clock before we reached our planter's house—White House Plantation. My small luggage was carried into my room by an old Negro in livery, who took great pains to assure me of my perfect welcome, and who turned out to be a most excellent valet. A low room hung with coloured mezzotints, windows covered with creepers, and an old-fashioned bedstead and quaint chairs, lodged me sumptuously; and after such toilette as was considered necessary by our host for a bachelor's party, we sat down to an excellent dinner, cooked by Negroes and served by Negroes, and aided by claret mellowed in Carolinian suns, and by Madeira brought down stairs cautiously, as in the days of Horace and Maecenas, from the cellar between the attic and the thatched roof.

Our party was increased by a neighboring planter, and after dinner the conversation returned to the old channel—all the frogs praying for a king—anyhow a prince—to rule over them. Our good host is anxious to get away to Europe where his wife and children are, and all he fears is being mobbed at New York, where Southerners are exposed to insult, though they may get off better in that respect than Black Republicans would down South. Some of our guests talked of the duels, and of famous hands with the pistol in these parts. The conversation had altogether very much the tone which would have probably characterized the talk of a group of Tory Irish gentlemen over their wine some sixty years ago, and very pleasant it was. Not a man—no, not one—will ever join the Union again! "Thank God!" they say, "we are freed from that tyranny at last."

April 23rd. The Negroes had but little to occupy them now. The children of both sexes, scantily clad, were fishing in the canals and stagnant waters, pulling out horrible-looking little catfish. They were so shy that they generally fled at our approach. The men and women were apathetic, neither seeking nor shunning us, and I found that their master knew nothing about them. It is only the servants engaged in household duties who are at all on familiar terms with their masters.

As the *Nina* starts down the river on her return voyage from Georgetown tonight, and Charleston Harbour may be blockaded at any time, I resolve to leave by her, in spite of many invitations and pressure from neighbouring planters.

Chapter XVIII

————▸◆◂————

April 24th. In the morning we found ourselves in chopping little seaway for which the *Nina* was particularly unsuited, laden as she was with provisions and produce. Eyes and glasses anxiously straining seawards for any trace of the blockading vessels. Every sail scrutinised, but no "Stars and Stripes" visible.

At three o'clock P.M., ran into Charleston harbour, and landed soon afterwards.

I saw General Beauregard in the evening; he was very lively and in good spirits, though he admitted he was rather surprised by the spirit displayed in the North. "A good deal of it is got up, however," he said, "and belongs to that washy sort of enthusiasm which is promoted by their lecturing and spouting." Beauregard is very proud of his personal strength, which for his slight frame is said to be very extraordinary, and he seemed to insist on it that the Southern men had more physical strength, owing to their mode of life and their education than their Northern "brethren." In the evening held a sort of *tabaks consilium* in the hotel, where a number of officers—Manning, Lucas, Chesnut, Calhoun, &c.— discoursed of the affairs of the nation. All my friends, except Trescot, I think were elated at the prospect of hostilities with the North, and overjoyed that a South Carolina regiment had already set out for the frontiers of Virginia.

April 25th. Sent off my letters by an English gentleman, who was taking dispatches from Mr. Bunch to Lord Lyons, as the post office is becoming a dangerous institution. We hear of letters being tampered with on both sides. Adams's Express Company, which acts as a sort of express post under certain conditions, is more trustworthy; but it is doubtful how long communications will be permitted to exist between the two hostile nations, as they may now be considered.

Dined with Mr. Petigru, who had most kindly postponed his dinner party till my return from the plantations, and met there General Beauregard, Judge King, and others, among whom, distinguished for their *esprit* and accomplishments, were Mrs. King and Mrs. Carson, daughters of my host. The dislike, which seems innate, to New England is universal, and varies only in the form of its expression. It is quite true Mr. Petigru is a decided Unionist, but he is the sole specimen of the genus in Charleston, and he is tolerated on account of his rarity. As the witty, pleasant old man trots down the street, utterly unconscious of the world around him, he is pointed out proudly by the Carolinians as an instance of forbearance on their part, and as a proof at the same time of popular unanimity of sentiment.

General Beauregard is apprehensive of an attack by the Northern "fanatics" before the South is prepared, and he considers they will carry out coercive measures most rigorously. He dreads the cutting of the levees, or high artificial works, raised along the whole course of the Mississippi, for many hundreds of miles above New Orleans, which the Federals may resort to in order to drown the plantations and ruin the planters.

We had a good-humoured argument in the evening about the ethics of burning the Norfolk Navy Yard. The Southerners consider the appropriation of the arms, moneys, and stores of the United States as rightful acts, inasmuch as they represent, according to them, their contribution, or a portion of it, to the national stock in trade. When a State goes out of the Union she should be permitted to carry her forts, armaments, arsenals, &c., along with her, and it was the property of Virginia at Norfolk.

April 26th. On the move again. Took our places in the

Charleston and Savannah Railway for Pocotaligo, which is the station for Barnwell Island. Our fellow-passengers were all full of politics—the pretty women being the fiercest of all—no! At least the good-looking were the most bitterly patriotic, as if they hoped to talk themselves into husbands by the most unfeminine expressions towards the Yankees.

The country is a dead flat, perforated by rivers and water-courses, over which the rail is carried on long and lofty trestle-work. But for the fine trees, the magnolias and live oak, the land-scape would be unbearably hideous, for there are none of the quaint, cleanly, delightful villages of Holland to relieve the monotonous level of rice swamps and wastes of land and water and mud. At the humble little stations there were invariably groups of horsemen waiting under the trees, and ladies with their black nurses and servants who had driven over in the odd-look-ing, old-fashioned vehicles which were drawn up in the shade. Those who were going on a long journey, aware of the utter barrenness of the land, took with them a viaticum and bottles of milk. The nurses and slaves squatted down by their side in the train, on perfectly well-understood terms. No one objected to their presence—on the contrary, the passengers treated them with a certain sort of special consideration, and they were on the happiest terms with their charges, some of which were in the absorbent condition of life, and dived their little white faces against the tawny bosom of their nurses with anything but re-luctance.

The train stopped, at 12:20, at Pocotaligo; and there we found Mr. Trescot and a couple of neighbouring planters, famous as fishers for "drum," of which more by-and-by.

Got into Trescot's gig, and plunged into a shady lane with woods on each side, through which we drove for some distance. The country, on each side and beyond, perfectly flat—all rice lands—few houses visible—scarcely a human being on the road—drove six or seven miles without meeting a soul. After a couple of hours or so, I should think, the gig turned up by an open gateway on a path or road made through a waste of rich black mud, "glorious for rice," and landed us at the door of a planter, Mr. Heyward, who came out and gave us a most hearty welcome, in the true Southern style. His house is charming, surrounded with trees, and covered with roses and creepers, through which birds and butterflies are flying. Mr. Heyward took it as a matter of course that we stopped to dinner, which we were by no means disinclined to do, as the day was hot, the road was dusty, and his reception frank and kindly. A fine specimen of the planter man; and, minus his broad-brimmed straw hat and loose clothing, not a bad representative of an English squire at home.

Chapter XIX

April 27th. Mrs. Trescot, it seems, spent part of her night in attendance on a young gentleman of colour, who was introduced into the world in a state of servitude by his poor chattel of a mother. Such kindly acts as these are more common than we may suppose; and it would be unfair to put a strict or unfair construction on the motives of slave owners in paying such attention to their property. Indeed, as Mrs. Trescot says, "When people talk of my having so many slaves, I always tell them it is the slaves who own me. Morning, noon, and night, I'm obliged to look after them, to doctor them, and attend to them in every way."

The planter's house is quite new, and was built by himself; the principal material being wood, and most of the work being done by his own Negroes. Such work as windowsashes and panelings, however, was executed in Charleston. A pretty garden runs at the back, and from the windows there are wide stretches of cotton fields visible, and glimpses of the river to be seen.

After breakfast our little party repaired to the river-side and sat under the shade of some noble trees waiting for the boat which was to bear us to the fishing grounds. The wind blew up stream, running with the tide, and we strained our eyes in vain for the boat. The river is here nearly a mile across—a noble estuary rather—with low banks lined with forests, into which the axe has made deep forays and clearings for cotton fields.

It would have astonished a stray English traveller, if, penetrating the shade, he had heard in such an out-of-the-way place familiar names and things spoken of by the three lazy persons who were stretched out—cigar in mouth—on the ant-haunted trunks which lay prostrate by the seashore. Mr. Trescot spent some time in London as *attaché* to the United States Legation, was a club man, and had a large circle of acquaintance among the young men about town, of whom he remembered many anecdotes and peculiarities, and little adventures. Since that time he was Under-Secretary of State in Mr. Buchanan's administration, and went out with Secession. He is the author of a very agreeable book on a dry subject, *The History of American Diplomacy,* which is curious enough as an unconscious exposition of the anti-British jealousies, and even antipathies, which have animated American statesmen since they were created.

April 28th. The church is a long way off, only available by a boat and then a drive in a carriage. In the morning a child brings in my water and boots—an intelligent, curly-headed creature, dressed in a sort of sack, without any particular waist, barefooted. I imagined it was a boy till it told me it was a girl. I asked if she was going to church, which seemed to puzzle her exceedingly; but she told me finally she would hear prayers from "uncle" in one of the cottages. The use of the words "uncle" and "aunt" for old people is very general. Is it because they have no fathers and mothers? In the course of the day, the child, who was fourteen or fifteen years of age, asked me "whether I would not buy her. She could wash and sew very well, and she thought missus wouldn't want much for her." The object she had in view leaked out at last. It was a desire to see the glories of Beaufort, of which she had heard from the fishermen; and she seemed quite wonderstruck when she was informed I did not live there, and had never seen it. She had never been outside the plantation in her life.

In the afternoon I took a short drive "to see a tree," which was not very remarkable, and looked in at the Negro quarters and the cotton mill. The old Negroes were mostly indoors, and came shambling out to the doors of their wooden cottages, making clumsy bows at our approach, but not expressing any interest or pleasure at the sight of their master and the strangers. They were shabbily clad; in tattered clothes, bad straw hats and felt bonnets, and broken shoes. The latter are expensive articles, and Negroes cannot dig without them. Trescot sighed as he spoke of the increase of price since the troubles broke out.

The huts stand in a row, like a street, each detached, with a poultry-house of rude planks behind it. The mutilations which the poultry undergo for the sake of distinction are striking. Some are deprived of a claw, others have the wattles cut, and tails and wings suffer in all ways. No attempt at any drainage or any convenience existed near them, and the same remark applies to very good houses of white people in the South. Heaps of oystershells, broken crockery, old shoes, rags, and feathers were found near each hut. The huts were all alike windowless, and the apertures, intended to be glazed some fine day, were generally filled up with a deal board. The roofs were shingle, and the whitewash which had once given the settlement an air of cleanliness was now only to be traced by patches which had escaped the action of the rain. I observed that many of the doors were fastened by a padlock and chain outside. "Why is that?" "The owners have gone out, and honesty is not a virtue they have towards each other. They would find their things stolen if they did not lock their doors." Mrs. Trescot, however, insisted on it that nothing could exceed the probity of the slaves in the house, except in regard to sweet things, sugar and the like; but money and jewels were quite safe. It is obvious that some reason must exist for this regard to the distinctions twixt *meum* and *tuum* in the case of masters and mistresses, when it does not guide their conduct towards each other, and I think it might easily be found in the fact that the Negroes could scarcely take money without detection. Jewels and jewellery would be of little value to them; they could not wear them, could not part with them. The system has made the white population a police against the black race, and the punishment is not only sure but grievous, such things as they can steal from each other are to be so readily traced.

On our return to the house, I found that Mr. Edmund Rhett, one of the active and influential political family of that name, had called—a very intelligent and agreeable gentleman, but one of the most ultra and violent speakers against the Yankees I have yet heard. He declared there were few persons in South Carolina who would not sooner ask Great Britain to take back the State than submit to the triumph of the Yankees. "We are an agricultural people, pursuing our own system, and working out our own destiny, breeding up women and men with some other purpose than to make them vulgar, fanatical, cheating Yankees— hypocritical, if as women they pretend to real virtue; and lying, if as men they pretend to be honest. We have gentlemen and gentlewomen in your sense of it. We have a system which enables us to reap the fruits of the earth by a race which we save from barbarism in restoring them to their real place in the world as labourers, whilst we are enabled to cultivate the arts, the graces, and accomplishments of life, to develop science, to apply ourselves to the duties of government, and to understand the affairs of the country."

This is a very common line of remark here. The Southerners also take pride to themselves, and not unjustly, for their wisdom in keeping in Congress those men who have proved themselves useful and capable. "We do not," they say, "cast able men aside at the caprices of a mob, or in obedience to some low party intrigue, and hence we are sure of the best men, and are served by gentlemen conversant with public affairs, far superior in every way to the ignorant clowns who are sent to Congress by the North. Look at the fellows who are sent out by Lincoln to insult foreign courts by their presence." I said that I understood Mr. Adams and Mr. Dayton were very respectable gentlemen, but I did not receive any sympathy; in fact, a neutral who attempts to moderate the violence of either side is very like an ice between two hot plates. Mr. Rhett is also persuaded that the Lord Chancellor sits on a cotton-bale. "You must recognise us, sir, before the end of October."

Chapter XX

———————▶◀▷◀———————

April 20th. This morning up at 6:00 A.M., bade farewell to our hostess and Barnwell Island, and proceeded with Trescot back to the Pocotaligo station, which we reached at 12:20. The country through which we passed was flat and flooded as usual, and the rail passed over dark deep rivers on lofty trestle-work, by pine wood and dogwood tree, by the green plantation clearing, with mud bank, dyke, and tiny canal mile by mile, the train stopping for the usual freight of ladies, and Negro nurses, and young planters, all very much of the same class, till at 3 o'clock

P.M., the cars rattled up alongside a large shed, and we were told we had arrived at Savannah.

Here was waiting for me Mr. Charles Green, who had already claimed me and my friend as his guests. The drive through such portion of Savannah as lay between the terminus and Mr. Green's house, soon satisfied my eyes that it had two peculiarities. In the first place, it had the deepest sand in the streets I have ever seen; and next, the streets wer composed of the most odd, quaint, green-windowed, many-coloured little houses I ever beheld, with an odd population of lean, sallow, ill-dressed unwholesome-looking whites, lounging about the exchanges and corners, and a busy, well-clad, gaily-attired race of Negroes, working their way through piles of children, under the shade of the trees which bordered all the streets. The fringe of green, and the height attained by the live oak, Pride of India, and magnolia, give a delicious freshness and novelty to the streets of Savannah, which is increased by the great number of squares and openings covered with something like sward, fenced round by white rail, and embellished with noble trees to be seen at every few hundred yards. It is difficult to believe you are in the midst of a city, and I was repeatedly reminded of the environs of a large Indian cantonment—the same kind of churches and detached houses, with their plantations and gardens not unlike. The wealthier classes, however, have houses of the New York Fifth Avenue character: one of the best of these, a handsome mansion of rich red sandstone, belonged to my host, who, coming out from England many years ago, raised himself by industry and intelligence to the position of one of the first merchants in Savannah. Italian statuary graced the hall; finely carved tables and furniture, stained glass, and pictures from Europe set forth the sitting-rooms; and the luxury of bathrooms and a supply of cold fresh water, rendered it an exception to the general run of Southern edifices. Mr. Green drove me through the town, which impressed me more than ever with its peculiar character. We visited Brigadier-General Lawton, who is charged with the defences of the place against

Balloon view of Washington, May, 1861

New Orleans around the time of Russell's visit

Portrait of Lincoln by Matthew Brady

The Capitol on the morning of Lincoln's inauguration, March 4, 1861

Lincoln's inaugural procession, 1861

Woodcut of Confederate batteries bombarding Fort Sumter, April 13, 1861

Portrait of Jefferson Davis, after a Brady photograph

Contemporary woodcut of the Battle of Bull Run, July 21, 1861

the expected Yankees, and found him just setting out to inspect a band of volunteers, whose drums we heard in the distance, and whose bayonets were gleaming through the clouds of Savannah dust, close to the statue erected to the memory of one Pulaski, a Pole, who was mortally wounded in the unsuccessful defence of the city against the British in the War of Independence. He turned back and led us into his house. The hall was filled with little round rolls of flannel. "These," said he, "are cartridges for cannon of various calibres, made by the ladies of Mrs. Lawton's 'cartridge class.'" There were more cartridges in the back parlour, so that the house was not quite a safe place to smoke a cigar in. The General has been in the United States Army, and has now come forward to head the people of this State in their resistance to the Yankees.

We took a stroll in the park, and I learned the news of the last few days. The people of the South, I find, are delighted at a snubbing which Mr. Seward has given to Governor Hicks of Maryland, for recommending the arbitration of Lord Lyons, and he is stated to have informed Governor Hicks that "our troubles could not be referred to foreign arbitration, least of all to that of the representatives of a European monarchy." The most terrible accounts are given of the state of things in Washington. Mr. Lincoln consoles himself for his miseries by drinking. Mr. Seward follows suit. The White House and capital are full of drunken border ruffians, headed by one Jim Lane of Kansas. But, on the other hand, the Yankees, under one Butler, a Massachusetts lawyer, have arrived at Annapolis, in Maryland, secured the *Constitution* man-of-war, and are raising masses of men for the invasion of the South all over the States. The most important thing, as it strikes me, is the proclamation of the Governor of Georgia, forbidding citizens to pay any money on account of debts due to Northerners, till the end of the war. General Robert E. Lee has been named Commander-in-Chief of the Forces of the Commonwealth of Virginia, and troops are flocking to that State from Alabama and other States. Governor Ellis has called out thirty thousand volunteers in North Carolina, and Governor Rector of Arkansas has seized the United States military stores at Napoleon. There is a rumor that Fort Pickens has been taken also, but it is very probably untrue. In Texas and Arkansas the United States regulars have not made an attempt to defend any of the forts.

April 30th. At 1:30 P.M., a small party started from Mr. Green's to visit the cemetery of Bonadventure, to which every visitor to Savannah must pay his pilgrimage; *difficiles aditus primos habet*—a deep sandy road which strains the horses and the carriages; but at last "the shell road" is reached—a highway several miles long, consisting of oyster-shells—the pride of Savannah, which eats as many oysters as it can to add to the length of this wonderful road. There is no stone in the whole of the vast alluvial ranges of South Carolina and maritime Georgia, and the only substance available for making a road is the oyster-shell. There is a tollgate at each end to aid the oyster-shells.

In the evening Mr. Green gave a dinner to some very agreeable people, Mr. Ward, the Chinese Minister—(who tried, by-the-by, to make it appear that his wooden box was the Pekin State carriage for distinguished foreigners)—Mr. Locke, the clever and intelligent editor of the principal journal in Savannah, Brigadier Lawton, one of the Judges, a Britisher, owner of the once renowned *America* which, under the name of *Camilla,* was now lying in the river (not perhaps without reference to a little speculation in running the blockade, hourly expected), Mr. Ward, and Commodore Tatnall, so well known to us in England for his gallant conduct in the Peiho affair, when he offered and gave our vessels aid, though a neutral, and uttered the exclamation in doing so,—in his dispatch at all events,—"that blood was thicker than water."

The Georgians are not quite so vehement as the South Carolinians in their hate of the Northerners; but they are scarcely less determined to fight President Lincoln and all his men.

Chapter XXI

———— ◆◀◄ ————

May Day. Not unworthy of the best effort of English fine weather before the change in the calendar robbed the poets of twelve days, but still a little warm for choice. When we got down to the river-side I found Commodore Tatnall and Brigadier Lawton in full uniform waiting for me.

I have been trying to persuade my friends here they will find very few Englishmen willing to take letters of marque and reprisal.

The steamer which was waiting to receive us had the Confederate flag flying, and Commodore Tatnall, pointing to a young officer in a naval uniform, told me he had just "come over from the other side," and that he had pressed hard to be allowed to hoist a Commodore or flag-officer's ensign in honour of the visit and of the occasion. I was much interested in the fine white-headed, blue-eyed, ruddy-cheeked old man—who suddenly found himself blown into the air by a great political explosion, and in doubt and wonderment was floating to shore, under a strange flag in unknown waters. He was full of anecdote too, as to strange flags in distant waters and well-known names. The gentry of Savannah had a sort of Celtic feeling towards him in regard of his old name, and seemed determined to support him.

He has served the Stars and Stripes for three-fourths of a long life—his friends are in the North, his wife's kindred are there, and so are all his best association—but his State has gone out. How could he fight against the country that gave him birth! The

United States is no country, in the sense we understand the words. It is a corporation or a body corporate for certain purposes, and a man might as well call himself a native of the common council of the city of London, or a native of the Swiss Diet, in the estimation of our Americans, as say he is a citizen of the United States; though it answers very well to say so when he is abroad, or for purposes of a legal character.

When I was venturing to point out to General Lawton the weakness of Fort Pulaski, placed as it is in low land, accessible to boats, and quite open enough for approaches from the city side, he said, "Oh, that is true enough. All our seacoast works are liable to that remark, but the Commodore will take care of the Yankees at sea, and we shall manage them on land." These people all make a mistake in referring to the events of the old war. "We beat off the British fleet at Charleston by the militia—ergo, we'll sink the Yankees now." They do not understand the nature of the new shell and heavy vertical fire, or the effect of projectiles from great distances falling into open works. The Commodore afterwards, smiling, remarked, "I have no fleet. Long before the Southern Confederacy has a fleet that can cope with the Stars and Stripes, my bones will be white in the grave."

May 3rd. I bade good-by to Mr. Green, who with several of his friends came down to see me off, at the terminus or depot of the Central Railway, on my way to Montgomery—and looking my last on Savannah, its squares and leafy streets, its churches, and institutes with a feeling of regret that I could not see more of them, and that I was forced to be content with the outer aspect of the public buildings.

From Savannah to Macon, 191 miles, the road passes through level country only partially cleared. That is, there are patches of forest still intruding on the green fields, where the jagged black teeth of the destroyed trees rise from above the maize and cotton. There were but few Negroes visible at work, nor did the land appear rich, but I was told the rail was laid along the most barren part of the country.

Among the passengers to whom I was introduced was the Bishop of Georgia, the Rev. Mr. Elliott, a man of exceeding fine presence, of great stature, and handsome face, with a manner easy and graceful, but we got on the unfortunate subject of slavery, and I rather revolted at hearing a Christian prelate advocating the institution on scriptural grounds.

This application of Biblical sanction and ordinance as the basis of slavery was not new to me, though it is not much known at the other side of the Atlantic. I had read in a work on slavery, that it was permitted by both the Scriptures and the Constitution of the United States, and that it must, therefore, be doubly right.

Whenever the Southern Confederacy shall achieve its independence—no matter what its resources, its allies, or its aims—it will have to stand face to face with civilised Europe on this question of slavery, and the strength which it derived from the aegis of the Constitution—"the league with the devil and covenant with Hell"—will be withered and gone.

The train halted at a snug little wood-embowered restaurant, surrounded by trellis and lattice-work, and in the midst of a pretty garden, which presented a marked contrast to the "surroundings" we had seen. The dinner, served by slaves, was good of its kind, and the charge not high. On tendering the landlord a piece of gold for payment, he looked at it with disgust, and asked, "Have you no Charleston money? No Confederate notes?" "Well, no! Why do you object to gold?" "Well, do you see, I'd rather have our own paper! I don't care to take any of the United States' gold. I don't want their stars and their eagles; I hate the sight of them." The man was quite sincere—my companion gave him notes of some South Carolina bank.

It was dark when the train reached Macon, one of the principal cities of the state. We drove to the best hotel, but the regular time for dinner-hour was over, and that for supper not yet come.

The landlord directed us to a subterranean restaurant, in which were a series of crypts closed by dirty curtains, where we made a very extraordinary repast, served by a half-clad little Negress, who watched us at the meal with great interest through the curtains—the service was of the coarsest description; thick French earthenware, the spoons of pewter, the knives and forks steel or iron, with scarce a pretext of being cleaned. On the doors were the usual warnings against pickpockets, and the customary internal police regulations and ukases. Pickpockets and gamblers abound in American cities and thrive greatly at the large hotels and the lines of railways.

Chapter XXII

May 4th. In the morning I took a drive about the city, which is loosely built in detached houses over a pretty undulating country covered with wood and fruit-trees. Many good houses of dazzling white, with bright green blinds, verandahs, and doors, stand in their own grounds or gardens. In the course of the drive I saw two or three signboards and placards announcing that "Smith & Co. advanced money on slaves, and had constant supplies of Virginian Negroes on sale or hire." These establishments were surrounded by high walls enclosing the slave-pens or large rooms, in which the slaves are kept for inspection. The train for Montgomery started at 9:45 A.M., and I had no time to stop and visit them.

It is evident we are approaching the Confederate capital, for the candidates for office begin to show, and I detected a printed testimonial in my room in the hotel.

The people are all hearty Secessionists here—the Bars and Stars are flying at the road-stations and from the pine-tops, and there are lusty cheers for Jeff Davis and the Southern Confederacy. Troops are flocking towards Virginia from the Southern States in reply to the march of volunteers from Northern States to Washington; but it is felt that the steps taken by the Federal Government to secure Baltimore have obviated any chance of successfully opposing the "Lincolnites" going through that city. There is a strong disposition on the part of the Southerners to believe they have many friends in the North, and they endeavour to attach a factious character to the actions of the Government by calling the volunteers and the war party in the North "Lincolnites," "Lincoln's Mercenaries," "Black Republicans," "Abolitionists," and the like. General Scott would, it was fondly believed, retire from the United States Army, and either remain neutral or take command under the Confederate flag, but now that it is certain he will not follow any of these courses, he is assailed in the foulest manner by the press and in private conversation. Heaven help the idol of a democracy!

At one of the junctions General Beauregard, attended by Mr. Manning, and others of his staff, got into the car, and tried to elude observation, but the conductors take great pleasure in unearthing distinguished passengers for the public, and the General was called on for a speech by the crowd of idlers. The General hates speech-making, he told me, and he had besides been bored to death at every station by similar demands. But a man must be popular or he is nothing. So, as next best thing, Governor Manning made a speech in the General's name, in which he dwelt on Southern Rights, Sumter, victory, and abolitiondom, and was carried off from the cheers of his auditors by the train in the midst of an unfinished sentence.

Towards evening, having thrown out some slight out-works

against accidental sallies of my fellow-passengers' saliva, I went to sleep, and woke up at 11 P.M. to hear we were in Montgomery. A very rickety omnibus took the party to the hotel, which was crowded to excess. The General and his friends had one room to themselves. Three gentlemen and myself were crammed into a filthy room which already contained two strangers, and as there were only three beds in the apartment it was apparent that we were intended to "double up considerably"; but after strenuous efforts, a little bribery and cajoling, we succeeded in procuring mattresses to put on the floor, which was regarded by our neighbors as proof of miserable aristocratic fastidiousness. Had it not been for the flies, the fleas would have been intolerable, but one nuisance neutralized the other. Then, as to food—nothing could be had in the hotel—but one of the waiters led us to a restaurant, where we selected from a choice bill of fare, which contained, I think, as many odd dishes as ever I saw, some unknown fishes, oyster-plants, 'possums, raccoons, frogs, and other delicacies, and, eschewing toads and the like, really made a good meal off dirty plates on a vile tablecloth, our appetites being sharpened by the best of condiments.

Colonel Pickett has returned up here, having made his escape from Washington just in time to escape arrest—travelling in disguise on foot through out-of-the-way places until he got among friends.

May 5th. Very warm, and no cold water, unless one went to the river. The hotel baths were not promising. This hotel is worse than Mill's House or Willard's. The feeding and the flies are intolerable. The house is full of Confederate Congressmen, politicians, colonels, and placemen with or without places, and a vast number of speculators, contractors, and the like, attracted by the embryo government. Among the visitors are many filibusterers, such as Henningsen, Pickett, Tochman, Wheat.* I hear a good deal about the association called the Knights of the Golden

* Since killed in action.

Circle, a Protestant association for securing the Gulf provinces and states, including—which has been largely developed by recent events—them in the Southern Confederacy, and creating them into an independent government.

May 6th. I forgot to say that yesterday before dinner I drove out with some gentlemen and the ladies of the family of Mr. George N. Sanders, once United States consul at Liverpool, now a doubtful man here, seeking some office from the Government, and accused by a portion of the press of being a Confederate spy —*Porcus de grege epicuri*—but a learned pig withal, and weather-wise, and mindful of the signs of the times, catching straws and whisking them upwards to detect the currents.

After breakfast I walked down with Senator Wigfall to the capitol of Montgomery—one of the true Athenian Yankee-ized structures of this novo-classic land, erected on a site worthy of a better fate and edifice. By an open cistern, on our way, I came upon a gentleman engaged in disposing of some living ebony carvings to a small circle, who had more curiosity than cash, for they did not at all respond to the energetic appeals of the auctioneer.

The sight was a bad preparation for an introduction to the legislative assembly of a Confederacy which rests on the institution as the cornerstone of the social and political arch which maintains it. But there they were, the legislators or conspirators, in a large room provided with benches and seats, and listening to such a sermon as a Balfour or Burley might have preached to his Covenanters—resolute and massive heads, and large frames— such men as must have a faith to inspire them.

The chaplain, a venerable old man, loudly invoked curses on the heads of the enemy, and blessings on the arms and councils of the New State. When he was done, Mr. Howell Cobb, a fat, double-chinned, mellow-eyed man, rapped with his hammer on the desk before the chair on which he sat as speaker of the assembly, and the house proceeded to business. I could fancy that, in all but garments, they were like the men who first conceived the great rebellion which led to the independence of this wonderful country—so earnest, so grave, so sober, and so vindictive.

The word "liberty" was used repeatedly in the short time allotted to the public transaction of business and the reading of documents; the Congress was anxious to get to its work, and Mr. Howell Cobb again thumped his desk and announced that the house was going into "secret session," which intimated that all persons who were not members should leave. I was introduced to what is called the floor of the house, and had a delegate's chair, and of course I moved away with the others, and with the disappointed ladies and men from the galleries, but one of the members, Mr. Rhett, I believe, said jokingly: "I think you ought to retain your seat. If the *Times* will support the South, we'll accept you as a delegate." I replied that I was afraid I could not act as a delegate to a Congress of Slave States. And, indeed, I had been much affected at the slave auction held just outside the hotel, on the steps of the public fountain, which I had witnessed on my way to the capitol. The auctioneer, who was an ill-favoured, dissipated-looking rascal, had his "article" beside him on, not in, a deal packing-case—a stout young Negro badly dressed and ill-shod, who stood with all his goods fastened in a small bundle in his hand, looking out at the small and listless gathering of men, who, whittling and chewing, had moved out from the shady side of the street as they saw the man put up.

A man in a cart, some volunteers in coarse uniform, a few Irish labourers in a long van, and four or five men in the usual black coat, satin waistcoat, and black hat, constituted the audience, whom the auctioneer addressed volubly: "A prime field-hand! Just look at him—good-natured, well-tempered; no marks, nary sign of bad about him! En-i-ne hunthered—only nine hunther-ed and fifty dol'rs for 'em! Why it's quite rad-aklous! Nine hundred and fifty dol'rs! I can't raly—That's good. Thank you, sir. Twenty-five bid—nine hun-therd and seventy-five dol'rs for this most useful hand." The price rose to one thousand dollars, at which the useful hand was knocked down to one of the black hats near me. The auctioneer and the Negro and his buyer all walked off together to settle the transaction, and the crowd moved away.

"That nigger went cheap," said one of them to a companion, as he walked towards the shade. "Yes, *Sirr!* Niggers is cheap now—that's a fact."

On my return, the Hon. W. M. Browne, Assistant Secretary of State, came to visit me—a cadet of an Irish family, who came to America some years ago, and having lost his money in land speculations, turned his pen to good account as a journalist, and gained Mr. Buchanan's patronage and support as a newspaper editor in Washington. There he became intimate with the Southern gentlemen, with whom he naturally associated in preference to the Northern members; and when they went out, he walked over along with them. He told me the Government had already received numerous—I think he said four hundred—letters from shipowners applying for letters of marque and reprisal. Many of these applications were from merchants in Boston, and other maritime cities in the New England States. He further stated that the President was determined to take the whole control of the Army, and the appointments to command in all ranks of officers into his own hands.

The press is fanning the flame on both sides: it would be difficult to say whether it or the telegraphs circulate lies most largely; but that as the papers print the telegrams they must have the palm. The Southerners are told there is a reign of terror in New York—that the 7th New York Regiment has been captured by the Baltimore people—that Abe Lincoln is always drunk—that General Lee has seized Arlington Heights, and is bombarding Washington. The New York people are regaled with similar stories from the South. The coincidence between the date of the skirmish at Lexington and the attack on the 6th

Massachusetts Regiment at Baltimore is not so remarkable as the fact that the first man who was killed at the latter place eighty-six years ago, was the direct descendant of the first of the colonists who was killed by the royal soldiery. Baltimore may do the same for the South which Lexington did for all the Colonies. Head-shaving, forcible deportations, tarring and feathering are recommended and adopted as specifics to produce conversion from erroneous opinions. The President of the United States has called into service of the Federal Government 42,000 volunteers, and increased the regular Army by 22,000 men, and the Navy by 18,000 men. If the South secedes, they ought certainly to take over with them some Yankee hotel keepers. This "Exchange" is in a frightful state—nothing but noise, dirt, drinking, wrangling.

Chapter XXIII

May 9th. Today the papers contain a proclamation by the President of the Confederate States of America, declaring a state of war between the Confederacy and the United States, and notifying the issue of letters of marque and reprisal. I went out with Mr. Wigfall in the forenoon to pay my respects to Mr. Jefferson Davis at the State Department. Mr. Seward told me that but for Jefferson Davis the Secession plot could never have been carried out. No other man of the party had the brain, or the courage and dexterity, to bring it to a successful issue. All the persons in the Southern States spoke of him with admiration, though their forms of speech and thought generally forbid them to be respectful to any one.

There before me was "Jeff Davis's State Department"—a large brick building, at the corner of a street, with a Confederate flag floating above it. The door stood open, and "gave" on a large hall white-washed, with doors plainly painted belonging to small rooms, in which was transacted the most important business, judging by the names written on sheets of paper and applied outside, denoting bureaus of the highest functions. A few clerks were passing in and out, and one or two gentlemen were on the stairs, but there was no appearance of any bustle in the building.

We walked straight upstairs to the first floor, which was surrounded by doors opening from a quadrangular platform. On one of these was written simply, "The President." Mr. Wigfall went in, and after a moment returned and said, "The President will be glad to see you; walk in, sir." When I entered, the President was engaged with four gentlemen, who were making some offer of aid to him. He was thanking them "in the name of the Government." Shaking hands with each, he saw them to the door, bowed them and Mr. Wigfall out, and turning to me said, "Mr. Russell, I am glad to welcome you here, though I fear your appearance is a symptom that our affairs are not quite prosperous," or words to that effect. He then requested me to sit down close to his own chair at his office-table, and proceeded to speak on general matters, adverting to the Crimean War and the Indian Mutiny, and asking questions about Sebastopol, The Redan, and the Siege of Lucknow.

I had an opportunity of observing the President very closely: he did not impress me as favorably as I had expected, though he is certainly a very different looking man from Mr. Lincoln. He is like a gentleman—has a slight, light figure, little exceeding middle height, and holds himself erect and straight. He was dressed in a rustic suit of slate-coloured stuff, with a black silk handkerchief round his neck; his manner is plain, and rather reserved and drastic; his head is well-formed, with a fine full forehead, square and high, covered with innumerable fine lines and wrinkles, features regular, though the cheek-bones are too high, and the jaws too hollow to be handsome; the lips are thin, flexible, and curved, the chin square, well-defined; the nose very regular, with wide nostrils; and the eyes deep set, large and full —one seems nearly blind, and is partly covered with a film, owing to excruciating attacks of neuralgia and tic. Wonderful to relate, he does not chew, and is neat and clean-looking, with hair trimmed and boots brushed. The expression of his face is anxious, he has a very haggard, care-worn, and pain-drawn look, though no trace of anything but the utmost confidence and greatest decision could be detected in his conversation. He asked me some questions respecting the route I had taken in the States.

I mentioned that I had seen great military preparations through the South, and was astonished at the alacrity with which the people sprang to arms. "Yes, sir," he remarked, and his tone of voice and manner of speech are rather remarkable for what are considered Yankee peculiarities, "in Eu-rope" (Mr. Seward also indulges in that pronunciation) "they laugh at us because of our fondness for military titles and displays. All your travellers in this country have commented on the number of generals, and colonels, and majors all over the States. But the fact is, we are a military people, and these signs of the fact were ignored. We are not less military because we have had no great standing armies. But perhaps we are the only people in the world where gentlemen go to a military academy, who do not intend to follow the profession of arms."

In the course of our conversation, I asked him to have the goodness to direct that a sort of passport or protection should be given to me, as I might possibly fall in with some guerilla leader on my way northwards, in whose eyes I might not be entitled to safe conduct. Mr. Davis said, "I shall give such instructions to the Secretary of War as shall be necessary. But, sir, you are among civilised, intelligent people who understand your position, and appreciate your character. We do not seek the sympathy of

England by unworthy means, for we respect ourselves, and we are glad to invite the scrutiny of men into our acts; as for our motives, we meet the eye of Heaven." I thought I could judge from his words that he had the highest idea of the French as soldiers, but that his feelings and associations were more identified with England, although he was quite aware of the difficulty of conquering the repugnance which exists to slavery.

Mr. Davis made no allusion to the authorities at Washington, but he asked me if I thought it was supposed in England there would be war between the two States? I answered that I was under the impression the public thought there would be no actual hostilities. "And yet you see we are driven to take up arms for the defence of our rights and liberties."

As I saw an immense mass of papers on his table, I rose and made my bow, and Mr. Davis, seeing me to the door, gave me his hand and said, "As long as you may stay among us you shall receive every facility it is in our power to afford to you, and I shall always be glad to see you." Colonel Wigfall was outside, and took me to the room of the Secretary of War, Mr. Walker, whom we found closeted with General Beauregard and two other officers in a room full of maps and plans. He is the kind of man generally represented in our types of a "Yankee"—tall, lean, straight-haired, angular, with fiery, impulsive eyes and manner— a ruminator of tobacco and a profuse spitter—a lawyer, I believe, certainly not a soldier; ardent, devoted to the cause, and confident to the last degree of its speedy success.

The news that two more States had joined the Confederacy, making ten in all, was enough to put them in good humour. "Is it not too bad these Yankees will not let us go our own way, and keep their cursed Union to themselves? If they force us to it, we may be obliged to drive them beyond the Susquehanna." Beauregard was in excellent spirits, busy measuring off miles of country with his compass, as if he were dividing empires.

From this room I proceeded to the office of Mr. Benjamin, the

Attorney-General of the Confederate States, the most brilliant perhaps of the whole of the famous Southern orators. He is a short, stout man, with a full face, olive-coloured, and most decidedly Jewish features, with the brightest large black eyes, one of which is somewhat diverse from the other, and a brisk, lively, agreeable manner, combined with much vivacity of speech and quickness of utterance. He is one of the first lawyers or advocates in the United States, and had a large practice at Washington, where his annual receipts from his profession were not less than £8,000 to £10,000 a year. But his love of the card-table rendered him a prey to older and cooler hands, who waited till the sponge was full at the end of the session, and then squeezed it to the last drop.

Mr. Benjamin is the most open, frank, and cordial of the Confederates whom I have yet met. In a few seconds he was telling me all about the course of Government with respect to privateers and letters of marque and reprisal, in order probably to ascertain what were our views in England on the subject. I observed it was likely the North would not respect their flag, and would treat their privateers as pirates. "We have an easy remedy for that. For any man under our flag whom the authorities of the United States dare to execute, we shall hang two of their people." "Suppose, Mr. Attorney-General, England, or any of the great powers which decreed the abolition of privateering, refuses to recognise your flag?" "We intend to claim, and do claim, the exercise of all the rights and privileges of an independent sovereign State, and any attempt to refuse us the full measure of those rights would be an act of hostility to our country." "But if England, for example, declared your privateers were pirates?" "As the United States never admitted the principle laid down at the Congress of Paris, neither have the Confederate States. If England thinks fit to declare privateers under our flag pirates, it would be nothing more or less than a declaration of war against us, and we must meet it as best we can." In fact,

Mr. Benjamin did not appear afraid of anything; but his confidence respecting Great Britain was based a good deal, no doubt, on his firm faith in her cotton interest and manufactures. "All this coyness about acknowledging a slave power will come right at last. We hear our commissioners have gone on to Paris, which looks as if they had met with no encouragement at London; but we are quite easy in our minds on this point at present."

Being invited to attend a levee or reception held by Mrs. Davis, the President's wife, I returned to the hotel to prepare for the occasion. On my way I passed a company of volunteers, 120 artillerymen, and three fieldpieces, on their way to the station for Virginia, followed by a crowd of "citizens" and Negroes of both sexes, cheering vociferously. The band was playing that excellent quick-step "Dixie." The men were stout, fine fellows, dressed in coarse grey tunics with yellow facings, and French caps. They were armed with smooth-bore muskets, and their knapsacks were unfit for marching, being waterproof bags slung from the shoulders. The guns had no caissons, and the shoeing of the troops was certainly deficient in soleing.

The modest villa in which the President lives is painted white —another "White House"—and stands in a small garden. The door was open. A coloured servant took in our names, and Mr. Browne presented me to Mrs. Davis, whom I could just make out in the *demi-jour* of a moderately-sized parlour, surrounded by a few ladies and gentlemen, the former in bonnets, the latter in morning dress *à la midi*. There was no affectation of state or ceremony in the reception. Mrs. Davis, whom some of her friends call "Queen Varina," is a comely, sprightly woman, verging on matronhood, of good figure and manners, well-dressed, lady-like, and clever, and she seemed a great favourite with those around her, though I did hear one of them say, "It must be very nice to be the President's wife, and be the first lady in the Confederate States." Mrs. Davis, whom the President C.S. married *en secondes noces,* exercised considerable social influence in Washington, where I met many of her friends. She was just now inclined to be angry, because the papers contained a report that a reward was offered in the North for the head of the arch rebel Jeff Davis. "They are quite capable, I believe," she said, "of such acts." There were not more than eighteen or twenty persons present, as each party came in and stayed only for a few moments, and, after a time, I made my bow and retired, receiving from Mrs. Davis an invitation to come in the evening, when I would find the President at home.

At sundown, amid great cheering, the guns in front of the State Department fired ten rounds, to announce that Tennessee and Arkansas had joined the Confederacy.

In the evening I dined with Mr. Benjamin and his brother-in-law, a gentleman of New Orleans, Colonel Wigfall coming in at the end of dinner. The New Orleans people of French descent, or "Creoles," as they call themselves, speak French in preference to English, and Mr. Benjamin's brother-in-law laboured considerably in trying to make himself understood in our vernacular. The conversation, Franco-English, very pleasant, for Mr. Benjamin is agreeable and lively. He is certain that the English law authorities must advise the Government that the blockade of the Southern ports is illegal so long as the President claims them to be ports of the United States. "At present," he said, "their paper blockade does no harm; the season for shipping cotton is over; but in October next, when the Mississippi is floating cotton by the thousands of bales, and all our wharves are full, it is inevitable that the Yankees must come to trouble with this attempt to coerce us." Mr. Benjamin walked back to the hotel with me, and we found our room full of tobacco-smoke, filibusters, and conversation, in which, as sleep was impossible, we were obliged to join. I resisted a vigorous attempt of Mr. G. N. Sanders and a friend of his to take me to visit a planter who had a beaver-dam some miles outside Montgomery.

Chapter XXIV

———— ▸◆◂ ————

May 8th. I tried to write, as I have taken my place in the steamer to Mobile tomorrow, and I was obliged to do my best in a room full of people, constantly disturbed by visitors. Early this morning, as usual, my faithful Wigfall comes in and sits by my bedside, and passing his hands through his locks, pours out his ideas with wonderful lucidity and of affectation of logic all his own. "We are a peculiar people, sir! You don't understand us, and you can't understand us, because we are known to you only by Northern writers and Northern papers, who know nothing of us themselves, or misrepresent what they do know. We are an agricultural people; we are a primitive but a civilised people. We have no cities—we don't want them. We have no literature—we don't need any yet. We have no press—we are glad of it. We do not require a press, because we go out and discuss all public questions from the stump with our people. We have no commercial marine—no navy—we don't want them. We are better without them. Your ships carry our produce, and you can protect your own vessels. We want no manufactures: we desire no trading, no mechanical or manufacturing classes. As long as we have our rice, our sugar, our tobacco, and our cotton, we can command wealth to purchase all we want from those nations with which we are in amity, and to lay up money besides. But with the Yankees we will never trade—never. Not one pound of cotton shall ever go from the South to their accursed cities; not one ounce of their steel or their manufactures shall ever cross our border." And so on. What the Senator who is preparing a bill for drafting the people into the army fears is that the North will begin active operations before the South is ready for resistance. "Give us till November to drill our men, and we shall be irresistible." He deprecates any offensive movement, and is opposed to an attack on Washington, which many journals here advocate.

Mr. Walker sent me over a letter recommending me to all officers of the Confederate States, and I received an invitation from the President to dine with him tomorrow, which I was much chagrined to be obliged to refuse. In fact, it is most important to complete my Southern tour speedily, as all mail communication will soon be suspended from the South, and the blockade effectually cuts off any communication by sea. Rails torn up, bridges broken, telegraphs down—trains searched—the war is begun.

I expressed a belief in a letter, written a few days after my arrival (March 27th), that the South would never go back into the Union. The North think that they can coerce the South, and I am not prepared to say they are right or wrong; but I am convinced that the South can only be forced back by such a conquest as that which laid Poland prostrate at the feet of Russia. It may be that such a conquest can be made by the North, but success must destroy the Union as it has been constituted in times past. A strong Government must be the logical consequence of victory, and the triumph of the South will be attended by a similar result, for which, indeed, many Southerners are very well disposed.

Neither party—if such a term can be applied to the rest of the United States, and to those States which disclaim the authority of the Federal Government—was prepared for the aggressive or resisting power of the other. Already the Confederate States perceive that they cannot carry all before them with a rush, while the North have learnt that they must put forth all their strength to make good a tithe of their lately uttered threats.

In the matter of slave-labour, South Carolina argues pretty much in the following manner: England and France (she says) require our products. In order to meet their wants, we must cultivate our soil. There is only one way of doing so. The white man cannot live on our land at certain seasons of the year; he cannot work in the manner required by the crops. He must, therefore, employ a race suited to the labour, and that is a race which will only work when it is obliged to do so. That race was imported from Africa, under the sanction of the law, by our ancestors, when we were a British colony, and it has been fostered by us, so that its increase here has been as great as that of the most flourishing people in the world. In other places, where its labour was not productive or imperatively essential, that race has been made free, sometimes with disastrous consequences to itself and to industry. But we will not make it free. We cannot do so. We hold that slavery is essential to our existence as producers of what Europe requires; nay more, we maintain it is in the abstract right in principle; and some of us go so far as to maintain that the only proper form of society, according to the law of God and the exigencies of man, is that which has slavery as its basis. As to the slave, he is happier far in his state of servitude, more civilised and religious, than he is or could be if free or in his native Africa. For this system we will fight to the end.

In the evening I paid farewell visits, and spent an hour with Mr. Toombs, who is unquestionably one of the most original, quaint, and earnest of the Southern leaders, and whose eloquence and power as a debater are greatly esteemed by his countrymen. He is something of an Anglo-maniac, and an Anglo-phobist—a combination not unusual in America—that is, he is proud of being connected with and descended from respectable English families, and admires our mixed constitution, whilst he is an enemy to what is called English policy, and is a strong pro-

[101]

slavery champion. Wigfall and he are very uneasy about the scant supply of gunpowder in the Southern States, and the difficulty of obtaining it.

In the evening had a little reunion in the bedroom as before —Mr. Wigfall, Mr. Keitt, an eminent Southern politician, Colonel Pickett, Mr. Browne, Mr. Benjamin, Mr. George Sanders, and others.

May the 9th. My faithful Wigfall was good enough to come in early, in order to show me some comments on my letters in the *New York Times.* It appears the papers are angry because I said that New York was apathetic when I landed, and they try to prove I was wrong by showing there was a "glorious outburst of Union feeling," after the news of the fall of Sumter.

Before my departure I had a little farewell leave—Mr. Toombs, Mr. Browne, Mr. Benjamin, Mr. Walker, Major Deas, Colonel Pickett, Major Calhoun, Captain Ripley, and others— who were exceedingly kind with letters of introduction and offers of service. Dined as usual on a composite dinner—Southern meat and poultry bad—at three o'clock, and at four P.M. drove down to the steep banks of the Alabama River, where the castle-like hulk of the *Southern Republic* was waiting to receive us. I bade good-by to Montgomery without regret.

Chapter XXV

———⋆◆⋆———

The vessel was nothing more than a vast wooden house, of three separate stories, floating on a pontoon which upheld the engine, with a dining-hall or saloon on the second story surrounded by sleeping-berths, and a nest of smaller rooms upstairs; on the metal roof was a "musical" instrument called a "calliope," played like a piano by keys, which acted on levers and valves, admitting steam into metal cups, where it produced the requisite notes—high, resonant, and not unpleasing at a moderate distance. It is 417 miles to Mobile, but at this season the steamer can maintain a good rate of speed, as there is very little cotton or cargo to be taken on board at the landings, and the stream is full.

The river is about 200 yards broad, and of the colour of chocolate and milk, with high, steep, wooded banks, rising so much above the surface of the stream that a person on the upper deck of the towering *Southern Republic,* cannot get a glimpse of the fields and country beyond. High banks and bluffs spring up to the height of 150 or even 200 feet above the river, the breadth of which is so uniform as to give the Alabama the appearance of a canal, only relieved by sudden bends and rapid curves. The surface is covered with masses of driftwood, whole trees, and small islands of branches. Now and then a sharp, black, fang-like projection standing stiffly in the current gives warning of a snag, but the helmsman, who commands the whole course of the river, from an elevated house amidships on the upper deck, can see these in time; and at night pine boughs are lighted in iron cressets at the bows to illuminate the water.

The captain, who was not particular whether his name was spelt Maher, or Meaher, or Meagher (*les trois se disent*), was evidently a character—perhaps a good one. One with a grey eye full of cunning and of some humour, strongly-marked features, and a very Celtic mouth of the Kerry type. He soon attached himself to me, and favoured me with some wonderful yarns, which I hope he was not foolish enough to think I believed. One relating to a wholesale destruction and massacre of Indians he narrated with evident gusto.

The management of the boat is dexterous,—as she approaches a landing-place, the helm is put hard over, to the screaming of the steam-pipe and the wild strains of "Dixie" floating out of the throats of the calliope, and as the engines are detached, one wheel is worked forward, and the other backs water, so she soon turns head up stream, and is then gently paddled up to the river bank, to which she is just kept up by steam—the plank is run ashore, and the few passengers who are coming in or out are lighted on their way by the flames of pine in an iron basket, swinging above the bow by a long pole. Then we see them vanishing into black darkness up the steps, or coming down clearer and clearer till they stand in the full blaze of the beacon which casts dark shadows on the yellow water. The air is glistening with fireflies, which dot the darkness with specks and points of flame, just as sparks fly through the embers of tinder or half-burnt paper.

Some of the landings were by far more important than others. There were some, for example, where an iron railroad was worked down the bank by windlasses for hoisting up goods; others where the Negroes half-naked leaped ashore, and rushing at piles of firewood, tossed them on board to feed the engine, which, all uncovered and open to the lower deck, lighted up the darkness by the glare from the stoke-holes, which cried forever

"Give, give!" as the Negroes ceaselessly thrust the pine-beams into their hungry maws. I could understand how easily a steamer can "burn up," and how hopeless escape would be under such circumstances. The whole framework of the vessel is of the lightest resinous pine, so raw that the turpentine oozes out through the paint; the hull is a mere shell. If the vessel once caught fire, all that could be done would be to turn her around, and run her to the bank, in the hope of holding there long enough to enable the people to escape into the trees; but if she were not near a landing, many must be lost; as the bank is steep down, the vessel cannot be run aground; and in some places the trees are in eight and ten feet of water. A few minutes would suffice to set the vessel in a blaze from stem to stern; and if there were cotton on board, the bales would burn almost like powder. The scene at each landing was repeated, with few variations, ten times till we reached Selma, 110 miles distance, at 11:30 at night.

May 10th. The cabin of one of these steamers, in the month of May, is not favourable to sleep. The wooden beams of the engines creak and scream "consumedly," and the great engines themselves throb as if they would break through their thin, pulse covers of pine,—and the whistle sounds, and the calliope shrieks out "Dixie" incessantly. So, when I was up and dressed, breakfast was over, and I had an opportunity of seeing the slaves on board, male and female, acting as stewards and stewardesses, at their morning meal, which they took with much good spirits and decorum. They were nicely dressed—clean and neat. I was forced to admit to myself that their Ashantee grandsires and grand-mothers, or their Kroo and Dahomey progenitors were certainly less comfortable and well clad, and that these slaves had other social advantages, though I could not recognise the force of the Bishop of Georgia's assertion that from slavery must come the sole hope of, and machinery for, the evangelisation of Africa. I

[105]

confess I would not give much for the influence of the stewards and stewardesses in Christionising the blacks.

Tonight, on the lower deck, amid wood faggots and barrels, a dance of Negroes was arranged by an enthusiast, who desired to show how "happy they were." That is the favorite theme of the Southerners; the gallant Captain Maher becomes quite eloquent when he points to Bully's prominent "yummy," and descants on the misery of his condition if he had been left to the precarious chances of obtaining such developments in his native land; then turns a quid, and, as if uttering some sacred refrain to the universal hymn of the South, says, "Yes, sir, they're the happiest people on the face of the airth!"

There was a fiddler, and also a banjo-player, who played uncouth music to the clumsiest of dances, which it would be insulting to compare to the worst Irish jig, and the men with immense gravity and great effusion of *sudor,* shuffled, and cut, and heeled and buckled to each other with an overwhelming solemnity, till the rum-bottle warmed them up to the lighter graces of the dance, when they became quite overpowering. "Yes, sir, jist look at them how they're enjoying it; they're the happiest people on the face of the airth." When "wooding" and firing up they don't seem to be in the possession of the same exquisite felicity.

May 11th. At early dawn the steamer went its way through a broad bay of snags bordered with driftwood, and with steam-trumpet and calliope announced its arrival at the quay of Mobile, which presented a fringe of tall warehouses, and shops alongside, over which were names indicating Scotch, Irish, English, many Spanish, German, Italian, and French owners; Captain Maher at once set off to his plantation, and we descended the stories of the walled castle to the beach, and walked on towards the "Battle House," so called from the name of its proprietor, for Mobile has not yet had its fight like New Orleans. The quays which usually, as we were told, are lined with stately hulls and a forest of masts, were deserted; although the port was not actually blockaded, there were squadrons of the United States ships at Pensacola on the east, and at New Orleans on the west.

The hotel, a fine building of the American stamp, was the seat of a Vigilance Committee, and as we put down our names in the book they were minutely inspected by some gentlemen who came out of the parlour. It was fortunate they did not find traces of Lincolnism about us, as it appeared by the papers they were busy deporting "Abolitionists" after certain preliminary processes supposed to

> Give them a rise, and open their eyes
> To a sense of their situation.

The citizens were busy in drilling, marching, and drum-beating, and the Confederate flag flew from every spire and steeple. The day was so hot that it was little more inviting to go out in the sun than it would be in the dog-days at Malaga, to which, by-the-by, Mobile bears some "kinder sorter" resemblance, but, nevertheless, I sallied forth, and had a drive on a shell road by the head of the bay, where there were pretty villarettes in charming groves of magnolia, orange-trees, and lime oaks. Wide streets of similar houses spring out to meet the country through sandy roads.

Many Mobilians called, and among them the mayor, Mr. Forsyth, in whom I recognised the most remarkable of the Southern Commissioners I had met at Washington. Mr. Magee, the acting British Consul, was also good enough to wait upon me, with offers of any assistance in his power. I hear he has most difficult questions to deal with, arising out of the claims of distressed British subjects, and disputed nationality. In the evening the Consul and Dr. Nott, a savant and physician of Mobile, well known to ethnologists for his work on the *Types of Mankind*, written cojointly with the late Mr. Gliddon, dined with me, and I learned from them that, notwithstanding the intimate commercial relations between Mobile and the great Northern cities,

[107]

the people here are of the most ultra-Secessionist doctrines. The wealth and manhood of the city will be devoted to repel the "Lincolnite mercenaries" to the last.

After dinner we walked through the city, which abounds in oyster saloons, drinking-houses, lager-beer and wine-shops, and gambling and dancing places. The market was well worthy of a visit—crowded with Negroes, mulattoes, quadroons, and mestizos of all sorts, Spanish, Italian, and French, speaking their own tongues, or a quaint *lingua franca,* and dressed in very striking and pretty costumes. The fruit and vegetable stalls displayed very fine produce, and some staples, remarkable for novelty, ugliness, and goodness. After our stroll we went into one of the great oyster saloons, and in a room upstairs had opportunity of tasting those great bivalvians in the form of natural fish puddings, fried in batter, roasted, stewed, deviled, broiled, and in many other ways, *plus* raw. I am bound to observe that the Mobile people ate them as if there was no blockade, as though oysters were a specific for political indigestions and civil wars; a fierce Marseillaise are they—living in the most foreign-looking city I have yet seen in the States. My private room in the hotel was large, well-lighted with gas, and exceedingly well-furnished in the German fashion, with French pendule and mirrors. The charge for a private room varies from 1£. to 1£. 5s. a day; the bedroom and board are charged separately, from 10s. 6d. to 12s. 6d. a day, but meals served in the private room are charged extra, and heavily too.

Chapter XXVI

———›•‹———

May 12th. Mr. Forsyth had been good enough to invite me to an excursion down the Bay of Mobile, to the forts built by Uncle Sam and his French engineers to sink his Britishers—now turned by "C.S.A." against the hated Stars and Stripes. The mayor and the principal merchants and many politicians—and are not all men politicians in America?—formed the party. If any judgment of men's acts can be formed from their words, the Mobilites, who are the representatives of the third greatest port of the United States, will perish ere they submit to the Yankees and people of New York. I have now been in North Carolina, South Carolina, Georgia, Alabama, and in none of these great States have I found the least indication of the Union sentiment, or of the attachment for the Union which Mr. Seward always assumed to exist in the South.

General Scott, who was a short time ago written of in the usual inflated style, to which respectable military mediocrity and success are entitled in the States, is now reviled by the Southern papers as an infamous hoary traitor and the like. If an officer prefers his allegiance to the United States' flag, and remains in the Federal service after his State has gone out, his property and his family and kindred are exposed to the gravest suspicion, and must prove their loyalty by extra zeal in the cause of Secession.

Our steamer, crowded to the sponsons, made little way against the tide; but at length, after nearly four hours' sail, we hauled up alongside a jetty at Fort Gaines, which is on the right hand or western exit of the harbour, and would command, were it finished, the light draft channel; it is now merely a shell of masonry, but Colonel Hardee, who has charge of the defences of Mobile, told me that they would finish it speedily.

The Colonel is an agreeable, delicate-looking man, scarcely of middle age, and is well-known in the States as the author of *The Tactics,* which is, however, merely a translation of the French manual of arms. He does not appear to be possessed of any great energy or capacity, but is, no doubt, a respectable officer.

Upon landing we found a small body of men on guard in the fort. A few cannon of moderate calibre were mounted on the sandhills and on the beach. We entered the unfinished work, and were received with a salute. The men felt difficulty in combining discipline with citizenship. They were "bored" with their sand-hill, and one of them asked me when I "thought them damned Yankees were coming." He wanted to touch off a few pills he knew "would be good for their complaint." I must say I could sympathise with the feelings of the young officer who said he would sooner have a day with the Lincolnites than a week with the mosquitoes, for which this locality is famous.

From Fort Gaines the steamer ran across to Fort Morgan, about three miles distant, passing in its way seven vessels, mostly British, at anchor, where hundreds may be seen, I am told, during the cotton season. This work has a formidable sea face, and may give great trouble to Uncle Sam, when he wants to visit his loving subjects in Mobile in his gunboats. It is the work of Bernard, I presume, and like most of his designs has a weak long base towards the land; but it is provided with a wet ditch and drawbridge, with demilunes covering the curtains, and has a regular bastioned trace. It has one row of casemates, armed with 32- and 42-pounders. The barbette guns are eight-inch and ten-inch guns; the external works at the salients are armed with howitzers and field-pieces, and as we crossed the drawbridge, a salute was fired from a field battery, on the flanking bastion, in our honour.

Inside the work was crammed with men, some of whom slept in the casemates—others in tents in the parade grounds and enceinte of the fort. They were Alabama Volunteers, and as sturdy a lot of fellows as every shouldered musket; dressed in homespun coarse grey suits, with blue and yellow worsted facings and stripes—to European eyes not very respectful to their officers, but very obedient, I am told, and very peremptorily ordered about, as I heard.

There were seven or eight hundred men in the work, and an undue proportion of officers, all of whom were introduced to the strangers in turn. The officers were a very gentlemanly, nice-looking set of young fellows, and some of them had just come over from Europe to take up arms for their State. I forget the name of the officer in command, though I cannot forget his courtesy, nor an excellent lunch he gave us in his casemate after a hot walk round the parapets, and some practice with solid shot from the barbette guns, which did not tend to make me think much of the greatly-be-praised Columbiads.

One of the officers named Maury, a relative of "deep-sea Maury," struck me as an ingenious and clever officer; the utmost harmony, kindliness, and devotion to the cause prevailed among the garrison, from the chief down to the youngest ensign. In its present state the Fort would suffer exceedingly from a heavy bombardment—the magazines would be in danger, and the traverses are inadequate. All the barracks and wooden buildings should be destroyed if they wish to avoid the fate of Sumter.

On our cruise homewards, in the enjoyment of a cold dinner, we had the inevitable discussion of the Northern and Southern contest. Mr. Forsyth, the editor and proprietor of the *Mobile Register,* is impassioned for the Cause, though he was not at one time considered a pure Southerner. There is difference of opinion relative to an attack on Washington. General St. George Cooke, commanding the Army of Virginia on the Potomac, declares there is no intention of attacking it, or any place outside the limits of that free and sovereign State. But then the conduct of the Federal Government in Maryland is considered by the more fiery Southerners to justify the expulsion of "Lincoln and his Myrmidons," "the Border Ruffians and Cassius M. Clay," from the capital. Butler has seized on the Relay House, on the junction of the Baltimore and Ohio Railroad, with the rail from Washington, and has displayed a good deal of vigour since his arrival at Annapolis. He is a Democrat, and a celebrated criminal lawyer in Massachusetts. Troops are pouring into New York, and are preparing to attack Alexandria, on the Virginia side, below Washington and the Navy Yard, where a large Confederate flag is flying, which can be seen from the President's window in the White House.

There is a secret soreness even here at the small effect produced in England compared with what they anticipated by the attack on Sumter; but hopes are excited that Mr. Gregory, who was travelling through the States some time ago, will have a strong party to support his forthcoming motion for a recognition of the South. The next conflict that takes place will be more bloody than that at Sumter. The gladiators are approaching—Washington, Annapolis, Pennsylvania are military departments, each with a chief and Staff, to which is now added that of Ohio, under Major G. B. McClellan, Major General of Ohio Volunteers at Cincinnati. The authorities on each side are busy administering oaths of allegiance.

The harbour of Charleston is reported to be under blockade by the *Niagara* steam frigate, and a force of United States' troops at St. Louis, Missouri, under Captain Lyon, has attacked and dispersed a body of State Militia under one Brigadier General Frost, to the intense indignation of all Mobile. The argument is that Missouri gave up the St. Louis Arsenal to the United States Government, and could take it back if she pleased, and was certainly competent to prevent the United States' troops stirring beyond the Arsenal.

Chapter XXVII

May 13th. I was busy making arrangements to get to Pensacola, and Fort Pickens, all day. The land journey was represented as being most tedious and exceedingly comfortless in all respects, through a waste of sand, in which we ran the chance of being smothered or lost. And then I had set my mind on seeing Fort Pickens as well as Pensacola, and it would be difficult, to say the least of it, to get across from an enemy's camp to the Federal fortress, and then return again. The United States' squadron blockaded the port of Pensacola, but I thought it likely they would permit me to run in to visit Fort Pickens, and that the Federals would allow me to sail thence across to General Bragg, as they might be assured I would not communicate any information of what I had seen in my character as neutral to any but the journal in Europe, which I represented, and in the interests of which I was bound to see and report all that I could as to the state of both parties. It was, at all events, worth while to make the attempt, and after a long search I heard of a schooner which was ready for the voyage at a reasonable rate, all things considered.

May 14th. Down to our yacht, the *Diana,* which is to be ready this afternoon, and saw her cleared out a little—a broad-beamed, flat-floored schooner, some fifty tons burthen, with a centre-board, badly caulked, and dirty enough—unfamiliar with paint. The skipper was a long-legged, ungainly young fellow, with long hair and an inexpressive face, just relieved by the twinkle of a very "Yankee" eye; but that was all of the hated creature about him, for a more earnest Seceder I never heard.

His crew consisted of three rough, mechanical sort of men and a Negro cook. Having freighted the vessel with a small stock of stores, a British flag, kindly lent by the acting Consul, Mr. Magee, and a tablecloth to serve as a flag of truce, our party, consisting of the gentlemen previously named, Mr. Ward, and a young artist, weighed from the quay of Mobile at five o'clock in the evening, with the manifest approbation of the small crowd who had assembled to see us off, the rumour having spread through the town that we were bound to see the great fight. The breeze was favourable and steady; at nine o'clock P.M., the lights of Fort Morgan were on our port beam, and for some time we were expecting to see the flash of a gun, as the skipper confidently declared they would never allow us to pass unchallenged.

With the first rays of the sun, Fort McRae, Fort Pickens, and the masts of the squadron were visible ahead.

On the land side on our left is Fort McRae, and on the end of the sand-bank, called Santa Rosa Island, directly opposite, rises the outline of the much-talked-of Fort Pickens. Through the glass the blockading squadron is seen to consist of a sailing frigate, a sloop, and three steamers; and as we are scrutinising them, a small schooner glides from under the shelter of the guardship, and makes towards us like a hawk on a sparrow. Hand over hand she comes, a great swaggering ensign at her peak, and a gun all ready at her bow; and rounding up alongside us, a boat, manned by four men, is lowered, an officer jumps in, and is soon under our counter. The officer, a bluff, sailor-like looking fellow, in a uniform a little the worse for wear, and wearing his beard as officers of the United States Navy generally do, fixed his eye upon the skipper—who did not seem quite at his ease, and had, indeed, confessed to us that he had been warned off by the *Oriental,* as the tender was named, only a short time before—

and said, "Hallo, sir, I think I have seen you before: what schooner is this?" "The *Diana* of Mobile." "I thought so." Stepping on deck, he said, "Gentlemen, I am Mr. Brown, Master in the United States Navy, in charge of the boarding schooner, *Oriental*." We each gave our names; whereupon Mr. Brown says, "I have no doubt it will be all right; be good enough to let me have your papers. And now, sir, make sail, and lie-to under the quarter of that steamer there, the *Powhatan*." The Captain did not look at all happy when the officer called his attention to the indorsement on his papers; nor did the Mobile party seem very comfortable when he remarked, "I suppose, gentlemen, you are quite well aware there is a strict blockade of this port?"

In half an hour the schooner lay under the guns of the *Powhatan,* which is a stumpy, thick-set, powerful steamer of the old paddle-wheel kind. We proceeded alongside in the cutter's boat, and were ushered into the cabin, where the officer commanding, Lieutenant David Porter, received us, begged us to be seated, then inquired into the object of our visit, which he communicated to the flagship by signal, in order to get instructions as to our disposal. Nothing could exceed his courtesy; and I was most favourably impressed by himself, his officers, and crew. He took me over the ship, which is armed with ten-inch Dahlgrens and an eleven-inch pivot gun, with rifled field-pieces and howitzers on the sponsons. Her boarding nettings were triced up, bows and weak portions padded with dead wood and old sails, and everything ready for action.

Lieutenant Porter has been in and out of the harbour examining the enemy's works at all hours of the night, and he has marked off on the chart, as he showed me, the bearings of the various spots where he can sweep or enfilade their works. The crew, all things considered, were very clean, and their personnel exceedingly fine.

We were not the only prize that was made by the *Oriental* this morning. A ragged little schooner lay at the other side of the

Powhatan, the master of which stood rubbing his knuckles into his eyes, and uttering dolorous expressions in broken English and Italian, for he was a noble Roman of Civita Vecchia. Lieutenant Porter let me into the secret. These small traders at Mobile, pretending great zeal for the Confederate cause, load their vessels with fruit, vegetables, and things of which they know the squadron is much in want, as well as the garrison of the Confederate forts. They set out with the most valiant intention of running the blockade, and are duly captured by the squadron, the officers of which are only too glad to pay fair prices for the cargoes. They return to Mobile, keep their money in their pockets, and declare they have been plundered by the Yankees. If they get in, they demand still higher prices from the Confederates, and lay claim to the most exalted patriotism.

By signal from the flagship *Sabine,* we were ordered to repair on board to see the senior officer, Captain Adams. Captain Adams, a grey-haired veteran of very gentle manners and great urbanity, received us in his cabin, and listened to my explanation of the cause of my visit with interest. About myself there was no difficulty; but he very justly observed he did not think it would be right to let the gentlemen from Mobile examine Fort Pickens, and then go among the Confederate camps.

Major Vogdes, an engineer officer from the fort, who happened to be on board, volunteered to take a letter from me to Colonel Harvey Browne, requesting permission to visit it; and I finally arranged with Captain Adams that the *Diana* was to be permitted to pass the blockade into Pensacola Harbour, and thence to return to Mobile, my visit to Pickens depending on the pleasure of the Commandant of the place. "I fear, Mr. Russell," said Captain Adams, "in giving you this permission, I expose myself to misrepresentation and unfounded attacks. Gentlemen of the press in our country care little about private character, and are, I fear, rather unscrupulous in what they say; but I rely upon your character that no improper use shall be made of this permission. You must hoist a flag of truce, as General Bragg, who commands over there, has sent me word he considers our blockade a declaration of war, and will fire upon any vessel which approaches him from our fleet."

In the course of conversation, whilst treating me to such man-of-war luxuries as the friendly officer had at his disposal, he gave be an illustration of the miseries of this cruel conflict—of the unspeakable desolation of homes, of the bitterness of feeling engendered in families. A Pennsylvanian by birth, he married long ago a lady of Louisiana, where he resided on his plantation till his ship was commissioned. He was absent on foreign service when the feud first began, and received orders at sea, on the South American station, to repair direct to blockade Pensacola. He has just heard that one of his sons is enlisted in the Confederate Army, and that two others have joined the forces in Virginia; and as he said sadly, "God knows, when I open my broadside, but that I may be killing my own children." But that was not all. One of the Mobile gentlemen brought him a letter from his daughter, in which she informs him that she has been elected vivandière to a New Orleans regiment, with which she intends to push on to Washington, and get a lock of old Abe Lincoln's hair; and the letter concluded with the charitable wish that her father might starve to death if he persisted in his wicked blockade.

The boat which took us from the *Powhatan* to the *Diana* was in charge of a young officer related to Captain Porter, who amused me by the spirit with which he bandied remarks about the Mobile men, who had now recovered their equanimity, and were indulging in what is called chaff about the blockade. "Well," he said, "you were the first to begin it; let us see whether you won't be the first to leave it off. I guess our Northern ice will pretty soon put out your Southern fire."

As we got abreast of Fort Pickens, I ordered tablecloth No. 1 to be hoisted to the peak; and through the glass I saw that our appearance attracted no ordinary attention from the garrison of Pickens close at hand on our right, and the more distant Confederates on Fort McRae and the sand-hills on our left. The latter work is weak and badly built, quite under the command of Pickens, but it is supported by the old Spanish fort of Barrancas upon high ground further inland, and by numerous batteries at the water-line, and partly concealed amid the woods which fringe the shore as far as the Navy Yard of Warrington, near Pensacola. The wind was light, but the tide bore us on towards the Confederate works. Arms glanced in the blazing sun where regiments were engaged at drill, clouds of dust rose from the sandy roads, horsemen riding along the beach, groups of men in uniform, gave a martial appearance to the place in unison with the black muzzles of the guns which peeped from the white sand batteries from the entrance of the harbour to the Navy Yard now close at hand. As at Sumter Major Anderson permitted the Carolinians to erect the batteries he might have so readily destroyed in the commencement, so the Federal officers here have allowed General Bragg to work away at his leisure, mounting cannon after cannon, throwing up earthworks, and strengthening his batteries, till he has assumed so formidale an attitude that I doubt very much whether the fort and the fleet combined can silence his fire.

The skipper went ashore with my letters to General Bragg, and speedily returned with an orderly, who brought permission for the *Diana* to come alongside the wharf. The Mobile gentlemen were soon on shore, eager to seek their friends; and in a few seconds the officer of the quartermaster-general's department on duty came on board to conduct me to the officers' quarters, whilst waiting for my reply from General Bragg.

The quartermaster conducted me through shady walks into one of the houses, then into a long room, and presented me *en masse* to a body of officers, mostly belonging to a Zouave regiment from New Orleans, who were seated at a very comfortable dinner, with abundance of champagne, claret, beer, and ice. They were all young, full of life and spirits, except three or four graver and older men, who were Europeans. One, a Dane, had fought against the Prussians and Schleswig-Holsteiners at Idstedt and Friederichstadt; another, an Italian, seemed to have been indifferently engaged in fighting all over the South American continent; a third, a Pole, had been at Comorn, and had participated in the revolutionary guerilla of 1848. From these officers I learned that Mr. Jefferson Davis, his wife, Mr. Wigfall, and Mr. Mallory, Secretary to the Navy, had come down from Montgomery, and had been visiting the works all day.

After dinner an aide-de-camp from General Bragg entered with a request that I would accompany him to the commanding officer's quarters. As the sand outside the Navy Yard was deep, and rendered walking very disagreeable, the young officer stopped a cart, into which we got, and were proceeding on our way, when a tall, elderly man, in a blue frock coat with a gold star on his shoulder, trousers with a gold stripe and gilt buttons, rode past, followed by an orderly, who looked more like a dragoon than anything I have yet seen in the States. "There's General Bragg," quoth the aide, and I was duly presented to the General, who reined up by the wagon. He sent his orderly off at once for a light cart drawn by a pair of mules, in which I completed my journey, and was safely decarted at the door of a substantial house surrounded by trees of lime, oak, and sycamore.

Lead horses and orderlies thronged the front of the portico, and gave it the usual headquarter-like aspect. General Bragg received me at the steps, and took me to his private room where we remained for a long time in conversation. He had retired from the United States army after the Mexican war—in which, by the way, he played a distinguished part, his name being generally coupled with the phrase "a little more grape, Captain Bragg," used in one of the hottest encounters of that campaign—to his plantation in Louisiana; but suddenly the Northern States declared their intention of using force to free and sovereign states, which were exercising their constitutional rights to secede from the Federal Union.

Neither he nor his family were responsible for the system of slavery. His ancestors found it established by law and flourishing, and had left him property, consisting of slaves, which was granted to him by the laws and constitution of the United States. Slaves were necessary for the actual cultivation of the soil in the South; Europeans and Yankees who settled there speedily became convinced of that; and if a Northern population were settled in Louisiana tomorrow, they would discover that they must till the land by the labour of the black race, and that the only mode of making the black race work was to hold them in a condition of involuntary servitude. "Only the other day, Colonel Harvey Browne, at Pickens, over the way, carried off a number of Negroes from Tortugas, and put them to work at Santa Rosa. Why? Because his white soldiers were not able for it." No. The North was bent on subjugating the South, and as long as he had a drop of blood in his body, he would resist such an infamous attempt.

Before supper General Bragg opened his maps, and pointed out to me in detail the position of all his works, the line of fire of each gun, and the particular object to be expected from its effects. "I know every inch of Pickens," he said, "for I happened to be stationed there as soon as I left West Point, and I don't think there is a stone in it that I am not as well acquainted with as Harvey Browne."

And so we bade good-by. "Tomorrow," said the General, "I will send down one of my best horses and Mr. Ellis, my aide-de-camp, to take you over all the works and batteries." As I rode home with my honest orderly beside instead of behind me, for he was of a conversational turn, I was much perplexed in my mind, endeavouring to determine which was right and which was wrong in this quarrel, and at last, as at Montgomery, I was forced to ask myself if right and wrong were geographical expressions depending for extension or limitation on certain conditions of climate and lines of latitude and longitude. Here was the General's orderly beside me, an intelligent middle-aged man, who had come to do battle with as much sincerity—aye, and religious confidence—as ever actuated old John Brown or any New England Puritan to make war against slavery. "I have left my old woman and the children to the care of the niggers; I have turned up all my cotton land and planted it with corn, and I don't intend to go back alive till I've seen the back of the last Yankee in our Southern States." "And are wife and children alone with the Negroes?" "Yes, sir. There's only one white man on the plantation, an overseer sort of chap." "Are not you afraid of the slaves rising?" "They're ignorant poor creatures, to be sure, but as yet they're faithful. Anyway, I put my trust in God, and I know He'll watch over the house while I'm away fighting for this good cause!" This man came from Mississippi, and had twenty-five slaves which represented a money value of at least £5,000. He was beyond the age of enthusiasm, and was actuated, no doubt, by strong principles, to him unquestionable and sacred.

Chapter XXVIII

May 16th. The noise of our arrival had gone abroad; haply the report of the good things with which the men of Mobile had laden the craft, for a few officers came aboard even at that early hour, and we asked two who were known to our friends to stay for breakfast. That meal, to which the Negro cook applied his whole mind and all the galley, consisted of an ugly-looking but well-flavoured fish from the waters outside us, fried ham and onions, biscuit, coffee, iced water and Bordeaux, served with charming simplicity.

Lieutenant Ellis, General Bragg's aide-de-camp, came on board at an early hour, in order to take me round the works, and I was soon on the back of the General's charger, safely ensconced between the raised pummel and cantle of a great brass-bound saddle, with emblazoned saddle-cloth and mighty stirrups of brass, fit for the fattest marshal that ever led an army of France to victory; but General Bragg is longer in the leg than the Duke of Malakhoff or Marshal Canrobert, and all my efforts to touch with my toe the wonderful supports which, in consonance with the American idea, dangled far beneath, were ineffectual.

I visited ten out of the thirteen batteries which General Bragg has erected against Fort Pickens. I saw but five heavy siege guns in the whole of the works among the fifty or fifty-five pieces with which they were armed. There may be about eighty altogether on the lines, which describe an arc of 135 degrees for about three miles round Pickens, at an average distance of a mile and one-third. I was rather interested with Fort Barrancas, built by the Spaniards long ago—an old work on the old plan, weakly armed, but possessing a tolerable command from the face of fire.

The working parties, as they were called—volunteers from Mississippi and Alabama, great long-bearded fellows in flannel shirts and slouched hats, uniformless in all save brightly burnished arms and resolute purpose—were lying about among the works, or contributing languidly to their completion.

Considerable improvements were in the course of execution; but the officers were not always agreed as to the work to be done. Captain A., at the wheelbarrows: "Now then, you men, wheel up these sandbags, and range them just at this corner." Major B.: "My good Captain A., what do you want the bags there for? Did I not tell you, these merlons were not to be finished till we had completed the parapet on the front?" Captain A.: "Well, Major, so you did, and your order made me think you know darned little about your business; and so I am going to do a little engineering of my own."

Altogether, I was quite satisfied General Bragg was perfectly correct in refusing to open his fire on Fort Pickens and on the fleet, which ought certainly to have knocked his works about his ears, in spite of his advantages of position, and of some well-placed mortar batteries among the brushwood, at distances from Pickens of twenty-five hundred and twenty-eight hundred yards. The magazines of the batteries I visited did not contain ammunition for more than one day's ordinary firing. The shot were badly cast, with projecting flanges from the mould, which would be very injurious to soft metal guns in firing. As to men, as in guns, the Southern papers had lied consumedly. I could not say how many were in Pensacola itself, for I did not visit the camp: at the outside guess of the numbers there was two thousand. I saw, however, all the camps here, and I doubt exceedingly if General Bragg—who at this time is represented to have any number from thirty thousand to fifty thousand men under his command—has eight thousand troops to support his batteries, or ten thousand, including Pensacola, all told.

On my return to headquarters I found General Bragg in his room, engaged writing an official letter in reply to my request to be permitted to visit Fort Pickens, in which he gave me full permission to do as I pleased. Not only this, but he had prepared a number of letters of introduction to the military authorities, and to his personal friends at New Orleans, requesting them to give me every facility and friendly assistance in their power. He asked me my opinion about the batteries and their armament, which I freely gave him *quantum valeat*. "Well," he said, "I think your conclusions are pretty just; but, nevertheless, some fine day I shall be forced to try the mettle of our friends on the opposite side." All I could say was, "May God defend the right." "A good saying, to which I say, Amen. And drink with you to it."

The schooner was all ready for sea, but the Mobile gentlemen had gone off to Pensacola, and as I did not desire to invite them to visit Fort Pickens—where, indeed, they would have most likely met with a refusal—I resolved to sail without them and to return to the Navy Yard in the evening, in order to take them back on our homeward voyage. "Now then, Captain, cast loose; we are going to Fort Pickens." The worthy seaman had by this time become utterly at sea, and did not appear to know whether he belonged to the Confederate States, Abraham Lincoln, or the British Navy. But this order roused him a little, and looking at me with all his eyes, he exclaimed, "Why, you don't mean to say you are going to make me bring the *Diana* alongside that darned Yankee Fort!" Our tablecloth, somewhat maculated with gravy, was hoisted once more to the peak, and, after some formalities between the guardians of the jetty and ourselves, the schooner canted round in the tideway, and with a fine light breeze ran down towards the Stars and Stripes.

"And now," said the skipper, "I think we'd best lie to—them cussed Yankees on the beach is shouting to us." And so they were. A sentry on the end of a wooden jetty sung out, "Hallo you there! Stand off or I'll fire," and "drew a bead-line on us." At the same time the skipper hailed, "Please to send a boat off to go ashore." "No, sir! Come in your own boat!" cried the officer of the guard. Our own boat! A very skiff of Charon! Leaky, rotten, lop-sided. We were a hundred yards from the beach, and it was to be hoped that with all its burthen, it could not go down in such a short row. As I stepped in, however, followed by my two companions, the water flew in as if forced by a pump, and when the sailors came after us the skipper said, through a mouthful of juice, "Deevid! pull your hardest, for there an't a more terrible place for sharks along the whole coast." Deevid and his friend pulled like men, and our hopes rose with the water in the boat and the decreasing distance to shore. They worked like Doggett's badgers, and in five minutes were out of "shark" depth and alongside the jetty, where Major Vogdes, Mr. Brown, of the *Oriental,* and an officer, introduced as Captain Barry of the United States artillery, were waiting to receive us.

If I were selecting a summer habitation I should certainly not choose Fort Pickens. It is, like all other American works I have seen, strong on the sea faces and weak towards the land. The outer gate was closed, but at a talismanic knock from Captain Barry, the wicket was thrown open by the guard, and we passed through a vaulted gallery into the parade-ground, which was full of men engaged in strengthening the place, and digging deep pits in the centre as shell traps. The men were United States regulars, not comparable in physique to the Southern volunteers, but infinitely superior in cleanliness and soldierly smartness. The officer on duty led me to one of the angles of the fort and turned in to a covered way, which had been ingeniously contrived by tilting up the gun platforms and beams of wood at an angle against the wall, and piling earth and sand banks against them for several feet in thickness. The casemates, which otherwise would have been exposed to a plunging fire in the rear, were thus effectually protected.

As it was approaching evening and I had seen everything in the fort, the hospital, casemates, magazines, bakehouses, tasted the rations, and drank the whiskey, I set out for the schooner, accompanied by Colonel Browne and Captain Barry and other officers, and picking up my friends at the bakehouse outside.

Having bidden our acquaintances good-by, we got on board the *Diana,* which steered towards the Warrington Navy Yard, to take the rest of the party on board. The sentries along the beach and on the batteries grounded arms, and stared with surprise as the *Diana,* with her tablecloth flying, crossed over from Fort Pickens, and ran slowly along the Confederate works.

Having been fourteen hours beating some twenty-seven miles,

I was landed at last at a wharf in the suburbs of the town about five o'clock in the evening. On my way to the Battle House I met seven distinct companies marching through the streets to drill, and the air was filled with sounds of bugling and drumming. In the evening a number of gentlemen called upon me to inquire what I thought of Fort Pickens and Pensacola, and I had some difficulty in parrying their very home questions, but at last adopted a formula which appeared to please them—I assured my friends I thought it would be an exceedingly tough business whenever the bombardment took place.

One of the most important steps which I have yet heard of has excited little attention, namely, the refusal of the officer commanding Fort MacHenry, at Baltimore, to obey the writ of *habeas corpus* issued by a judge of that city for the person of a soldier of his garrison.

Chapter XXIX

━━━━◆◆◄

May 18th. An exceedingly hot day, which gives bad promise of comfort for the Federal soldiers, who are coming, as the Washington Government asserts, to put down the rebellion in these quarters. The mosquitoes are advancing in numbers and force.

I dined at Dr. Nott's, and met Judge Campbell, who has resigned his high post as one of the Judges of the Supreme Court of the United States, and explained his reasons for doing so in a letter, charging Mr. Seward with treachery, dissimulation, and falsehood. He seemed to me a great casuist rather than a profound lawyer, and to delight in subtle distinctions and technical abstractions; but I had the advantage of hearing from him at great length the whole history of the Dred Scott case, and a recapitulation of the arguments used on both sides, the force of which, in his opinion, was irresistibly in favor of the decision of the Court. Mr. Forsyth, Colonel Hardee, and others were of the company.

As to Dr. Nott, his studies have induced him to take a purely materialist view of the question of slavery, and, according to him, questions of morals and ethics, pertaining to its consideration, ought to be referred to the cubic capacity of the human cranium—the head that can take the largest charge of snipe-shot will eventually dominate in some form or other over the head of inferior capacity. Dr. Nott detests slavery, but he does not see what is to be done with the slaves, and how the four millions of Negroes are to be prevented from becoming six, eight, or ten million, if their growth is stimulated by high prices for Southern produce.

May 20th. I left Mobile in the steamer *Florida* for New Orleans this morning at eight o'clock. She was crowded with passengers in uniform. In my cabin was a notice of the rules and regulations of the steamer. No. 6 was as follows: "All slave servants must be cleared at the Custom House. Passengers having slaves will please report as soon as they come on board."

The approach to New Orleans is indicated by large hamlets and scattered towns along the seashore, hid in the piny woods, which offer a retreat to the merchants and their families from the fervid heat of the unwholesome city in summer time. As seen from the sea, these sanitary settlements have a picturesque effect, and an air of charming freshness and lightness. There are detached villas of every variety of architecture in which timber can be constructed, painted in the brightest hues—greens, and blues, and rose tints—each embowered in magnolias and rhododendrons. From every garden a very long and slender pier, terminated by a bathing-box, stretches into the shallow sea; and the general aspect of these houses, with the light domes and spires of churches rising above the lines of white railings set in the dark green of the pines, is light and novel. To each of these cities there is a jetty, at two of which we touched, and landed newspapers, received or discharged a few bales of goods, and were off again.

After dinner there was some slight difficulty among the military gentlemen, though whether of a political or personal character I could not determine; but it was much aggravated by the appearance of a six-shooter on the scene, which, to my no small perturbation, was presented in a right line with my berth, out of the window of which I was looking at the combatants. I am happy to say the immediate delivery of the fire was averted by an amicable arrangement that the disputants should meet at the St. Charles Hotel at twelve o'clock on the second day after their arrival, in order to fix time, place, and conditions of a more orthodox and regular encounter.

At night the steamer entered a dismal canal, through a swamp which is infamous as the most mosquito-haunted place along the infested shore; the mouths of the Mississippi themselves being quite innocent, compared to the entrance of Lake Pontchartrain. When I woke up at daylight, I found the vessel lying alongside a wharf with a railway train alongside, which is to take us to the city of New Orleans, six miles distant.

A village of restaurants or "restaurats" as they are called here, and of bathing-boxes, has grown up around the terminus; all the names of the owners, the notices and the sign-boards, being French. Outside the settlement the railroad passes through a swamp, like an Indian jungle, through which the overflowings of the Mississippi creep in black currents. The spires of New Orleans rise above the underwood and semi-tropical vegetation of this swamp. Nearer to the city lies a marshy plain, in which flocks of cattle, up to the belly in the soft earth, are floundering among the clumps of vegetation. The nearer approach to New Orleans by rail lies through a suburb of exceedingly broad lanes, lined on each side by rows of miserable mean one-storied houses, inhabited, if I am to judge from the specimens I saw, by a miserable and sickly population.

A great number of the men and women had evident traces of Negro blood in their veins, and of the purer-blooded whites many had the peculiar look of the fishy-fleshy population of the Levantine towns, and all were pale and lean. The railway terminus is marked by a dirty, barrack-like shed in the city. Selecting one of the numerous tumble-down hackney carriages which crowded the street outside the station, I directed the man to drive me to the house of Mr. Mure, the British consul, who had been kind enough to invite me as his guest for the period of my stay in New Orleans.

The streets are badly paved, as those of most of the American cities, if not all that I have ever been in, but in other respects they are more worthy of a great city than are those of New York. There is an air thoroughly French about the people—cafés, restaurants, billiard rooms abound, with oyster and lager-beer saloons interspersed. The shops are all *magazins;* the people in the streets are speaking French, particularly the Negroes, who are going out shopping with their masters and mistresses, exceedingly well dressed, noisy, and not unhappy-looking.

The streets are full of Turcos, Zouaves, Chasseurs; walls are covered with placards of volunteer companies: there are Pickwick rifles, La Fayette, Beauregard, MacMahon guards, Irish, German, Italian, and Spanish, and native volunteers, among whom the Meagher rifles, indignant with the gentleman from whom they took their name, because of his adhesion to the North, are going to rebaptise themselves and to seek glory under one more auspicious. Tailors are busy night and day making uniforms. I went into a shop with the consul for some shirts—the mistress and all her seamstresses were busy preparing flags as hard as the sewing machine could stitch them, and could attend to no business for the present.

May 23rd. I dined with Major Ranney, the president of one of the railways, with whom Mr. Ward was stopping. Among the company were Mr. Eustis, son-in-law of Mr. Slidell; Mr. Morse, the Attorney-General of the State; Mr. Moise, a Jew, supposed to have considerable influence with the governor, and a vehement politician; Messrs. Hunt, and others. The table was excellent, and the wines were worthy of the reputation which our host enjoys, in a city where Sallusts and Luculli are said to abound. One of the slave servants who waited at table, an intelligent yellow "boy," was pointed out to me as a son of General Andrew Jackson.

Chapter XXX

May 24th. A great budget of news today, which with the events of the week may be briefly enumerated. The fighting has actually commenced between the United States steamers off Fortress Monroe, and the Confederate battery erected at Sewall's Point— both sides claim a certain success. The Confederates declare they riddled the steamer, and that they killed and wounded a number of the sailors. The captain of the vessel says he desisted from want of ammunition, but believes he killed a number of the rebels, and knows he had no loss himself. Beria Magoffin, governor of the sovereign state of Kentucky, has warned off both Federal and Confederate soldiers from his territory. The Confederate Congress has passed an act authorising persons indebted to the United States, except Delaware, Maryland, Kentucky, Missouri, and the district of Columbia, to pay the amount of their debts to the

Confederate Treasury. The State Convention of North Carolina has passed an Ordinance of Secession. Arkansas has sent its delegates to the Southern Congress. Several Southern vessels have been made prizes by the blockading squadron; but the event which causes the greatest excitement and indignation here, was the seizure, on Monday, by the United States' marshals, in every large city throughout the Union, of the telegraphic dispatches of the last twelve months.

At half-past four, I went down by train to the terminus on the lake where I had landed, and dined with Mr. Eustis, Mr. Johnson, an English merchant, Mr. Josephs, a New Orleans lawyer, and Mr. Hunt. The dinner was worthy of the reputation of the French cook. The terrapin soup excellent, though not comparable, as Americans assert, to the best turtle. The creature from which it derives its name is a small tortoise, the flesh is boiled somewhat in the manner of turtle, but the soup abounds in small bones, and the black paws with the white nail-like stumps projecting from them, found amongst the *disjecta membra,* are not agreeable to look upon. The bouillabaisse was unexceptionable, the soft crab worthy of every commendation, but the best dish was, unquestionably, the pompano, an odd fish, something like an unusually ugly John Dory, but possessing admirable qualities in all that makes fish good.

May 25th. Virginia has indeed been invaded by the Federals. Alexandria has been seized. It is impossible to describe the excitement and rage of the people; they take, however, some consolation in the fact that Colonel Ellsworth, in command of a regiment of New York Zouaves, was shot by J. T. Jackson, the landlord of an inn in the city, called the Marshal House. Ellsworth, on the arrival of his regiment in Alexandria, proceeded to take down the Secession flag, which had been long seen from the President's windows. He went out upon the roof, cut it from the staff, and was proceeding with it downstairs, when a man rushed out of a room, levelling a double-barrelled gun, shot Colonel Ellsworth dead, and fired the other barrel at one of his men, who had struck at the piece when the murderer presented it at the Colonel. Almost instantaneously, the Zouave shot Jackson in the head, and as he was falling dead thust his sabre bayonet through his body. Strange to say, the people of New Orleans consider Jackson was completely right in shooting the Federal colonel, and maintain that the Zouave, who shot Jackson, was guilty of murder. Their theory is that Ellsworth had come over with a horde of ruffianly abolitionists, or, as the Richmond *Examiner* has it, "the band of thieves, robbers and assassins, in the pay of Abraham Lincoln, commonly known as the United States' Army," to violate the territory of a sovereign state, in order to execute their bloody and brutal purposes, and that he was in the act of committing a robbery, by taking a flag which did not belong to him, when he met his righteous fate.

In the evening I visited Mr. Slidell, whom I found at home with his family, Mrs. Slidell and her sister Madame Beauregard, wife of the general, two very charming young ladies, daughters of the house, and a parlour full of fair companions, engaged, as hard as they could, in carding lint with their fair hands. Among the company was Mr. Slidell's son, who had just travelled from school at the North, under a feigned name, in order to escape violence at the hands of the Union mobs which are said to be insulting and outraging every Southern man. The conversation, as is the case in most creole domestic circles, was carried on in French. I rarely met a man whose features have a greater *finesse* and firmness of purpose than Mr. Slidell's; his keen grey eye is full of life, his thin, firmly-set lips indicate resolution and passion. Mr. Slidell, though born in a Northern state, is perhaps one of the most determined disunionists in the Southern Confederacy; he is not a speaker of note, nor a ready stump orator, nor an able writer; but he is an excellent judge of mankind, adroit, persevering, and subtle, full of device, and fond of intrigue; one of those men who, unknown almost to the outer world, organises and sustains a faction, and exalts it into the position of a party—what is called here a "wire-puller." Mr. Slidell is to the South something greater than Mr. Thurlow Weed has been to his party in the North. He, like every one else, is convinced that recognition must come soon; but, under any circumstances, he is quite satisfied the government and independence of the Southern Confederacy are as completely established as those of any power in the world. Mr. Slidell and the members of his family possess *naïveté,* good sense, and agreeable manners; and the regrets I heard expressed in Washington society at their absence had every justification.

May 26th. When the Congress at Montgomery adjourned, the other day, they resolved to meet on the 20th of July at Richmond, which thus becomes the capital of the Confederacy. The city is not much more than one hundred miles south of Washington, with which it was in communication by rail and river; and the selection must cause a collision between the two armies in front of the rival capitals. The seizure of the Norfolk Navy Yard by the Confederates rendered it necessary to reinforce Fortress Monroe; and for the present the Potomac and the Chesapeake are out of danger.

The military precautions taken by General Scott, and the movements attributed to him to hold Baltimore and to maintain his communications between Washington and the North, afford evidence of judgment and military skill. The Northern papers are clamouring for an immediate advance of their raw levies to Richmond, which General Scott resists.

In one respect the South has shown greater sagacity than the North. Mr. Jefferson Davis having seen service in the field, and having been Secretary of War, perceived the dangers and inefficiency of irregular levies, and therefore induced the Montgomery Congress to pass a bill which binds volunteers to serve during the war, unless sooner discharged, and reserves to the President of the Southern Confederacy the appointment of staff and field officers, the right of veto to battalion officers elected by each company, and the power of organising companies of volunteers into squadrons, battalions and regiments.

May 27th. "Charges of abolitionism" appear in the reports of police cases in the papers every morning; and persons found guilty not of expressing opinions against slavery, but of stating their belief that the Northerners will be successful, are sent to prison for six months. The accused are generally foreigners, or belong to the lower orders, who have got no interest in the support of slavery. The moral persuasion of the lasso, of tarring and feathering, head-shaving, ducking, and horse-ponds, deportation on rails, and similar ethical processes, are highly in favor.

May 28th. I dined with a large party at the Lakes, who had invited me as their guest, among whom were Mr. Slidell, Governor Hebert, Mr. Hunt, Mr. Norton, Mr. Fellows, and others. I observed in New York that every man had his own solution to the cause of the present difficulty, and contradicted plumply his neighbor the moment he attempted to propound his own theory. Here I found every one agreed as to the righteousness of the quarrel, but all differed as to the best mode of action for the South to pursue. Nor was there any approach to unanimity as the evening waxed older. Incidentally we had wild tales of Southern life, some good songs, curiously intermingled with political discussions, and what the Northerners call hifalutin talk.

When I was in the Consulate today, a tall and well-dressed, but not very prepossessing-looking man, entered to speak to Mr. Moore on business, and was introduced to me at his own request. His name was mentioned incidentally tonight, and I heard a passage in his life not of an agreeable character, to say the least of it. A good many years ago there was a ball at New Orleans, at which this gentleman was present; he paid particular attention to a lady who, however, preferred the society of one of the company, and in the course of the evening an altercation occurred respecting an engagement to dance, in which violent language

[134]

was exchanged, and a push or blow given by the favoured partner to his rival, who left the room, and, as it is stated, proceeded to a cutler's shop, where he procured a powerful dagger-knife. Armed with this, he returned, and sent in a message to the gentleman with whom he had quarrelled. Suspecting nothing, the latter came into the ante-chamber, the assassin rushed upon him, stabbed him to the heart, and left him weltering in his blood. Another version of the story was that he waited for his victim till he came into the cloak-room, and struck him as he was in the act of putting on his overcoat. After a long delay, the criminal was tried. The defence put forward on his behalf was that he had seized a knife in the heat of the moment when the quarrel took place, and had slain his adversary in a moment of passion; but evidence, as I understand, went strongly to prove that a considerable interval elapsed between the time of the dispute and the commission of the murder. The prisoner had the assistance of able and ingenious counsel; he was acquitted. His acquittal was mainly due to the judicious disposition of a large sum of money; each juror, when he retired to dinner previous to consulting over the verdict, was enabled to find the sum of $1,000 under his plate; nor was it clear that the judge and sheriff had not participated in the bounty; in fact, I heard a dispute as to the exact amount which it is supposed the murderer had to pay. He now occupies, under the Confederate Government, the post at New Orleans which he lately held as representative of the Government of the United States.

May 29th. Dined in the evening with M. Aristide Miltenberger, where I met His Excellency Mr. Moore, the Governor of Louisiana, his military secretary, and a small party.

It is a strange country, indeed; one of the evils which afflicts the Louisianians, they say, is the preponderance and influence of South Carolinian Jews, and Jews generally, such as Moise, Mordecai, Josephs, and Judah Benjamin, and others. The subtlety and keenness of the Caucasian intellect give them a high place among a people who admire ability and dexterity, and are at the same time reckless of means and averse to labour. The Governor is supposed to be somewhat under the influence of the Hebrews, but he is a man quite competent to think and act for himself—a plain, sincere ruler of a slave state, and an upholder of the patriarchal institution. After dinner we accompanied Madame Milten-berger (who affords in her own person a very complete refutation of the dogma that American women furnish no examples of the charms which surround their English sisters in the transit from the prime of life toward middle age), in a drive along the shell road to the lake and canal; the most remarkable object being a long wall lined with a glorious growth of orange trees; clouds of mosquitoes effectually interfered with an enjoyment of the drive.

Chapter XXXI

———— ►◄►◄◄ ————

June 1st. The respectable people of the city are menaced with two internal evils in consequence of the destitution caused by the stoppage of trade with the North and with Europe. The municipal authorities, for want of funds, threaten to close the city schools, and to disband the police; at the same time, employers refuse to pay their workmen on the ground of inability. The British Consulate was thronged today by Irish, English, and Scotch, entreating to be sent North or to Europe. The stories told by some of these poor fellows were most pitiable, and were vouched for by facts and papers; but Mr. Moore has no funds at his disposal to enable him to comply with their prayers. Nothing remains for them but to enlist. For the third or fourth time I heard cases of British subjects being forcibly carried off to fill the ranks of so-called volunteer companies and regiments. In some instances they have been knocked down, bound, and confined in barracks, till in despair they consented to serve. Those who have friends aware of their condition were relieved by the interference of the Consul; but there are many, no doubt, thus coerced and placed in involuntary servitude without his knowledge.

The great commercial community of New Orleans, which now feels the pressure of the blockade, depends on the interference of the European Powers next October. They have among them men who refuse to pay their debts to Northern houses, but they deny that they intend to repudiate, and promise to pay all who are not black Republicans when the war is over. Repudiation is a word out of favour, as they feel the character of the Southern States and of Mr. Jefferson Davis himself has been much injured in Europe by the breach of honesty and honour of which they have been guilty; but I am assured on all sides that every State will eventually redeem all its obligations. Meantime, money here is fast vanishing. Bills on New York are worth nothing, and bills on England are at eighteen per cent discount from the par value of gold; but the people of this city will endure all this and much more to escape from the hated rule of the Yankees.

Through the present gloom come the rays of a glorious future, which shall see a grand slave confederacy enclosing the Gulf in its arms, and swelling to the shores of the Potomac and Chesapeake, with the entire control of the Mississippi and a monopoly of the great staples on which so much of the manufacture and commerce of England and France depend. They believe themselves, in fact, to be masters of the destiny of the world. Cotton is king —not along king, but czar; and coupled with the gratification and profit to be derived from this mighty agency, they look forward with intense satisfaction to the complete humiliation of their hated enemies in the New England States, to the destruction of their usurious rival New York, and to the impoverishment and ruin of the states which have excited their enmity by personal liberty bills, and have outraged and insulted them by harbouring abolitionists and an anti-slavery press.

Having made some purchases, and paid all my visits, I returned to prepare for my voyage up the Mississippi and visits to several planters on its banks—my first being to Governor Roman.

Chapter XXXII

June 2nd. My good friend the Consul was up early to see me off; and we drove together to the steamer *J. L. Cotten.*

On arriving at the steamer I found a considerable party of citizens assembled to see off their friends. Governor Roman's son apologised to me for his inability to accompany me up the river, as he was going to the drill of his company of volunteers.

The aspect of New Orleans from the river is marred by the very poor houses lining the quays on the levee.

As we were now floating nine feet higher than the level of the streets, we could look down upon a sea of flat roofs and low wooden houses, painted white, pierced by the domes and spires of churches and public buildings. Grass was growing in many of these streets. At the other side of the river there is a smaller city of shingle-roofed houses, with a background of low timber.

The steamer stopped continually at various points along the levee, discharging commissariat stores, parcels, and passengers; and after a time glided up into the open country, which spread beneath us for several miles at each side of the banks, with a continuous background of forest. All this part of the river is called the Coast, and the country adjacent is remarkable for its fertility. The sugar plantations are bounded by lines drawn at right angles to the banks of the river, and extending through the forest. The villas of the proprietors are thickly planted in the midst of the green fields, with the usual porticoes, pillars, verandahs, and green blinds; and in the vicinity of each are rows of whitewashed huts, which are the slave quarters. These fields, level as a billiard-table, are of the brightest green with crops of maize and sugar.

At half-past three P.M. the steamer ran alongside the levee at the right bank, and discharged me at "Cahabanooze," in the Indian tongue, or "The ducks' sleeping-place," together with an English merchant of New Orleans, M. La Ville Beaufevre, son-in-law of Governor Roman, and his wife. The Governor was waiting to receive us in the levee, and led the way through a gate in the paling which separated his ground from the roadside, towards the house, a substantial, square, two-storied mansion, with a verandah all round it, embosomed amid venerable trees, and surrounded by magnolias. By way of explaining the proximity of his house to the river, M. Roman told me that a considerable portion of the garden in front had a short time ago been carried off by the Mississippi; nor is he at all sure the house itself will not share the same fate; I hope sincerely it may not. My quarters were in a detached house, complete in itself, containing four bedrooms, library, and sitting-room, close to the mansion, and surrounded, like it, by fine trees.

After we had sat for some time in the shade of the finest group, M. Roman, or, as he is called, the Governor—once a captain always a captain—asked me whether I would like to visit the slave quarters. I assented, and the Governor led the way to a high paling at the back of the house, inside which the scraping of the fiddles was audible. As we passed the back of the mansion some young women flitted past in snow-white dresses, crinolines, pink sashes, and gaudily coloured handkerchiefs on their heads, who were, the Governor told me, the domestic servants going off to a dance at the sugar-house; he lets his slaves dance every Sunday. The American planters who are not Catholics, although they do not make the slaves work on Sunday except there is something to do, rarely grant them the indulgence of a dance, but a few permit them some hours of relaxation on each Saturday afternoon.

We entered, by a wicket gate, a square enclosure, lined with Negro huts, built of wood. They are not furnished with windows —a wooden slide or grating admits all the air a Negro desires. There is a partition dividing the hut into two departments, one of which is used as the sleeping-room, and contains a truckle bedstead and a mattress stuffed with cotton wool, or the hair-like fibres of dried Spanish moss. The wardrobes of the inmates hang from nails or pegs driven into the wall. The other room is furnished with a dresser, on which are arranged a few articles of crockery and kitchen utensils. Sometimes there is a table in addition to the plain wooden chairs, more or less dilapidated, constituting the furniture—a hearth, in connection with a brick chimney outside the cottage, in which, hot as the day may be, some embers are sure to be found burning. The ground round the huts was covered with litter and dust, heaps of old shoes, fragments of clothing and feathers, amidst which pigs and poultry were recreating. Curs of low degree scampered in and out of the shade, or around two huge dogs, *chiens de garde,* which are let loose at night to guard against the precincts; belly-deep, in a pool of stagnant water, thirty or forty mules were swinking in the sun and enjoying their day of rest.

The huts of the Negroes engaged in the house are separated from those of the slaves devoted to field-labour out of doors by a wooden paling. I looked into several of the houses, but somehow or other I felt a repugnance, I dare say unjustifiable, to

[140]

examine the pentralia, although invited—indeed, urged to do so by the Governor. It was not that I expected to come upon anything dreadful, but I could not divest myself of some regard for the feelings of the poor creatures, slaves though they were, who stood by, shy, curtseying, and silent, as I broke in upon their family circle, felt their beds, and turned over their clothing. What right had I to do so?

Swarms of flies, tin cooking utensils attracting them by remnants of molasses, crockery, broken and old, on the dressers, more or less old clothes were found in all the huts; not a sign of ornament or decoration was visible; not the most tawdry print, image of Virgin or Saviour; not a prayerbook or printed volume. The slaves are not encouraged, or indeed permitted to read, and some communities of slave-owners punish heavily those attempting to instruct them.

It struck me more and more, however, as I examined the expression of the faces of the slaves, that deep dejection is the prevailing, if not universal, characteristic of the race. Here there were abundant evidences that they were all well treated; they had good clothing of its kind, food, and a master who wittingly could do them no injustice, as he is, I am sure, incapable of it. Still, they all looked sad, and even the old woman who boasted that she had held her old owner in her arms when he was an infant did not smile cheerfully, as the nurse at home would have done at the sight of her ancient charge.

In the evening several officers of M. Alfred Roman's company and neighbouring planters dropped in, and we sat out in the verandah, illuminated by the flashing fireflies, and talking politics. I was struck by the profound silence which reigned all around us, except a low rushing sound, like that made by the wind blowing over cornfields, which came from the mighty river before us. Nothing else was audible but the sound of our own voices and the distant bark of a dog. After the steamer which bore us had passed on, I do not believe a single boat floated up or down the stream, and but one solitary planter, in his gig or buggy, traversed the road, which lay between the garden palings and the bank of the great river.

Mr. Forstall maintains the South can raise an enormous revenue by a small direct taxation; whilst the North, deprived of Southern resources, will refuse to pay taxes at all, and will accumulate enormous debts, inevitably leading to its financial ruin. He, like every Southern man I have as yet met, expresses unbounded confidence in Mr. Jefferson Davis. I am asked invariably, as the second question from a stranger, "Have you seen our President, sir? Don't you think him a very able man?" This unanimity in the estimate of his character, and universal confidence in the head of the State, will prove of incalculable value in a civil war.

Chapter XXXIII

----·◄••►·----

June 3rd. At five o'clock this morning, having been awakened an hour earlier by a wonderful chorus of riotous mockingbirds, my old Negro attendant brought in my bath of Mississippi water, which, Nile-like, casts down a strong deposit, and becomes as clear, if not so sweet, after standing. "Le seigneur vous attend"; and already I saw, outside my window, the Governor mounted on a stout cob, and a nice chestnut horse waiting, led by a slave. Early as it was, the sun felt excessively hot, and I envied the Governor his slouched hat as we rode through the fields, crisp with dew. In a few minutes our horses were traversing narrow alleys between the tall fields of maize, which rose far above our heads. This corn, as it is called, is the principal food of the Negroes; and every planter lays down a sufficient quantity to afford him, on the average, a supply all the year round. Outside this spread vast fields, hedgeless, wall-less, and unfenced, where the green cane was just learning to wave its long shoots in the wind—a lake of bright green sugar-sprouts, along the margin of which, in the distance, rose an unbroken boundary of forest, two miles in depth, up to the swampy morass, all to be cleared and turned into arable land in process of time. From the river front to this forest, the fields of rich loam, unfathomable, and yielding from one to one and a half hogsheads of sugar per acre under cultivation, extend for a mile and a half in depth. In the midst of this expanse white dots were visible. Those are the gangs of hands at work—we will see what they are at presently. When the Indian corn is not good, peas are sowed, alternately, between the stalks, and are considered to be of much benefit; and when the cane is bad, corn is sowed with it, for the same object. Before we came up to the gangs we passed a cart on the road containing a large cask, a bucket full of molasses, a pail of hominy, or boiled Indian corn, and a quantity of tin pannikins. The cask contained water for the Negroes, and the other vessels held the materials for their breakfast; in addition to which, they generally have each a dried fish. The food was ample, and looked wholesome; such as any labouring man would be well content with.

We returned to the house in time for breakfast, for which our early cup of coffee and biscuit and the ride had been good preparation. Here was old France again. One might imagine a lord of the seventeenth century in his hall, but for the black faces of the servitors and the strange dishes of tropical origin. There was the old French abundance, the numerous dishes and efflorescence of napkins, and the long-necked bottles of Bordeaux, with a steady current of pleasant small talk.

The Americans, not unmindful of the aid to which, at the end of the War of Independence, their efforts were merely auxiliary, delight, even in the North, to exalt France above her ancient rival; but, as if to show the innate dissimilarity of the two races, the French creoles exhibit towards the New Englanders and the North an animosity, mingled with contempt, which argues badly for a future amalgamation or reunion. As the South Carolinians declare, they would rather return to their allegiance under the English monarchy, so the Louisianians, although they have no sentiment in common with the people of republican and imperial France, assert they would far sooner seek a connection with the old country than submit to the yoke of the Yankees.

At six A.M., Moise came to ask me if I should like a glass of absinthe, or anything stomachic. At breakfast was Doctor Laporte, formerly a member of the Legislative Assembly of France, who was exiled by Louis Napoleon; in other words, he was ordered to give in his adhesion to the new *régime,* or to take a passport for abroad. He preferred the latter course, and now, true Frenchman, finding the Emperor has aggrandised France and added to her military reputation, he admires the man on whom but a few years ago he lavished the bitterest hate.

The carriage is ready, and the word farewell is spoken at last. M. Alfred Roman, my companion, has traveled in Europe, and learned philosophy; is not so orthodox as many of the gentlemen I have met who indulge in ingenious hypotheses to comfort the consciences of the anthropoproprietors. The Negro skull won't hold as many ounces of shot as the white man's. Potent proof that the white man has a right to sell and to own the creature! He is plantigrade, and curved as to the tibia! Cogent demonstration that he was made expressly to work for the arch-footed, straight-tibiaed Caucasian. He has a *rete mucosum* and a coloured pigment! Surely he cannot have a soul of the same colour as that of an Italian or a Spaniard, far less of a flaxen-haired Saxon! See these peculiarities in the frontal sinus—in sinciput or occiput! Can you doubt that the being with a head of that shape was made only to till, hoe, and dig for another race? Besides, the Bible says that he is a son of Ham, and prophecy must be carried out in the rice-swamps, sugar-canes, and maize-fields of the Southern Confederation. It is flat blasphemy to set yourself against it. Our Saviour sanctions slavery because he does not say a word against it, and it is very likely that St. Paul was a slave-owner. Had cotton and sugar been known, the apostle might have been a planter! Furthermore, the Negro is civilised by being carried away from Africa and set to work, instead of idling in native inutility. What hope is there of Christianising the African races, except by the agency of the apostles from New Orleans, Mobile, or Charleston, who sing the sweet songs of Zion with such vehemence, and clamour so fervently for baptism in the waters of the "Jawdam?"

As we drove on the storm gathered overhead, and the rain fell in torrents—the Mississippi flowed lifelessly by—not a boat on its broad surface.

At last we reached Governor Manning's place, and went to the house of the overseer, a large, heavy-eyed old man.

"This rain will do good to the corn," said the overseer. "The niggers has had sceerce nothin' to do leetly, as they'eve clearied out the fields pretty well."

At the ferry-house I was attended by one stout young slave, who was to row me over. Two flat-bottomed skiffs lay on the bank. The Negro groped under the shed, and pulled out a piece of wood like a large spatula, some four feet long, and a small round pole a little longer. "What are those?" quoth I. "Dem's oars, Massa," was my sable ferryman's brisk reply. "I'm very sure they are not; if they were spliced they might make an oar between them." "Golly, and dat's the trute, Massa." "Then go and get oars, will you?" While he was hunting about we entered the shed at the ferry for shelter from the rain. We found "a solitary woman sitting" smoking a pipe by the ashes on the hearth, blear-eyed, low-browed and morose—young as she was. She never said a word nor moved as we came in, sat and smoked, and looked through her gummy eyes at chickens about the size of sparrows, and at a cat not larger than a rat which ran about on the dirty floor. A little girl, some four years of age, not over-dressed—indeed, half naked,—crawled out from under the bed, where she had hid on our approach. As she seemed incapable of appreciating the use of a small piece of silver presented to her —having no precise ideas in coinage or toffy—her parent took the obolus in charge, with unmistakable decision; but still the lady would not stir a step to aid our guide, who now insisted on the "key ov de oar-house." The little thing sidled off and hunted it out from the top of the bedstead, and when it was found, and the boat was ready, I was not sorry to quit the company of the silent woman in black. The boatman pushed his skiff, in shape a snuffer-dish, some ten feet long and a foot deep, into the water —there was a good deal of rain in it. I got in too, and the conscious waters immediately began vigorously spurting through the cotton wadding wherewith the craft was caulked. Had we gone out into the stream we should have had a swim for it, and they do say that the Mississippi is the most dangerous river in the known world for that healthful exercise. "Why! deuce take you" (I said at least that, in my wrath), "don't you see the boat is leaky?" "See it now for true, Massa. Nobody able to tell dat till Massa get in, though." Another skiff proved to be more staunch. I bade good-bye to my friend Roman, and sat down in my boat, which was forced by the Negro against the stream close to the bank, in order to get a good start across to the other side. The view from my lonely position was curious, but not at all picturesque. The world was bounded on both sides by a high bank, which constricted the broad river, just as if one were sailing down an open sewer of enormous length and breadth. Above the bank rose the tops of tall trees and the chimneys of sugar-houses, and that was all to be seen save the sky.

A quarter of an hour brought us to the levee on the other side. I ascended the bank, and across the road, directly in front, appeared a carriage gateway and wickets of wood, painted white, in a line of palings of the same material, which extended up and down the road far as the eye could see, and guarded wide-spread fields of maize and sugar-cane. An avenue lined with trees, with branches close set, drooping and overarching a walk paved with red brick, led to the house, the porch of which was visible at the extremity of the lawn, with clustering flowers, rose jessamine, and creepers clinging to the pillars supporting the verandah. The view from the belvedere on the roof was one of the most striking of its kind in the world.

If an English agriculturist could see six thousand acres of the finest land in one field, unbroken by hedge or boundary, and covered with the most magnificent crops of tasseling Indian corn and sprouting sugar-cane, as level as a billiard-table, he would surely doubt his senses. But here is literally such a sight—six thousand acres, better tilled than the finest patch in all the Lothians, green as Meath pastures, which can be turned up for a hundred years to come without requiring manure, of depth practically unlimited, and yielding an average profit on what is sold off it of at least £20 an acre, at the old prices and usual yield of sugar. Rising up in the midst of the verdure are the white lines of the Negro cottages and the plantation offices and sugar-houses, which look like large public edifices in the distance. My host was not ostentatiously proud in telling me that, in the year 1857, he had purchased this estate for £300,000, and an adjacent property, of eight thousand acres, for £150,000, and that he had left Belfast in early youth, poor and unfriended, to seek his fortune, and indeed scarcely knowing what fortune meant, in the New World. In fact, he had invested in these purchases the greater part, but not all, of the profits arising from the business in New Orleans, which he inherited from his master; of which there still remained a solid nucleus in the shape of a great woolen magazine and country house. He is not yet fifty years of age, and his confidence in the great future of sugar induced him to embark this enormous fortune in an estate which the blockade has stricken with paralysis. I cannot doubt, however, that he regrets he did not invest his money in a certain great estate in the North of Ireland, which he had nearly decided on buying. Six thousand acres on this one estate all covered with sugar-cane, and sixteen thousand acres more of Indian corn, to feed the slaves; these were great possessions, but not less than eighteen thousand acres still remained, covered with brake and forest, and swampy, to be reclaimed and turned into gold. As easy to persuade the owner of such wealth that slavery is indefensible as to have convinced the Norman baron that the Saxon churl who tilled his lands ought to be his equal.

Chapter XXXIV

June 5th. The smart Negro who waited on me this morning spoke English. I asked him if he knew how to read and write. "We must not do that, sir." "Where were you born?" "I were raised on the plantation, Massa, but I have been to New Orleans"; and then he added, with an air of pride, "I s'pose, sir, Massa Burnside not take less than fifteen hundred for me." Downstairs to breakfast, the luxuries of which are fish, prawns, and red meat which has been sent for to Donaldsonville by boat rowed down by an old Negro. Breakfast over, I walked down to the yard, where the horses were waiting, and proceeded to visit the saccharine principality. Mr. Seal, the overseer of this portion of the estate, was my guide, if not philosopher and friend.

Mr. Seal conducted me to a kind of forcing-house, where the

young Negroes are kept in charge of certain old crones too old for work, whilst their parents are away in the cane and Indian corn. A host of children of both sexes were seated in the verandah of a large wooden shed, or playing around it, very happily and noisily. I was glad to see the boys and girls of nine, ten, and eleven years of age were at this season, at all events, exempted from the cruel fate which befalls poor children of their age in the mining and manufacturing districts of England. At the sight of the overseer the little ones came forward in tumultuous glee, babbling out, "Massa Seal," and evidently pleased to see him.

As a jolly agriculturist looks at his yearlings or young beeves, the kindly overseer, lolling in his saddle, pointed with his whip to the glistening fat ribs and corpulent paunches of his woolly-headed flock. "There's not a plantation in the State," quoth he, "can show such a lot of young niggers. The way to get them right is not to work the mothers too hard when they are near their time; to give them plenty to eat, and not to send them to the fields too soon." He told me the increase was about five per cent per annum. The children were quite sufficiently clad, ran about round us, patted the horses, felt our legs, tried to climb up on the stirrup, and twinkled their black and ochry eyes at Massa Seal. Some were exceedingly fair. He talked about their colour and complexion quite openly; nor did it seem to strike him that there was any particular turpitude in the white man who had left his offspring as slaves on the plantation.

June 6th. My chattel Joe, *adscriptus mihi domino,* awoke me to a bath of Mississippi water with huge lumps of ice in it, to which he recommended a mint-julep as an adjunct. It was not here that I was first exposed to an ordeal of mint julep, for in the early morning a stranger in a Southern planter's house may expect the offer of a glassful of brandy, sugar, and peppermint beneath an island of ice—an obligatory panacea for all the evils of climate. After it has been disposed of, Pompey may come up again with glass number two: "Massa say fever very bad this morning—much dew." It is possible that the degenerate Anglo-Saxon stomach has not the fine tone and temper of that of an Hibernian friend of mine, who considered the finest thing to counteract the effects of a little excess was a tumbler of hot whisky and water the moment the sufferer opened his eyes in the morning. Therefore, the kindly offering may be rejected. But on one occasion before breakfast the Negro brought up mint julep number three, the acceptance of which he enforced by the emphatic declaration, "Massa says, sir, you had better take this, because it'll be the last he make before breakfast."

Breakfast is served: there is on the table a profusion of dishes —grilled fowl, prawns, eggs and ham, fish from New Orleans, potted salmon from England, preserved meats from France, claret, iced water, coffee and tea, varieties of hominy, mush, and African vegetable preparations. Then come the newspapers, which are perused eagerly with ejaculations, "Do you hear what they are doing now—infernal villains! that Lincoln must be mad!" and the like.

Chapter XXXV

June 7th. The Confederate issue of ten millions sterling, in bonds payable in twenty years, is not sufficient to meet the demands of Government; and the four millions of small Treasury notes, without interest, issued by Congress, are being rapidly absorbed. Whilst the Richmond papers demand an immediate movement on Washington, the journals of New York are clamouring for an advance upon Richmond. The planters are called upon to accept the Confederate bonds in payment of the cotton to be contributed by the States.

Extraordinary delusions prevail on both sides. The North believe that battalions of scalping Indian savages are actually stationed at Harper's Ferry. One of the most important movements has been made by Major-General McClellan, who has marched a force into western Virginia from Cincinnati, has occupied a portion of the line of the Baltimore and Ohio railway, which was threatened with destruction by the Secessionists; and has already advanced as far as Grafton. General McDowell has been appointed to the command of the Federal forces in Virginia. Every day regiments are pouring down from the North to Washington. General Butler, who is in command at Fortress Monroe, has determined to employ Negro fugitives, whom he has called "Contrabands," in the works about the fort, feeding them, and charging the cost of their keep against the worth of their services; and Mr. Cameron, the Secretary of War, has ordered him to refrain from surrendering such slaves to their masters.

Mr. Jefferson Davis has arrived at Richmond. At sea the Federal steamers have captured a number of Southern vessels; and some small retaliations have been made by the Confederate privateers. The largest mass of the Confederate troops have assembled at a place called Manassas Junction, on the railway from western Virginia to Alexandria.

The Northern papers are filled with an account of a battle at Philippi, and a great victory, in which not less than two of their men were wounded and two were reported missing as the whole casualties, but Napoleon scarcely expended so much ink over Austerlitz as is absorbed on this glory in the sensation headings of the New York papers.

After breakfast I accompanied a party of Mr. Burnside's friends to visit the plantations of Governor Manning, close at hand. One plantation is as like another as two peas. We had the same paths through tasseling corn, high above our heads, or through wastes of rising sugar-cane; but the slave quarters on Governor Manning's were larger, better built, and more comfortable-looking than any I have seen.

Chapter XXXVI

June 10th. At last *venit summa dies et ineluctabile tempus.* I had seen as much as might be of the best phase of the great institution—less than I could desire of a most exemplary, kind-hearted, clear-headed, honest man. In the calm of a glorious summer evening we crossed the Father of Waters, waving an adieu to the good friend who stood on the shore, and turning our backs to the home we had left behind us.

June 11th. Before noon the steamer hauled alongside a stationary hulk at Baton Rouge, which once "walked the waters" by the aid of machinery, but which was now used as a floating hotel, depot and storehouse—315 feet long, and fully thirty feet on the upper deck above the level of the river. The *Acadia* stopped, and I disembarked. Here were my quarters till the boat for Natchez should arrive.

Precisely at seven o'clock on Wednesday morning the *Mary T.* came alongside, and soon afterward bore me on to Natchez, through scenery which became wilder and less cultivated as she got upwards. Of the fifteen hundred steamers on the river, not a tithe are now in employment, and the owners of these profitless flotillas are "in a bad way." It was late at night when the steamer arrived at Natchez, and next morning early I took shelter in another engineless steamer beside the bank of the river at Natchez-under-the-Hill, which was thought to be a hotel by its owners.

In the morning I asked for breakfast. "There is nothing for breakfast; go to Curry's on shore." Walk up hill to Curry's—a bar-room occupied by a waiter and flies. "Can I have any breakfast?" "No, sir-ree; it's over half an hour ago." "Nothing to eat at all?" "No, sir." "Can I get some anywhere else?" "I guess not." It had been my belief that a man with money in his pocket could not starve in any country *soi-disant* civilised.

My hunger was assuaged by Mr. Marshall, who drove me to his comfortable mansion through a country like the wooded parts of Sussex, abounding in fine trees, and in the only lawns and park-like fields I have yet seen in America.

After dinner, my host took me out to visit a wealthy planter, who has raised and armed a cavalry corps at his own expense. We were obliged to get out of the carriage at a narrow lane and walk toward the encampment on foot in the dark; a sentry stopped us, and we observed that there was a semblance of military method in the camp. The captain was walking up and down in the verandah of the poor hut, for which he had abandoned his home. A book of tactics—Hardee's—lay on the table of his little room. Our friend was full of fight, and said he would give all he had in the world to the cause. But the day before, a party of horse, composed of sixty gentlemen in the district, worth from £20,000 to £50,000 each, had started for war in Virginia. Everything to be seen or heard testifies to the great zeal and resolution with which the South have entered upon the quarrel. But they hold the power of the United States and the loyalty of the North to the Union at far too cheap a rate.

Chapter XXXVII

▶◀◀◀

Friday, June 14th. Last night with my good host from his plantation to the great two-storied steamer *General Quitman,* at
Natchez. She was crowded with planters, soldiers and their
families, and as the lights shone out of her windows, looked like
a walled castle blazing from double lines of embrasures.

Before noon we were in sight of Vicksburg, which is situated
on a high bank or bluff on the left bank of the river, about 400
miles above New Orleans and some 120 miles from Natchez.

Mr. MacMeekan, the proprietor of the "Washington," declares himself to have been the pioneer of hotels in the Far West;
but he has now built himself this huge caravanserai, and rests
from his wanderings. We entered the dining saloon, and found
the tables closely packed with a numerous company of every
condition in life from generals and planters down to soldiers in
the uniform of privates. At the end of the room there was a long
table on which the joints and dishes were brought hot from the
kitchen to be carved by the Negro waiters, male and female, and
as each was brought in the proprietor, standing in the centre of
the room shouted out with a loud voice, "Now, then, here is a
splendid goose! Ladies and gentlemen, don't neglect the goose
and applesauce! Here's a piece of beef that *I* can recommend!
Upon my honour you will never regret taking a slice of the beef.
Oyster pie! Oyster pie! Never was better oyster pie seen in Vicksburg. Run about, boys, and take orders. Ladies and gentlemen,

[154]

just look at that turkey! Who's for turkey?"—and so on, wiping the perspiration from his forehead and combating with the flies.

When dinner was over, the mayor and several gentlemen of the city were good enough to request that I would attend a meeting at a room in the railway station, where some of the inhabitants of the town had assembled. Accordingly I went to the terminus and found a room filled with gentlemen. Large china bowls, blocks of ice, bottles of wine and spirits, and boxes of cigars were on the table, and all the materials for a symposium.

The company discussed recent events, some of which I learned for the first time. Dislike was expressed to the course of the authorities in demanding Negro labour for the fortifications along the river, and uneasiness was expressed respecting a Negro plot in Arkansas; but the most interesting matter was Judge Taney's protest against the legality of the President's course in suspending the writ of *habeas corpus* in the case of Merriman. The lawyers who were present at this meeting were delighted with his argument, which insists that Congress alone can suspend the writ, and that the President cannot legally do so.

The news of the defeat of an expedition from Fortress Monroe against a Confederate post at Great Bethel, has caused great rejoicing. The accounts show that there was the grossest mismanagement on the part of the Federal officers. The Northern papers particularly regret the loss of Major Winthrop, aide-de-camp to General Butler, a writer of promise. At four o'clock P.M. I bade the company farewell, and the train started for Jackson. The line runs through a poor clay country, cut up with gullies and water-courses made by violent rain.

There were a number of volunteer soldiers in the train; and their presence no doubt attracted the girls and women, who waved flags and cheered for Jeff Davis and States' Rights.

At six o'clock the train stopped in the country at a railway crossing by the side of a large platform. On the right was a common, bounded by a few detached wooden houses, separated by palings from each other, and surrounded by rows of trees. In front of the station were two long wooden sheds, which, as the signboard indicates, were exchanges or drinking saloons; and beyond these again were visible some rudimentary streets of straggling houses, above which rose three pretentious spires and domes, resolved into insignificance by nearer approach. This was Jackson.

Jackson proper consists of strings of wooden houses, with white porticoes and pillars a world too wide for their shrunk rooms, and various religious and other public edifices, of the hydrocephalic order of architecture, where vulgar cupola and exaggerated steeple tower above little bodies far too feeble to support them. There are of course a monster hotel and blazing barrooms—the former celebrated as the scene of many a serious difficulty, out of some of which the participators never escaped alive. The streets consist of rows of houses such as I have seen at Macon, Montgomery, and Baton Rouge; and as we walked towards the Capital or State-house there were many more invitations "to take a drink" addressed to my friend and me than we were able to comply with. Our steps were bent to the State-house, which is a pile of stone, with open colonnades, and an air of importance at a distance which a nearer examination of its dilapidated condition does not confirm. Mr. Pettus, the Governor of the State of Mississippi, was in the Capital; and on sending in our cards, we were introduced to his room, which certainly was of more than republican simplicity. The apartment was surrounded with some commonglass cases, containing papers and odd volumes of books; the furniture, a table or desk, and a few chairs and a ragged carpet; the glass in the windows cracked and broken; the walls and ceiling discoloured by mildew.

The Governor is a silent man, of abrupt speech but easy of access; and, indeed, whilst we were speaking, strangers and soldiers walked in and out of his room, looked around them, and acted in all respects as if they were in a public house, except in

[156]

ordering drinks. This grim, tall, angular man seemed to me such a development of public institutions in the South as Mr. Seward was in a higher phase in the North. For years he hunted deer and trapped in the forest of the Far West, and lived in a Natty Bumpo or David Crockett state of life; and he was not ashamed of the fact when taunted with it during his election contest, but very rightly made the most of his independence and his hard work.

The pecuniary honours of his position are not very great as Governor of the enormous State of Mississippi. He has simply an income of £800 a year and a house provided for his use; he is not only quite contented with what he has, but believes that the society in which he lives is the highest development of civilised life, notwithstanding the fact that there are more outrages on the person in his State, nay, more murders perpetrated in the very capital, than were known in the worst days of Mediaeval Venice or Florence; indeed, as a citizen said to me, "Well, I think our average in Jackson is a murder a month"; but he used a milder name for the crime.

The Governor conversed on the aspect of affairs, and evinced that wonderful confidence in his own people which, whether it arises from ignorance of the power of the North, or a conviction of greater resources, is to me so remarkable. "Well, sir," said he, dropping a portentous plug of tobacco just outside the spittoon, with the air of a man who wished to show he could have hit the centre if he liked, "England is no doubt a great country, and has got fleets and the like of that, and may have a good deal to do in Eu-*rope;* but the sovereign State of Mississippi can do a great deal better without England than England can do without her."

June 16th. When my work was over I walked out and sat in the shade with a gentleman whose talk turned upon the practices of the Mississippi duello.

I learned many valuable facts. I was warned, for example, against the impolicy of trusting to small-bored pistols or to pocket six-shooters in case of a close fight, because suppose you hit your man mortally he may still run in upon you and rip you up with a bowie knife before he falls dead; whereas if you drive a good heavy bullet into him, or make a hole in him with a "Derringer" ball, he gets faintish and drops at once.

Many illustrations, too, were given of the value of practical lessons of this sort. One particularly struck me. If a gentleman with whom you are engaged in altercation moves his hand towards his breeches pocket, or behind his back, you must smash him or shoot him at once, for he is either going to draw his six-shooter, to pull out a bowie knife, or to shoot you through the lining of his pocket. The latter practice is considered rather ungentlemanly, but it has been somewhat more honoured lately in the observance than in the breach.

Our host gave me an early dinner, at which I met some of the citizens of Jackson, and at six o'clock I proceeded by the train for Memphis. The carriages were, of course, full of soldiers or volunteers, bound for a large camp at a place called Corinth, who made night hideous by their song and cries, stimulated by enormous draughts of whiskey and a proportionate consumption of tobacco, by teeth and by fire. The heat in the carriages added to the discomforts arising from these causes, and from great quantities of biting insects in the sleeping places.

June 17th. If it was any consolation to me that the very noisy and very turbulent warriors of last night were exceedingly sick, dejected, and crestfallen this morning, I had it to the full. Their cries for water were incessant to allay the internal fires caused by "forty rod" and "sixty rod," as whiskey is called, which is supposed to kill people at those distances.

The victory at Big or Little Bethel has greatly elated these men, and they think they can walk all over the Northern States. It was a relief to get out of the train for a few minutes at a station called Holly Springs, where the passengers breakfasted at a dirty table on most execrable coffee, corn bread, rancid butter, and very dubious meats, and the wild soldiers outside made the most of their time, as they had recovered from their temporary depression by this time, and got out on the tops of the carriages, over which they performed tumultuous dances to the music of their band, and the great admiration of the surrounding Negrodom. Their demeanour is very unlike that of the unexcitable staid people of the North.

The enthusiasm for the Southern cause among all the people is most remarkable—the sight of the flag waving from the carriage windows drew all the population of the hamlets and the workers in the field, black and white, to the side of the carriages to cheer for Jeff Davis and the Southern Confederacy, and to wave whatever they could lay hold of in the air.

At the station of Grand Junction, north of Holly Springs, which latter is 210 miles north of Jackson, several hundreds of our warrior friends were turned out in order to take the train northeastward for Richmond, Virginia. The 1st Company, seventy rank and file, consisted of Irishmen armed with sporting rifles without bayonets. Five-sixths of the 2nd Company were all Americans. The 4th Company were almost all Irish. Some were in green, others were in grey; the Americans who were in blue had not yet received their arms. When the word "Fix bayonets" was given by the officer, a smart keen-looking man, there was an astonishing hurry and tumult in the ranks.

"Now then, Sweeny, where are yes dhriven me to? It is out of the redjmint amongst the officers yer shovin' me?"

"Sullivan, don't ye hear we're to fix beenits?"

"Sarjent, jewel, wud yes ayse the shtrap of me baynit?"

"If ye prod me wid that agin, I'll let dayloite into ye."

The officer, reading, "Number twenty-three, James Phelan." No reply.

Officer again, "Number twenty-three, James Phelan."

Voice from the rank, "Shure, captain, and faix Phelan's gone, he wint at the last depot."

[159]

"Number forty, Miles Corrigan."

Voice further on, "He's the worse for drink in the cars, yer honour, and says he'll shoot us if we touch him;" and so on.

But these fellows were, nevertheless, the material for fighting and for marching after proper drill and with good officers, even though there was too large a proportion of old men and young lads in the ranks. To judge from their dress these recruits came from the labouring and poorest classes of whites. The officers affected a French cut and bearing with indifferent success, and in the luggage vans there were three foolish young women with slop-dress imitation clothes of the vivandière type, who, with dishevelled hair, dirty faces, and dusty hats and jackets, looked sad, sorry, and absurd. Their notions of propriety did not justify them in adopting straps, boots, and trousers, and the rest of the tawdry ill-made costume looked very bad indeed.

On approaching Memphis the line ascends towards the bluff of the Mississippi, and farms of a better appearance come in sight on the side of the rail; but after all I do not envy the fate of the man who, surrounded by slaves and shut out from the world, has to pass his life in this dismal region, be the crops ever so good.

It was 1:40 P.M. when the train arrived at Memphis. I was speedily on my way to the Gayoso House, so called after an old Spanish ruler of the district, which is situated in the street on the bluff, which runs parallel with the course of the Mississippi. This resuscitated Egyptian city is a place of importance, and extends for several miles along the high bank of the river, though it does not run very far back. The streets are at right angles to the principal thoroughfares, which are parallel to the stream; and I by no means expected to see the lofty stores, warehouses, rows of shops, and handsome buildings on the broad esplanade along the river, and the extent and size of the edifices public and private in this city, which is one of the developments of trade and commerce created by the Mississippi. Memphis contains nearly thirty thousand inhabitants, but many of them are foreigners, and there is a nomad draft into and out of the place, which abounds in haunts for Bohemians, drinking and dancing saloons, and gaming rooms. And this strange kaleidoscope of Negroes and whites of extremes of civilisation in its American development, and of the semi-savage degraded by his contact with the white; of enormous steamers on the river, which bears equally the dug-out or canoe of the black fisherman; the rail, penetrating the inmost recesses of swamps, which on either side of it remain no doubt in the same state as they were centuries ago; the roll of heavily-laden wagons through the streets; the rattle of omnibuses and all the phenomena of active commercial life before our eyes, included in the same scope of vision which takes in at the other side of the Mississippi lands scarcely yet settled, though the march of empire has gone thousands of miles beyond them, amuses but perplexes the traveller in this new land.

The evening was so exceedingly warm that I was glad to remain within the walls of my darkened bedroom. All the six hundred and odd guests whom the Gayoso House is said to accommodate were apparently in the passage at one time. At present it is the headquarters of General Gideon J. Pillow, who is charged with the defences of the Tennessee side of the river, and commands a considerable body of troops around the city and in the works above. The house is consequently filled with men in uniform, belonging to the General's staff or the various regiments of Tennessee troops.

The Governors and the Legislatures of the States view with dislike every action on the part of Mr. Davis which tends to form the State troops into a national army.

On hearing of my arrival, General Pillow sent his aide-de-camp to inform me that he was about starting in a steamer up the river, to make an inspection of the works and garrison at Fort Randolph, and at other points where batteries had been erected to command the stream, supported by large levies of

Tennesseans. The aide-de-camp conducted me to the General, whom I found in his bedroom, fitted up as an office, littered with plans and papers. Before the Mexican War General Pillow was a flourishing solicitor, connected in business with President Polk, and commanding so much influence that when the expedition was formed he received the nomination of Brigadier-General of Volunteers. He served with distinction, and was severely wounded at the battle of Chapultepec, and at the conclusion of the campaign he retired into civil life, and was engaged directing the work of his plantation till this great rebellion summoned him once more to the field.

General Pillow is a small, compact, clear-complexioned man, with short grey whiskers, cut in the English fashion, a quick eye, and a pompous manner of speech; and I had not been long in his company before I heard of Chapultepec and his wound, which causes him to limp a little in his walk, and gives him inconvenience in the saddle. He wore a round black hat, plain blue frock coat, dark trousers, and brass spurs on his boots; but no signs of military rank. The General ordered carriages to the door, and we went to see the batteries on the bluff or front of the esplanade, which are intended to check any ship attempting to pass down the river from Cairo, where the Federals under General Prentiss have entrenched themselves, and are understood to meditate an expedition against the city. A parapet of cotton bales, covered with tarpaulin, has been erected close to the edge of the bank of earth, which rises to heights varying from sixty to one hundred feet almost perpendicularly from the waters of the Mississippi, with zigzag roads running down through it to the landing-places. This parapet could offer no cover against vertical fire, and is so placed that well-directed shell into the bank below it would tumble it all into the water. The zigzag roads are barricaded with weak planks, which would be shivered to pieces by boat-guns; and the assaulting parties could easily mount through these covered ways to the rear of the parapet, and up to the very centre of the esplanade.

The blockade of the river at this point is complete; not a boat is permitted to pass either up or down. At the extremity of the esplanade, on an angle of the bank, an earthen battery, mounted with six heavy guns, has been thrown up, which has a fine command of the river; and the General informed me he intends to mount sixteen guns in addition, on a prolongation of the face of the same work.

The inspection over, we drove down a steep road to the water beneath, where the *Ingomar,* a large river steamer, now chartered for the service of the State of Tennessee, was lying to receive us. The vessel was crowded with troops—all volunteers, of course—about to join those in camp. Great as were their numbers, the proportion of the officers was inordinately large, and the rank of the greater number preposterously high. It seemed to me as if I was introduced to a battalion of colonels, and that I was not permitted to pierce to any lower strata of military rank. I counted seventeen colonels, and believe the number was not then exhausted.

General Clarke, of Mississippi, who had come over from the camp at Corinth, was on board, and I had the pleasure of making his acquaintance. He spoke with sense and firmness of the present troubles, and dealt with the political difficulties in a tone of moderation which bespoke a gentleman and a man of education and thought. He also had served in the Mexican War, and had the air and manner of a soldier. With all his quietness of tone, there was not the smallest disposition to be traced in his words to retire from the present contest, or to consent to a reunion with the United States under any circumstances whatever. Another general, of a very different type, was among our passengers—a dirty-faced, frightened-looking young man, of some twenty-three or twenty-four years of age, redolent of tobacco, his chin and shirt slavered by its foul juices, dressed in a green cutaway

[163]

coat, white jean trousers, strapped under a pair of prunella slippers, in which he promenaded the deck in an Agag-like manner, which gave rise to a suspicion of bunions or corns. This strange figure was topped by a tremendous black felt sombrero, looped up at one side by a gilt eagle, in which was stuck a plume of ostrich feathers, and from the other side dangled a heavy gold tassel. This decrepit young warrior's name was Ruggles or Struggles, who came from Arkansas, where he passed, I was informed, for "quite a leading citizen."

Chapter XXXVIII

June 18th. On looking out of my cabin window this morning I found the steamer fast alongside a small wharf, above which rose, to the height of 150 feet, at an angle of 45 degrees, the rugged bluff already mentioned. The wharf was covered with commissariat stores and ammunition. Three heavy guns, which some men were endeavouring to sling to rude bullock carts, in a manner defiant of all the laws of gravitation, seemed likely to go slap into the water at every moment; but of the many great strapping fellows who were lounging about, not one gave a hand to the working party. A dusty track wound up the hill to the brow, and there disappeared; and at the height of fifty feet or so above the level of the river two earthworks had been rudely erected in an ineffective position. The volunteers who were lounging about the edge of the stream were dressed in different ways, and had no uniform.

General Pillow proceeded on shore after breakfast, and we

mounted the coarse cart-horse chargers which were in waiting at the jetty to receive us. It is scarcely worth while to transcribe from my diary a description of the works, which I sent over at the time to England. Certainly, a more extraordinary maze could not be conceived, even in the dreams of a sick engineer— a number of mad beavers might possibly construct such dams. They were so ingeniously made as to prevent the troops engaged in their defence from resisting the enemy's attacks, or getting away from them when the assailants had got inside—most difficult and troublesome to defend, and still more difficult for the defenders to leave, the latter perhaps being their chief merit.

The General ordered some practice to be made with round shot down the river. An old forty-two pound carronade was loaded with some difficulty, and pointed at a tree about seventeen hundred yards—which I was told, however, was not less than twenty-five hundred yards—distant. The General and his staff took their posts on the parapet to the leeward, and I ventured to say, "I think, General, the smoke will prevent your seeing the shot." To which the General replied, "No, sir," in a tone which indicated, "I beg you to understand I have been wounded in Mexico, and know all about this kind of thing." "Fire," the string was pulled, and out of the touch-hole popped a piece of metal with a little chirrup. "Darn these friction tubes! I prefer the linstock and match," quoth one of the staff, *sotto voce,* "but General Pillow will have us use friction tubes made at Memphis, that are'nt worth a cuss." Tube No. 2, however, did explode, but where the ball went no one could say, as the smoke drifted right into our eyes.

The General then moved to the other side of the gun, which was fired a third time, the shot falling short in good line, but without any ricochet. Gun No. 3 was next fired. Off went the ball down the river, but off went the gun, too, and with a frantic leap it jumped, carriage and all, clean off the platform. Nor was it at all wonderful, for the poor old-fashioned chamber carronade had been loaded with a charge and a solid shot heavy enough to make it burst with indignation. Most of us felt relieved when the firing was over, and, for my own part, I would much rather have been close to the target than to the battery.

The volunteers were mostly engaged at drill in distinct companies, but by order of the General some seven or eight hundred of them were formed into line for inspection. Many of these men were in their shirt sleeves, and the awkwardness with which they handled their arms showed that, however good they might be as shots, they were bad hands at manual platoon exercise; but such great strapping fellows, that, as I walked down the ranks, there were few whose shoulders were not above the level of my head, excepting here and there a weedy old man or a growing lad. They were armed with old pattern percussion muskets, no two clad alike, many very badly shod, few with knapsacks, but all provided with a tin water flask and a blanket. These men have been only five weeks enrolled, and were called out by the State of Tennessee, in anticipation of the vote of Secession.

I could get no exact details as to the supply of food, but from the Quartermaster-General I heard that each man had from ¾ to 1¼ pounds of meat and a sufficiency of bread, sugar, coffee, and rice daily; however, these military Olivers "asked for more." Neither whiskey nor tobacco was served out to them, which to such heavy consumers of both must prove one source of dissatisfaction. The officers were plain, formerly planters, merchants, lawyers, and the like—energetic, determined men, but utterly ignorant of the most rudimentary parts of military science.

Having gone down the lines of these motley companies, the General addressed them in a harangue in which he expatiated on their patriotism, on their courage, and the atrocity of the enemy, in an odd farrago of military and political subjects. But the only matter which appeared to interest them much was the announcement that they would be released from work in another day or so, and that Negroes would be sent to perform all that was required. This announcement was received with the words, "Bully for us!" and "That's good." And when General Pillow wound up with florid peroration by assuring them, "When the hour of danger comes I will be with you," the effect was by no means equal to his expectations. The men did not seem to care much whether General Pillow was with them or not at such an eventful moment; and, indeed, all dusty as he was in his plain clothes he did not look very imposing, or give one an idea that he would contribute much to the means of resistance. However, one of the officers called out, "Boys, three cheers for General Pillow."

What they may do in the North I know not, but certainly the Southern soldiers cannot cheer, and what passes muster for that jubilant sound is a shrill ringing scream with a touch of the Indian war-whoop in it. As these cries ended, a stentorian voice shouted out, "Who cares for General Pillow?" No one answered; whence I inferred the General would not be very popular until the niggers were actually at work in the trenches.

In the afternoon we returned to Memphis. Here I was obliged to cut short my Southern tour, though I would willingly have stayed to have seen the most remarkable social and political changes the world has probably ever witnessed. The necessity of my position obliged me to return northwards—unless I could write, there was no use in my being on the spot at all. By this time the Federal fleets have succeeded in closing the ports, if not effectually, so far as to render the carriage of letters precarious, and the route must be at best devious and uncertain.

Mr. Jefferson Davis was, I was assured, prepared to give me every facility at Richmond to enable me to know and to see all that was most interesting in the military and political action of the New Confederacy; but of what use could this knowledge be if I could not communicate it to the journal I served?

Much, therefore, as I desired to go to Richmond, where I was urged to repair by many considerations, and by the earnest appeals of those around me, I felt it would be impossible, notwithstanding the interest attached to the proceedings there, to perform my duties in a place cut off from all communication with the outer world; and so I decided to proceed to Chicago, and thence to Washington, where the Federals had assembled a large army, with the purpose of marching upon Richmond, in obedience to the cry of nearly every journal of influence in the Northern cities.

My resolution was mainly formed in consequence of the intelligence which was communicated to me at Memphis, and I told General Pillow that I would continue my journey to Cairo, in order to get within the Federal lines. As the river was blockaded, the only means of doing so was to proceed by rail to Columbus, and thence to take a steamer to the Federal position; and so, whilst the General was continuing his inspection, I rode to the telegraph office, in one of the camps, to order my luggage to be prepared for departure as soon as I arrived, and thence went on board the steamer, where I sat down in the cabin to write my last dispatch from Dixie.

The saloon in which I was sitting afforded abundant evidence of the vigour with which the South are entering upon the contest. Men of every variety and condition of life had taken up arms against the cursed Yankee and the black Republican—there was not a man there who would not have given his life for the rare pleasure of striking Mr. Lincoln's head off his shoulders, and yet to a cold European the scene was almost ludicrous.

Along the covered deck lay tall Tennesseans, asleep, whose plumed felt hats were generally the only indications of their martial calling, for few indeed had any other signs of uniform, except the rare volunteers, who wore stripes of red and yellow cloth on their trousers, or leaden buttons, and discoloured worsted braid and facings on their jackets. The afterpart of the saloon deck was appropriated to General Pillow, his staff, and officers. The approach to it was guarded by a sentry, a tall, good-looking young fellow, in a grey flannel shirt, grey trousers, fastened with a belt and a brass buckle, inscribed U.S., which came from some plundered Federal arsenal, and a black wide-awake hat, decorated with a green plume. His Enfield rifle lay beside him on the deck, and, with great interest expressed on his face, he leant forward in his rocking chair to watch the varying features of a party squatted on the floor, who were employed in the national game of "euchre." As he raised his eyes to examine the condition of the cigar he was smoking, he caught sight of me, and by the simple expedient of holding his leg out across my chest, and calling out, "Hallo! where are you going to?" brought me to a standstill—whilst his captain, who was one of the happy euchreists, exclaimed, "Now, Sam, you let nobody go in there."

I was obliged to explain who I was, whereupon the sentry started to his feet, and said, "Oh! indeed, you are Russell that's been in that war with the Rooshians. Well, I'm very much pleased to know you. I shall be off sentry in a few minutes; I'll just ask you to tell me something about that fighting." He held out his hand, and shook mine warmly as he spoke. There was not the smallest intention to offend in his manner; but, sitting down again, he nodded to the captain, and said, "It's all right! it's Pillow's friend—that's Russell of the London *Times*." The game of euchre was continued—and indeed it had been perhaps all night—for my last recollection on looking out of my cabin was a number of people playing cards on the floor and on the tables all down the saloon, and of shouts of "Eukerr!" "Ten dollars, you don't!" "I'll lay twenty on this!" and so on; and with break-fast the sport seemed to be fully revived.

By-and-by, a number of sick men were brought down on lit-ters, and placed here and there along the deck. As there was a considerable misunderstanding between the civilian and military doctors, it appeared to be understood that the best way of arrang-ing it was not to attend to the sick at all, and unfortunate men suffering from fever and dysentery were left to roll and groan, and lie on their stretchers, without a soul to help them. I had a medicine chest on board, and I ventured to use the lessons of my experience in such matters, administered my quinine, James's Powder, calomel, and opium, *secundum meam artem,* and nothing could be more grateful than the poor fellows were for the small mark of attention. "Stranger, remember, if I die," gasped one great fellow, attenuated to a skeleton by dysentery, "that I am Robert Tallon, of Tishomingo County, and that I died for States' Right; see, now, they put that in the papers, won't you? Robert Tallon died for States' Rights," and so he turned round on his blanket.

Presently the General came on board, and the *Ingomar* proceeded on her way back to Memphis. General Clarke, to whom I mentioned the great neglect from which the soldiers were suffering, told me he was afraid the men had no medical attendance in camp. All the doctors, in fact, wanted to fight, and as they were educated men, and generally connected with respectable families, or had political influence in the State, they aspired to be colonels at the very least, and to wield the sword instead of the scalpel.

Chapter XXXIX

June 19th. By the time I had arrived at the station my clothes were covered with a fine alluvial deposit in a state of powder; the platform was crowded with volunteers moving off for the wars, and I was obliged to take my place in a carriage full of Confederate officers and soldiers who had a large supply of whiskey, which at that early hour they were consuming as a prophylactic against the influence of the morning dews, which hereabouts are of such a deadly character that, to be quite safe from their influence, it appears to be necessary, judging from the examples of my companions, to get as nearly drunk as possible. Whiskey, by-the-by, is also a sovereign specific against the bites of rattlesnakes. All the dews of the Mississippi and the rattle-snakes of the prairie might have spent their force or venom in vain on my companions before we had got as far as Union City.

The portion of Tennessee through which the rail runs is exceedingly uninteresting, and looks unhealthy; the clearings occur at long intervals in the forest, and the unwholesome popu-lation, who came out of their low shanties, situated amidst black-ened stumps of trees or fields of Indian corn, did not seem prosperous or comfortable.

The names of the stations show that a savant has been ram-bling about the district. Here is Corinth, which consists of a wooden grog-shop and three log shanties; the acropolis is repre-sented by a grocery store, of which the proprietors, no doubt, have gone to the wars, as their names were suspiciously Milesian, and the doors and windows were fastened; but occasionally the names of the stations on the railway boards represented towns and villages, hidden in the wood some distance away, and Mum-mius might have something to ruin if he marched off the track but not otherwise.

The city of Troy was still simpler in architecture than the Grecian capitol. The Dardanian towers were represented by a timber house, in the verandah of which the American Helen was seated, in the shape of an old woman smoking a pipe, and she certainly could have set the Palace of Priam on fire much more readily than her prototype.

Numerous were the invitations to stop, which I received from the officers. "Why not stay with us, sir; what can a gentleman want to go among black Republicans and Yankees for?" It is quite obvious that my return to the Northern States is regarded with some suspicion; but I am bound to say that my explanation of the necessity of the step was always well received, and satisfied my Southern friends that I had no alternative. A special correspondent, whose letters cannot get out of the country in which he is engaged, can scarcely fulfil the purpose of his mission; and I used to point out, good-humouredly, to these gentlemen that until they had either opened the communication with the North, or had broken the blockade, and established steam communication with Europe, I must seek my base of operations elsewhere.

In those border states the coming war promises to produce the greatest misery; they will be the scenes of hostile operations; the population is divided in sentiment; the greatest efforts will be made by each side to gain the ascendancy in the state, and to crush the opposite faction, and it is not possible to believe that Kentucky can maintain a neutral position, or that either Federals or Confederates will pay the smallest regard to the proclamation of Governor McGoffin, and to his empty menaces.

At Columbus the steamer was waiting to convey us up to Cairo, and I congratulated myself on the good fortune of arriving in time for the last opportunity that will be afforded of proceeding northward by this route. General Pillow on the one hand, and General Prentiss on the other, have resolved to blockade the Mississippi, and as the facilities for Confederates going up to Columbus and obtaining information of what is happening in the Federal camps cannot be readily checked, the general in command of the port to which I am bound has intimated that the steamers must cease running. It was late in the day when we entered once more on the Father of Waters, which is here just as broad, as muddy, as deep, and as wooded as it is at Baton Rouge, or Vicksburg.

Columbus is situated on an elevated spur or elbow of land projecting into the river. The steamer which lay at the wharf, or rather the wooden piles in the bank which afforded a resting-place for the gangway, carried no flat, and on board presented traces of better days, a list of refreshments no longer attainable, and a bill of fare utterly fanciful. About twenty passengers came on board, most of whom had a distracted air, as if they were doubtful of their journey. The captain was surly, the office-keeper petulant, the crew morose, and, perhaps, only one man on board, a stout Englishman, who was purser or chief of the vic-tualling department, seemed at all inclined to be communicative. At dinner he asked me whether I thought there would be a fight, but as I was oscillating between one extreme and the other, I considered it right to conceal my opinion even from the steward of the Mississippi boat; and, as it happened, the expression of it would not have been of much consequence one way or the other, for it turned out that our friend was of very stern stuff. "This war," he said, "is all about niggers; I've been sixteen years in the country, and I never met one of them yet was fit to be any-thing but a slave; I know the two sections well, and I tell you, sir, the North can't whip the South, let them do their best; they may ruin the country, but they'll do no good."

In about two hours or so the captain pointed out to me a tall building and some sheds, which seemed to arise out of a wide reach in the river. "That's Cairey," said he, "where the Unionists have their camp," and very soon the Stars and Stripes were visible, waving from a lofty staff, at the angle of low land formed by the junction of the Mississippi and Ohio.

A more desolate woebegone looking place, now that all trade and commerce had ceased, cannot be conceived; but as the southern terminus of the central Illinois railway, it displayed a very different scene before the war broke out.

With the exception of the large hotel, which rises far above the levee of the river, the public edifices are represented by a church and spire, and the rest of the town by a line of shanties and small houses, the rooms and upper stories of which are just visible above the embankment. The stream, formed by the united efforts of the Mississippi and the Ohio, did not appear to gain much breadth, and each of the confluents looked as large as its product with the other. Three steamers lay alongside the wooden wharves projecting from the embankment, which was also lined by some flatboats. Sentries paraded the gangways as the steamer made fast along the shore, but no inquiry was directed to any of the passengers, and I walked up the levee and proceeded straight to the hotel, which put me very much in mind of an effort made by speculating proprietors to create a watering-place on some lifeless beach. In the hall there were a number of officers in United States uniforms, and the lower part of the hotel was, apparently, occupied as a military bureau; finally, I was shoved into a small dungeon, with a window opening out on the angle formed by the two rivers, which was lined with sheds and huts and terminated by a battery.

These camps are such novelties in the country, and there is such romance in the mere fact of a man living in a tent, that people come far and wide to see their friends under such extraordinary circumstances, and the hotel at Cairo was crowded by men and women who had come from all parts of Illinois to visit their acquaintances and relations belonging to the state troops encamped at this important point. The *salle à manger,* a long and lofty room on the ground floor, which I visited at supper time, was almost untenable by reason of heat and flies: nor did I find that the free Negroes, who acted at attendants, possessed any advantages over their enslaved brethren a few miles lower down the river; though their freedom was obvious enough in their demeanour and manners.

I was introduced to General Prentiss, an agreeable person, without anything about him to indicate the soldier. He gave me a number of newspapers, the articles in which were principally occupied with a discussion of Lord John Russell's speech on American affairs. Much as the South found fault with the British minister for the views he had expressed, the North appears much more indignant, and denounces in the press what the journalists are pleased to call "the hostility of the Foreign Minister to the United States." Soon after nightfall I retired to my room and battled with mosquitoes till I sank into sleep and exhaustion, and abandoned myself to their mercies; perhaps, after all, there were not more than a hundred or so, and their united efforts could not absorb as much blood as would be taken out by one leech, but then their horrible acrimony, which leaves a wreck behind in the place where they have banqueted, inspires the utmost indignation, and appears to be an indefensible prolongation of the outrage of the original bite.

June 20th. I am living among "abolitionists, cut-throats, Lincolnite mercenaries, foreign invaders, assassins, and plundering Dutchmen." Such, at least, the men of Columbus tell me the garrison at Cairo consists of. Down below me are "rebels, conspirators, robbers, slave breeders, wretches bent upon destroying the most perfect government on the face of the earth, in order to perpetuate an accursed system, by which human beings are held in bondage and immortal souls consigned to perdition."

After breakfast I went down about the works, which fortify the bank of mud, in the shape of a V, formed by the two rivers— a flèche with a ditch, scarp, and counter-scarp. Some heavy pieces cover the end of the spit at the other side of the Mississippi, at Bird's Point. On the side of Missouri there is a field entrenchment, held by a regiment of Germans, Poles, and Hungarians, about one thousand strong, with two field batteries. The sacred soil of Kentucky, on the other side of the Ohio, is tabooed by Beriah Magoffin, but it is not possible for the belligerents to stand so close face to face without occupying either Columbus or Hickman. The thermometer was at one hundred degrees soon after breakfast, and it was not wonderful to find that the men in Camp Defiance, which is the name of the cantonment on the mud between the levees of the Ohio and Mississippi, were suffering from diarrhea and fever.

In the evening there was a review of three regiments, forming a brigade of some twenty-eight hundred men, who went through their drill, advancing in columns of company, moving *en échelon*, changing front, deploying into line on the centre company, very creditably. It was curious to see what a start ran through the men during the parade when a gun was fired from the battery close at hand, and how their heads turned towards the river; but the steamer which had appeared round the bend hoisted the private signs by which she was known as a friend, and tranquillity was restored.

Chapter XL

————————►◄◄◄————————

June 21st. In the afternoon the General drove me round the camps in company with Mr. Washburne, Member of Congress from Illinois, his staff and a party of officers.

At each station the officers came out of their tents, shook hands all round, and gave an unfailing invitation to get down and take a drink, and the guns on the General's approach fired salutes, as though it was a time of profoundest peace. Powder was certainly more plentiful than in the Confederate camps, where salutes are not permitted unless by special order on great occasions.

The General remained for some time in the camp of the Chicago light artillery, which was commanded by a fine young Scotchman of the Saxon genus Smith, who told me that the privates of his company represented a million and a half of dollars in property. Their guns, horses, carriages, and accoutrements were all in the most creditable order, and there was an air about the men and about their camp which showed they did not belong to the same class as the better disciplined Hungarians of Milotzky close at hand.

Whilst we were seated in Captain Smith's tent, a number of the privates came forward, and sang the "Star-Spangled Banner" and a patriotic song, to the air of "God Save the Queen," and the rest of the artillerymen, and a number of stragglers from the other camps, assembled and then formed line behind the singers. When the chorus was over there arose a great shout for Washburne, and the honourable Congressman was fain to come forward and make a speech, in which he assured his hearers of a very speedy victory and the advent of liberty all over the land. Then "General Prentiss" was called for; and as citizen soldiers command their Generals on such occasions, he too was obliged to speak, and to tell his audience "the world had never seen any men more devoted, gallant, or patriotic than themselves." "Oglesby" was next summoned, and the tall, portly, good-humoured old man stepped to the front, and with excellent tact and good sense, dished up in the Buncombe style, told them the time for making speeches had passed, indeed it had lasted too long; and although it was said there was very little fighting when there was much talking, he believed too much talking was likely to lead to a great deal more fighting than any one desired to see between citizens of the United States of America, except their enemies, who, no doubt, were much better pleased to see Americans fighting each other than to find them engaged in any other employment.

With the exception of the foreign officers, and some of the staff, there are very few of the colonels, majors, captains, or lieutenants who know anything of their business. The men do not care for them and never think of saluting them. A regiment of Germans was sent across from Bird's Point this evening for plundering and robbing the houses in the district in which they were quartered.

June 22nd. The heat drove me in among the flies of the crowded hotel, where Brigadier Prentiss is planning one of those absurd expeditions against a Secessionist camp at Commerce, in the State of Missouri, about two hours' steaming up the river and some twelve or fourteen miles inland. Cairo abounds in Secessionists and spies, and it is needful to take great precautions lest the expedition be known; but, after all, stores must be got ready, and put on board the steamers, and preparations must be made which cannot be concealed from the world. At dusk seven hundred men, supported by a six-pounder fieldpiece, were put on board the *City of Alton,* on which they clustered like bees in a swarm, and as the huge engine laboured up and down against the stream, and the boat swayed from side to side, I felt a considerable desire to see General Prentiss chucked into the stream for his utter recklessness in cramming on board one huge tinder-box, all fire and touchwood, so many human beings, who, in event of an explosion, or a shot in the boiler, or of a heavy musketry fire on the banks, would have been converted into a great slaughterhouse. One small boat hung from her stern and although there were plenty of river flats and numerous steamers, even the horses belonging to the fieldpiece were crammed in among the men along the deck.

At night there was a kind of *émeute* in camp. The day, as I have said, was excessively hot, and on returning to their tents and huts from evening parade the men found the contractor who supplies them with water had not filled the barrels; so they forced the sentries, broke barracks after hours, mobbed their officers, and streamed up to the hotel, which they surrounded, calling "water, water," in chorus. The General came out, and got up on a rail: "Gentlemen," said he, "it is not my fault you are without water. It's your officers who are to blame, not me." ("Groans for the Quartermaster," from the men.) "If it is the fault of the contractor, I'll see that he is punished. I'll take steps at once to see that the matter is remedied. And now, gentlemen, I hope you'll go back to your quarters"; and the gentlemen took it into their heads very good-humouredly to obey the suggestion, fell in, and marched back two deep to their huts.

Chapter XLI

June 23rd. The latest information which I received today is of a nature to hasten my departure for Washington; it can no longer be doubted that a battle between the two armies assembled in the neighbourhood of the capital is imminent.

At four o'clock in the evening I started by train on the famous Central Illinois line from Cairo to Chicago.

The carriages were tolerably well filled with soldiers, and in addition to them there were a few unfortunate women, undergoing deportation to some less moral neighbourhood.

A considerable number of towns, formed by accretions of small stores and drinking places, called magazines, round the original shed wherein live the station master and his assistants, mark the course of the railway. Some are important enough to possess a bank, which is generally represented by a wooden hut, with a large board nailed in front, bearing the names of the president and cashier, and announcing the success and liberality of the management. The stores are also decorated with large signs, recommending the names of the owners to the attention of the public, and over all of them is to be seen the significant announcement, "Cash for produce."

One of my friends argues that as slavery is at the base of

Secession, it follows that States or portions of States will be disposed to join the Confederates or the Federalists just as the climate may be favourable or adverse to the growth of slave produce. Thus in the mountainous parts of the border States of Kentucky and Tennessee, in the northwestern part of Virginia, vulgarly called the pan handle, and in the pine woods of North Carolina, where white men can work at the rosin and naval store manufactories, there is a decided feeling in favour of the Union; in fact, it becomes a matter of isothermal lines.

Next morning, just at dawn, I woke up and got out on the platform of the carriage, which is the favourite resort of smokers and their antithetics, those who love pure fresh air, notwithstanding the printed caution "It is dangerous to stand on the platform"; and under the eye of early morn saw spread around a flat sea-like expanse not yet warmed into colour and life by the sun. The line was no longer guarded from daring Secessionists by soldiers' outposts, and small camps had disappeared. The train sped through the centre of the great verdant circle as a ship through the sea, leaving the rigid iron wake behind it tapering to a point at the horizon, and as the light spread over it the surface of the crisping corn waved in broad undulations beneath the breeze from east to west. This is the prairie indeed. Hereabouts it is covered with the finest crops, some already cut and stacked. Looking around one could see church spires rising in the distance from the white patches of houses, and by degrees the tracks across the fertile waste became apparent, and then carts and horses were seen toiling through the rich soil.

A large species of partridge or grouse appeared very abundant, and rose in flocks from the long grass at the side of the rail or from the rich carpet of flowers on the margin of the corn fields. They sat on the fence almost unmoved by the rushing engine, and literally swarmed along the line. These are called "prairie chickens" by the people and afford excellent sport.

The scene now began to change gradually as we approached

Chicago, the prairie subsided into swampy land, and thick belts of trees fringed the horizon; on our right glimpses of the sea could be caught through openings in the wood—the inland sea on which stands the Queen of the Lakes. Michigan looks broad and blue as the Mediterranean. Large farmhouses stud the country, and houses which must be the retreat of merchants and citizens of means; and when the train, leaving the land altogether, dashes out on a pier and causeway built along the borders of the lake, we see lines of noble houses, a fine boulevard, a forest of masts, huge isolated piles of masonry, the famed grain elevators by which so many have been hoisted to fortune, churches and public edifices, and the apparatus of a great city; and just at nine o'clock the train comes to a standstill in the spacious station of the Central Illinois Company, and in half an hour more I am in comfortable quarters at the Richmond House, where I find letters waiting for me, by which it appears that the necessity for my being in Washington in all haste no longer exists. The wary General who commands the Army is aware that the advance to Richmond, for which so many journals are clamouring, would be attended with serious risk at present, and the politicians must be content to wait a little longer.

Chapter XLII

I have already seen so many statements respecting my sayings, my doings, and my opinions, in the American papers, that I have resolved to follow a general rule, with few exceptions indeed, which prescribes as the best course to pursue, not so much an indifference to these remarks as a fixed purpose to abstain from the hopeless task of correcting them. The "Quicklys" of the press are incorrigible. Commerce may well be proud of Chicago. I am not going to reiterate what every Crispinus from the old country has said again and again concerning this wonderful place—not one word of statistics, of corn elevators, of shipping, or of the piles of buildings raised from the foundation by ingenious applications of screws. Nor am I going to enlarge on the splendid future of that which has so much present prosperity, or on the benefits to mankind opened up by the Illinois Central Railway. It is enough to say that by the borders of this lake there has sprung up in thirty years a wonderful city of fine streets, luxurious hotels, handsome shops, magnificent stores, great warehouses, extensive quays, capacious docks; and that as long as corn holds its own, and the mouths of Europe are open, and her hands full, Chicago will acquire greater importance, size, and wealth with every year. The only drawback, perhaps, to the comfort of the money-making inhabitants, and of the stranger within the gates, is to be found in the clouds of dust and in the unpaved streets and thoroughfares, which give anguish to horse and man.

I spent three days here writing my letters and repairing the wear and tear of my Southern expedition; and although it was hot enough, the breeze from the lake carried health and vigour to the frame, enervated by the sun of Louisiana and Mississippi.

I could not satisfy myself whether there was, as I have been told, a peculiar state of feeling in Chicago, which induced many people to support the Government of Mr. Lincoln because they believed it necessary for their own interests to obtain decided advantages over the South in the field, whilst they were opposed *totis viribus* to the genius of emancipation and to the views of the black Republicans. But the genius and eloquence of the little giant have left their impress on the facile mould of democratic thought; and he who argued with such acuteness and ability last March in Washington, in his own study, against the possibility, or at least the constitutional legality, of using the national forces, and the militia and volunteers of the Northern States, to subjugate the Southern people, carried away by the great bore which rushed through the placid North when Sumter fell, or perceiving his inability to resist its force, sprang to the crest of the wave, and carried to excess the violence of the Union reaction.

Whilst I was in the South I had seen his name in Northern papers with sensation headings and descriptions of his magnificent crusade for the Union in the West. I had heard his name reviled by those who had once been his warm political allies, and his untimely death did not seem to satisfy their hatred. His old foes in the North admired and applauded the sudden apostasy of their eloquent opponent, and were loud in lamentations over his loss. Imagine, then, how I felt when visiting his grave at Chicago, seeing his bust in many houses, or his portrait in all the shop windows, I was told that the enormously wealthy community of which he was the idol were permitting his widow to live in a state not far removed from penury.

"Senator Douglas, sir," observed one of his friends to me, "died of bad whiskey. He killed himself with it while he was stumping for the Union all over the country."

Chapter XLIII

At eight o'clock on the morning of the 27th I left Chicago for Niagara, which was so temptingly near that I resolved to make a detour by that route to New York.

It was dusk when we reached the steam ferryboat at Detroit,

which took us across to Windsor; but through the dusk I could perceive the Union Jack waving above the unimpressive little town which bears a name to be respected by British ears. The customs' inspections seemed very mild; and I was not much impressed by the representative of the British crown, who, with a brass button on his coat and a very husky voice, exercised his powers on behalf of Her Majesty at the landing-place at Windsor.

All night we travelled. A long day through a dreary, ill-settled, pine-wooded, half-cleared country, swarming with mosquitoes and biting flies, and famous for fevers. Just about daybreak the train stopped.

"Now, then," said an English voice; "now, then, who's for Clifton Hotel? All passengers leave cars for this side of the Falls." Consigning our baggage to the commissioner of the Clifton, my companion, Mr. Ward, and myself resolved to walk along the banks of the river to the hotel, which is some two miles and a half distant, and set out whilst it was still so obscure that the outline of the beautiful bridge which springs so lightly across the chasm, filled with furious hurrying waters, hundreds of feet below, was visible only as is the tracery of some cathedral arch through the dim light of the cloister.

It was distressing to find that Niagara was surrounded by the paraphernalia of a fixed fair. I had looked forward to a certain degree of solitude. It appeared impossible that man could cockneyfy such a maginificent display of force and grandeur in nature. But, alas! it is haunted by what poor Albert Smith used to denominate "harpies." The hateful race of guides infest the precincts of the hotels, waylay you in the lanes, and prowl about the unguarded moments of reverie. There are miserable little peepshows and photographers, bird stuffers, shell polishers, collectors of crystals, and proprietors of natural curiosity shops.

Next to the purveyors of curiosities and hotel keepers, the Indians, who live in a village at some distance from Niagara, reap the largest profit from the crowds of visitors who repair annually to the Falls. They are a harmless and by no means elevated race of semi-civilized savages, whose energies are expended on whiskey, feather fans, bark canoes, ornamental moccasins, and carved pipe stems. I had arranged for an excursion to see them in their wigwams one morning, when the news was brought to me that General Scott had ordered, or been forced to order, the advance of the Federal troops encamped in front of Washington, under the command of McDowell, against the Confederates, commanded by Beauregard, who was described as occupying a most formidable position, covered with entrenchments and batteries in front of a ridge of hills, through which the railway passes to Richmond.

The New York papers represent the Federal army to be of some grand indefinite strength, varying from 60,000 to 120,000 men, full of fight, admirably equipped, well disciplined, and provided with an overwhelming force of artillery. General Scott, I am very well assured, did not feel such confidence in the result of an invasion of Virginia that he would hurry raw levies and a rabble of regiments to undertake a most arduous military operation.

July 2nd. At about nine A.M., the train reached New York, and in driving to the house of Mr. Duncan, who accompanied me from Niagara, the first thing which struck me was the changed aspect of the streets. Instead of peaceful citizens, men in military uniforms thronged the pathways, and such multitudes of United States flags floated from the windows and roofs of the houses as to convey the impression that it was a great holiday festival.

As long as there was a chance that the struggle might not take place, the merchants of New York were silent, fearful of offending their Southern friends and connections, but inflicting infinite damage on their own government and misleading both sides. Their sentiments, sympathies, and business bound them with the South; and, indeed, till "the glorious uprising," the South believed New York was with them, as might be credited from the tone of some organs in the press, and I remember hearing it said by Southerners in Washington, that it was very likely New York would go out of the Union!

The change in manner, in tone, in argument, is most remarkable. I met men today who last March argued coolly and philosophically about the right of Secession. They are now furious at the idea of such wickedness—furious with England because she does not deny their own famous doctrine of the sacred right of insurrection. "We must maintain our glorious Union, sir." "We must have a country." "We cannot allow two nations to grow up on this Continent, sir." "We must possess the entire control of the Mississippi." These "musts," and "can'ts," and "won'ts," are the angry utterances of a spirited people who have had their will so long that they at last believe it is omnipotent. Assuredly, they will not have it over the South without a tremendous and long-sustained contest, in which they must put forth every exertion, and use all the resources and superior means they so abundantly possess.

Chapter XLIV

July 3rd. Nearly four months since I went by this road to Washington. The change which has since occurred is beyond belief. Men were then speaking of place under Government, of compromises between North and South, and of peace; now they only talk of war and battle. Ever since I came out of the South, and could see the newspapers, I have been struck by the easiness of the American people, by their excessive credulity. Whether they wish it or not, they are certainly deceived. Not a day has passed without the announcement that the Federal troops were moving, and that "a great battle was expected" by somebody unknown, at some place or other.

I could not help observing the arrogant tone with which writers of stupendous ignorance on military matters write of the operations which they think the Generals should undertake. They demand that an army, which has neither adequate transport, artillery, nor cavalry, shall be pushed forward to Richmond to crush out Secession, and at the same time their columns teem with accounts from the Army, which prove that it is not only ill-disciplined, but that it is ill-provided. A general outcry has been raised against the War Department and the contractors, and it is openly stated that Mr. Cameron, the Secretary, has not clean hands.

Coming so recently from the South, I can see the great difference which exists between the two races, as they may be called, exemplified in the men I have seen, and those who are in the train going towards Washington. These volunteers have none of the swashbuckler bravado, gallant-swaggering air of the Southern men. They are staid, quiet men, and the Pennsylvanians, who are on their way to join their regiment in Baltimore, are very inferior in size and strength to the Tennesseans and Carolinians.

Below Philadelphia, from Havre-de-Grace all the way to Baltimore, and then on to Washington, the stations on the rail were guarded by soldiers, as though an enemy were expected to destroy the bridges and to tear up the rails. Wooden bridges and causeways, carried over piles and embankments, are necessary, in consequence of the nature of the country; and at each of these a small camp was formed for the soldiers who have to guard the approaches. Sentinels are posted, pickets thrown out, and in the open field by the wayside troops are to be seen moving, as though

[187]

a battle was close at hand. In one word, we are in the State of Maryland. By these means alone are communications maintained between the North and the capital. As we approach Baltimore the number of sentinels and camps increase, and earthworks have been thrown up on the high grounds commanding the city. The display of Federal flags from the public buildings and some shipping in the river was so limited as to contrast strongly with those symbols of Union sentiments in the Northern cities.

Since I last passed through this city the streets have been a scene of bloodshed. The conductor of the car on which we travelled from one terminus to the other, along the street railway, pointed out the marks of the bullets on the walls and in the window frames. "That's the way to deal with the Plug Uglies," exclaimed he; a name given popularly to the lower classes called Rowdies in New York.

It is about forty miles from Baltimore to Washington, and at every quarter of a mile for the whole distance a picket of soldiers guarded the rails. Camps appeared on both sides, larger and more closely packed together; and the rays of the setting sun fell on countless lines of tents as we approached the unfinished dome of the Capitol. On the Virginian side of the river, columns of smoke rising from the forest marked the site of Federal encampments across the stream. The fields around Washington resounded with the words of command and tramp of men, and flashed with wheeling arms. Parks of artillery studded the waste ground, and long trains of white-covered wagons filled up the open spaces in the suburbs of Washington.

To me all this was a wonderful sight. As I drove up Pennsylvania Avenue I could scarce credit that busy thoroughfare—all red, white, and blue with flags, filled with dust from galloping chargers and commissariat carts; the sidewalks thronged with people, of whom a large proportion carried sword or bayonet; shops full of life and activity—was the same as that through which I had driven the first morning of my arrival. Washington now, indeed, is the capital of the United States; but it is no longer the scene of beneficent legislation and of peaceful government. It is the representative of armed force engaged in war—menaced whilst in the very act of raising its arm by the enemy it seeks to strike.

To avoid the tumult of Willard's, I requested a friend to hire apartments and drove to a house in Pennsylvania Avenue, close to the War Department, where he had succeeded in engaging a sitting room about twelve feet square, and a bedroom to correspond, in a very small mansion, next door to a spirit merchant's. At the Legation I saw Lord Lyons, and gave him a brief account of what I had seen in the South.

The relations of the United States Government with Great Britain have probably been considerably affected by Mr. Seward's failure in his prophecies. As the Southern Confederacy develops its power, the Foreign Secretary assumes higher ground, and becomes more exacting and defiant. In these hot summer days, Lord Lyons and the members of the Legation dine early, and enjoy the cool of the evening in the garden: so after a while I took my leave, and proceeded to Gautier's. On my way I met Mr. Sumner, who asked me for Southern news very anxiously, and in the course of conversation with him I was confirmed in my impressions that the feeling between the two countries was not as friendly as could be desired.

Congress met today, merely for the purpose of forming itself into a regular body, and there was no debate or business of public importance introduced. Mr. Wilson gave me to understand, however, that some military movements of the utmost importance might be expected in a few days, and that General McDowell would positively attack the rebels in front of Washington. The Confederates occupy the whole of northern Virginia, commencing from the peninsula above Fortress Monroe on the right or east, and extending along the Potomac, to the extreme verge of the State, by the Baltimore and Ohio Railway. This immense

[189]

line, however, is broken by great intervals, and the army with which McDowell will have to deal may be considered as detached, covering the approaches to Richmond, whilst its left flank is protected by a corps of observation, stationed near Winchester, under General Jackson. A Federal corps is being prepared to watch the corps and engage it, whilst McDowell advances on the main body. To the right of this again, or further west, another body of Federals, under General McClellan, is operating in the valleys of the Shenandoah and in western Virginia; but I did not hear any of these things from Mr. Wilson, who was, I am sure, in perfect ignorance of the plans, in a military sense, of the general. I sat at Mr. Sumner's desk, and wrote the final paragraphs of a letter describing my impressions of the South in a place but little disposed to give a favourable colour to them.

Chapter XLV

All the population of Washington had turned out in their best to listen to the military bands, the music of which was rendered nearly inaudible by the constant discharge of fireworks. The camp of the 12th New York presented a very pretty and animated scene. The men liberated from duty were enjoying themselves out and inside their tents, and the sutlers' booths were driving a roaring trade. I was introduced to Colonel Butterfield, commanding the regiment, who was a merchant of New York; but notwithstanding the training of the counting-house, he looked very much like a soldier, and had got his regiment very fairly in hand. In compliance with a desire of Professor Henry, the Colonel had prepared a number of statistical tables in which the nationality, height, weight, breadth of chest, age, and other particulars respecting the men under his command were entered. I looked over the book, and as far as I could judge, but two out of twelve of the soldiers were native-born Americans, the rest being Irish, German, English, and European-born generally. According to the commanding officer they were in the highest state of discipline and obedience. He had given them leave to go out as they pleased for the day, but at tattoo only fourteen men out of one thousand were absent, and some of those had been accounted for by reports that they were incapable of locomotion owing to the hospitality of the citizens.

The sounds in Washington tonight might have led one to believe the city was carried by storm. Constant explosion of firearms, fireworks, shouting, and cries in the streets, which combined with the heat and the abominable odours of the undrained houses and mosquitoes to drive sleep far away.

July 5th. The Congress met today to hear the President's Message read. Somehow or other there is not such anxiety and eagerness to hear what Mr. Lincoln has to say as one could expect on such a momentous occasion. The President has, it is said, written much of it in his own fashion, which has been revised and altered by his Ministers; but he has written it again and repeated himself, and after many struggles a good deal of pure Lincolnism goes down to Congress.

At a little after half past eleven I went down to the Capitol. Pennsylvania Avenue was thronged as before, but on approaching Capitol Hill, the crowd rather thinned away, as though they shunned, or had no curiosity to hear, the President's Message. One would have thought that, where every one who could get in was at liberty to attend the galleries in both Houses, there would have been an immense pressure from the inhabitants and strangers in the city, as well as from the citizen soldiers, of which such multitudes were in the street; but when I looked up from the

[191]

floor of the Senate, I was astonished to see that the galleries were not more than three parts filled. There is always a ruinous look about an unfinished building when it is occupied and devoted to business. The Capitol is situated on a hill, one face of which is scarped by the road, and has the appearance of being formed of heaps of rubbish.

All the encaustics and the white marble and stone staircases suffer from tobacco juice, though there is a liberal display of spittoons at every corner. The official messengers, doorkeepers, and porters wear no distinctive badge or dress. No policemen are on duty, as in our Houses of Parliament; no soldiery, gendarmerie, or *sergents-de-ville* in the precincts; the crowd wanders about the passages as it pleases, and shows the utmost propriety, never going where it ought not to intrude.

It was a hot day; but there was no excuse for the slop coats and light-coloured clothing and felt wide-awakes worn by so many Senators in such a place. They gave the meeting an aspect of a gathering of bakers or millers: nor did the constant use of the spittoons beside their desks, their reading of newspapers and writing letters during the despatch of business, or the hurrying to and fro of the pages of the House between the seats, do anything but derogate from the dignity of the assemblage, and, according to European notions, violate the respect due to a Senate Chamber.

The House of Representatives exaggerates all the peculiarities I have observed in the Senate, but the debates are not regarded with so much interest as those of the Upper House; indeed, they are of far less importance. Strong-minded statesmen and officers—Presidents or Ministers—do not care much for the House of Representatives.

July 6th. I breakfasted with Mr. Bigelow this morning, to meet General McDowell, who commands the Army of the Potomac, now so soon to move. He came in without an aide-de-camp, and on foot, from his quarters in the city. He is a man about forty years of age, square and powerfully built, but with rather a stout and clumsy figure and limbs, a good head covered with close-cut thick dark hair, small light-blue eyes, short nose, large cheeks and jaws, relieved by an iron-grey tuft somewhat of the French type, and affecting in dress the style of our gallant allies. His manner is frank, simple, and agreeable, and he did not hesitate to speak with great openness of the difficulties he had to contend with, and the imperfection of all the arrangements of the Army.

As an officer of the regular army he has a thorough contempt for what he calls "political generals"—the men who use their influence with President and Congress to obtain military rank, which in time of war places them before the public in the front of events, and gives them an appearance of leading in the greatest of all political movements. Nor is General McDowell enamoured of volunteers, for he served in Mexico, and has from what he saw there formed rather an unfavourable opinion of their capabilities in the field. He is inclined, however, to hold the Southern troops in too little respect; and he told me that the volunteers from the slave states, who entered the field full of exultation and boastings, did not make good their words, and that they suffered especially from sickness and disease, in consequence of their disorderly habits and dissipation. His regard for old associations was evinced in many questions he asked me about Beauregard, with whom he had been a student at West Point, where the Confederate commander was noted for his studious and reserved habits, and his excellence in feats of strength and athletic exercises.

The General walked back with me as far as my lodgings, and I observed that not one of the many soldiers he passed in the streets saluted him though his rank was indicated by his velvet collar and cuffs, and a gold star on the shoulder strap.

July 7th. Mr. Bigelow invited me to breakfast, to meet Mr. Senator King, Mr. Olmsted, Mr. Thurlow Weed, a Senator from Missouri, a West Point professor, and others. It was indicative of

[193]

the serious difficulties which embarrass the action of the Government to hear Mr. Wilson, the Chairman of the Military Committee of the Senate, inveigh against the officers of the regular army, and attack West Point itself. Whilst the New York papers were lauding General Scott and his plans to the skies, the Washington politicians were speaking of him as obstructive, obstinate, and prejudiced—unfit for the times and the occasion.

General Scott refused to accept cavalry and artillery at the beginning of the levy, and said that they were not required; now he was calling for both arms most urgently. The officers of the regular army had followed suit. Although they were urgently pressed by the politicians to occupy Harper's Ferry and Manassas, they refused to do either, and the result is that the enemy have obtained invaluable supplies from the first place, and are now assembled in force in a most formidable position at the second. Everything as yet accomplished has been done by political generals—not by the officers of the regular army. Butler and Banks saved Baltimore in spite of General Scott. There was an attempt made to cry up Lyon in Missouri; but in fact it was Frank Blair, the brother of the Postmaster-General, who had been the soul and body of all the actions in that State. The first step taken by McClellan in western Virginia was atrocious—he talked of slaves in a public document as property. Butler, at Monroe, had dealt with them in a very different spirit, and had used them for State purposes under the name of contraband. One man alone displayed powers of administrative ability, and that was Quartermaster Meigs; and unquestionably from all I heard, the praise was well bestowed.

Chapter XLVI

————◄•►————

July 8th. As a consequence of the magnificent conceptions which were entertained by the founders regarding the future dimensions of their future city, Washington is all suburb and no city. The road to the Long Bridge passes by a four-sided shaft of blocks of white marble, contributed, with appropriate mottoes, by the various States, as a fitting monument to Washington. It is not yet completed, and the materials lie in the field around, just as the Capitol and the Treasury are surrounded by the materials for their future and final development. Further on, is the red, and rather fantastic, pile of the Smithsonian Institute, and then the road makes a dip to the bridge, past some squalid little cottages, and the eye reposes on the shore of Virginia, rising in successive folds, and richly wooded, up to a moderate height from the water. Through the green forest leaves gleams the white canvas of the tents, and on the highest ridge westward rises an imposing structure, with a portico and colonnade in front, and belongs by descent, through Mr. Custis, from the wife of George Washington, to General Lee, Commander-in-Chief of the Confederate Army. It is now occupied by General McDowell as his headquarters, and a large United States flag floats from the roof, which shames even the ample proportions of the many Stars and Stripes rising up from the camps in the trees.

At the bridge there was a post of volunteer soldiers. The sentry on duty was sitting on a stump, with his firelock across his knees, reading a newspaper. He held out his hand for my pass, which was in the form of a letter, written by General Scott, and ordering all officers and soldiers of the Army of the Potomac to permit me to pass freely without let or hindrance, and recommending me to the attention of Brigadier-General McDowell and all officers under his orders. "That'll do, you may go," said the sentry. "What pass is that, Abe?" inquired a non-commissioned officer. "It's from General Scott, and says he's to go wherever he likes." "I hope you'll go right away to Richmond, then, and get Jeff Davis's scalp for us," said the patriotic sergeant.

At the other end of the bridge a weak *tête de pont*, commanded by a road-work further on, covered the approach, and turning to the right I passed through a maze of camps, in front of which the various regiments, much better than I had expected to find them, broken up into small detachments, were learning elementary drill. A considerable number of the men were Germans, and the officers were for the most part in a state of profound ignorance of company drill, as might be seen by their confusion and inability to take their places when the companies faced about, or moved from one flank to the other. They were by no means equal in size or age, and with some splendid exceptions, were inferior to the Southern soldiers. The camps were dirty, no latrines—the tents of various patterns—but on the whole they were well castramentated.

It would scarcely be credited, were I not told it by General McDowell, that there is no such thing procurable as a decent map of Virginia. He knows little or nothing of the country before him, more than the general direction of the main roads, which are bad at the best; and he can obtain no information, inasmuch as the enemy are in full force all along his front, and he has not a cavalry officer capable of conducting a reconnaissance, which would be difficult enough in the best hands, owing to the dense woods which rise up in front of his lines, screening the enemy completely. The Confederates have thrown up very heavy batteries at Manassas, about thirty miles away, where the railway from the West crosses the line to Richmond, and I do not think General McDowell much likes the look of them, but the cry for action is so strong the President cannot resist it.

The most absurd rumours were flying about the staff, one of whom declared very positively that there was going to be a compromise, and that Jeff Davis had made an overture for peace. The papers are filled with accounts of an action in Missouri, at a place called Carthage, between the Federals commanded by Colonel Sigel, consisting for the most part of Germans, and the Confederates under General Parsons, in which the former were obliged to retreat, although it is admitted the State troops were miserably armed, and had most ineffective artillery, whilst their opponents had every advantage in both respects, and were commanded by officers of European experience.

July 9th. I had the honour of dining with General Scott, who has moved to new quarters, near the War Department, and met General Frémont, who is designated, according to rumor, to take command of an important district in the West, and to clear the right bank of the Mississippi and the course of the Missouri. "The Pathfinder" is a strong Republican and Abolitionist, whom the Germans delight to honour—a man with a dreamy deep blue eye, a gentlemanly address, pleasant features, and an active frame, but without the smallest external indication of extraordinary vigour, intelligence, or ability; if he has military genius, it must come by intuition, for assuredly he has no professional acquirements or experience. Two or three members of Congress, and the General's staff, and Mr. Bigelow, completed the company. The General has become visibly weaker since I first saw him. He walks down to his office, close at hand, with difficulty; returns a short time before dinner, and reposes; and when he has dismissed his guests at an early hour, or even before he does so, stretches himself on his bed, and then before midnight rouses himself to look at dispatches or to transact any necessary busi-

[197]

ness. In case of an action it is his intention to proceed to the field in a light carriage, which is always ready for the purpose with horses and driver; nor is he unprepared with precedents of great military commanders who have successfully conducted engagements under similar circumstances.

July 10th. Today was spent in a lengthy excursion along the front of the camp in Virginia, round by the chain bridge which crosses the Potomac about four miles from Washington.

The Government have been coerced, as they say, by the safety of the Republic, to destroy the liberty of the press, which is guaranteed by the Constitution, and this is not the first instance in which the Constitution of the United States will be made *nominis umbra.* The telegraph, according to General Scott's order, confirmed by the Minister of War, Simon Cameron, is to convey no dispatches respecting military movements not permitted by the General; and today the newspaper correspondents have agreed to yield obedience to the order, reserving to themselves a certain freedom of detail in writing their dispatches, and relying on the Government to publish the official accounts of all battles very speedily. They will break this agreement if they can, and the Government will not observe their part of the bargain. The freedom of the press, as I take it, does not include the right to publish news hostile to the cause of the country in which it is published; neither can it involve any obligation on the part of Government to publish any dispatches which may be injurious to the party they represent.

I just got into the House in time to hear Mr. Vallandigham, who is an ultra-Democrat, and very nearly a Secessionist, conclude a well-delivered argumentative address. He is a tall, slight man, of a bilious temperament, with light flashing eyes, dark hair and complexion, and considerable oratorical power. "Deem me ef I wouldn't just ride that Vallandiggaim on a reay-al," quoth a citizen to his friend, as the speaker sat down amid a few feeble expressions of assent.

[198]

July 12th. There are rumours that the Federals, under Brigadier McClellan, who have advanced into western Virginia, have
gained some successes; but so far it seems to have no larger
dimensions than the onward raid of one clan against another in
the Highlands.

July 13th. I have had a long day's ride through the camps of
the various regiments across the Potomac, and at this side of it,
which the weather did not render very agreeable to myself or
the poor hack that I had hired for the day, till my American
Quatermaine gets me a decent mount.

In the first place, there are not, I should think, 30,000 men
of all sorts available for the campaign. The papers estimate it at
any number from 50,000 to 100,000, giving the preference to
75,000. In the next place, their artillery is miserably deficient;
they have not, I should think, more than five complete batteries,
or six batteries, including scratch guns, and these are of different
calibres, badly horsed, miserably equipped, and provided with
the worst set of gunners and drivers which I, who have seen the
Turkish field guns, ever beheld. They have no cavalry, only a
few scarecrow-men, who would dissolve partnership with their
steeds at the first serious combined movement, mounted in high
saddles, on wretched mouthless screws, and some few regulars
from the frontiers, who may be good for Indians, but who would
go over like ninepins at a charge from Punjaubee irregulars.
Their transport is tolerably good, but inadequate; they have no
carriage for reserve ammunition; the commissariat drivers are
civilians, under little or no control; the officers are unsoldierly-
looking men; the camps are dirty to excess; the men are dressed
in all sorts of uniforms; and from what I hear, I doubt if any
of these regiments have ever performed a brigade evolution
together, or if any of the officers know what it is to deploy a
brigade from column into line. They are mostly three months'
men, whose time is nearly up. They were rejoicing today over
the fact that it was so, and that they had kept the enemy from

Washington "without a fight." And it is with this rabblement that the North propose not only to subdue the South but according to some of their papers, to humiliate Great Britain, and conquer Canada afterwards.

Major-General McClellan—I beg his pardon for styling him Brigadier—has really been successful. By a very well-conducted and rather rapid march, he was enabled to bring superior forces to bear on some raw levies under General Garnett (who came over with me in the steamer), which fled after a few shots, and were utterly routed, when their gallant commander fell, in an abortive attempt to rally them by the banks of the Cheat River. In this "great battle" McClellan's loss is less than thirty killed and wounded, and the Confederates' loss is less than one hundred. But the dispersion of such guerilla bands has the most useful effect among the people of the district; and McClellan has done good service, especially as his little victory will lead to the discomfiture of all Secessionists in the valley of the Kenawha, and in the valley of western Virginia. I left Washington this afternoon, with the Sanitary Commissioners, for Baltimore, in order to visit the Federal camps at Fortress Monroe, to which we proceeded down the Chesapeake the same night.

Chapter XLVII

July 14th. At six o'clock this morning the steamer arrived at the wharf under the walls of Fortress Monroe, which presented a very different appearance from the quiet of its aspect when first I saw it, some months ago. Camps spread around it, the parapets lined with sentries, guns looking out towards the land, lighters and steamers alongside the wharf, a strong guard at the end of the pier, passes to be scrutinised and permits to be given. I landed with the members of the Sanitary Commission, and repaired to a very large pile of buildings, called "The Hygeia Hotel," for once on a time Fortress Monroe was looked upon as the resort of the sickly, who required bracing air and an abundance of oysters; it is now occupied by the wounded in the several actions and skirmishes which have taken place, particularly at Bethel; and it is so densely crowded that we had difficulty in procuring the use of some small dirty rooms to dress in. As the business of the Commission was principally directed to ascertain the state of the hospitals, they considered it necessary in the first instance to visit General Butler, the commander of the post, who has been recommending himself to the Federal Government by his activity ever since he came down to Baltimore, and the whole body marched to the fort, crossing the drawbridge after some parley with the guard, and received permission, on the production of passes, to enter the court.

It was quite refreshing to the eye to see the cleanliness of the regulars—their white gloves and belts, and polished buttons, contrasted with the slovenly aspect of the volunteers; but, as far as the material went, the volunteers had by far the best of the comparison. The civilians who were with me did not pay much attention to the regulars, and evidently preferred the volunteers, although they could not be insensible to the magnificent drum major who led the band of the regulars. Presently General Butler came out of his quarters, and walked down the lines, followed by a few officers. He is a stout, middle-aged man, strongly built, with coarse limbs, his features indicative of great shrewdness and craft, his forehead high, the elevation being in some degree due perhaps to the want of hair; with a strong obliquity of vision, which may perhaps have been caused by an injury, as the eyelid hangs with a peculiar droop over the organ.

The General, whose manner is quick, decided, and abrupt, but not at all rude or unpleasant, at once acceded to the wishes of the Sanitary Commissioners, and expressed his desire to make my stay at the fort as agreeable and useful as he could. "You can first visit the hospitals in company with these gentlemen, and then come over with me to our camp, where I will show you everything that is to be seen. I have ordered a steamer to be in readiness to take you to Newport News." He speaks rapidly, and either affects or possesses great decision. The Commissioners accordingly proceeded to make the most of their time in visiting the Hygeia Hotel, being accompanied by the medical officers of the garrison.

The rooms, but a short time ago occupied by the fair ladies of Virginia, when they came down to enjoy the sea breezes, were now crowded with Federal soldiers, many of them suffering from the loss of limb or serious wounds, others from the worst form of camp disease.

The Americans were fighting for the combined excellences and strength of the States of New England, and the rest of the Federal power over the Confederates, for they could not in their heart of hearts believe the Old Union could be restored by force of arms.

At the end of our promenade round the ramparts, Lieutenant Butler, the General's nephew and aide-de-camp came to tell us the boat was ready, and we met His Excellency in the courtyard, whence we walked down to the wharf. On our way, General Butler called my attention to an enormous heap of hollow iron lying on the sand, which was the Union gun that is intended to throw a shot of some 350 pounds weight or more, to astonish the Confederates at Sewall's Point opposite, when it is mounted. This gun, if I mistake not, was made after the designs of Captain Rodman, of the United States artillery, who in a series of remarkable papers, the publication of which has cost the country a large sum of money, has given us the results of long-continued

[202]

investigations and experiments on the best method of cooling masses of iron for ordnance purposes, and of making powder for heavy shot. The piece must weigh about twenty tons, but a similar gun, mounted on an artificial island called the Rip Raps, in the Channel opposite the fortress, is said to be worked with facility. The Confederates have raised some of the vessels sunk by the United States officers when the Navy Yard at Gosport was destroyed, and as some of these are to be converted into rams, the Federals are preparing their heaviest ordnance to try the effect of crushing weights at low velocities against their sides, should they attempt to play any pranks among the transport vessels. The General said: "It is not by these great masses of iron this contest is to be decided: we must bring sharp points of steel, directed by superior intelligence." Hitherto General Butler's attempts at Big Bethel have not been crowned with success in employing such means.

A vivacious, prying man, this Butler, full of bustling life, self-esteem, revelling in the exercise of power. In the course of our rounds we were joined by Colonel Phelps, who was formerly in the United States Army, and saw service in Mexico, but retired because he did not approve of the manner in which promotions were made, and who only took command of a Massachusetts regiment because he believed he might be instrumental in striking a shrewd blow or two in this great battle of Armageddon—a tall, saturnine, gloomy, angry-eyed, sallow man, soldier-like too, and one who places old John Brown on a level with the great martyrs of the Christian world.

At the tea table there were no additions to the General's family; he therefore spoke without any reserve. Going over the map, he explained his views in reference to future operations, and showed cause, with more military acumen than I could have expected from a gentleman of the long robe, why he believed Fortress Monroe was the true base of operations against Richmond.

I have been convinced for some time that if a sufficient force could be left to cover Washington, the Federals should move against Richmond from the Peninsula, where they could form their depots at leisure, and advance, protected by their gun-boats, on a very short line which offers far greater facilities and advantages than the inland route from Alexandria to Richmond, which, difficult in itself from the nature of the country, is exposed to the action of a hostile population, and, above all, to the danger of constant attacks by the enemies' cavalry, tending more or less to destroy all communication with the base of the Federal operations.

The threat of seizing Washington led to a concentration of the Union troops in front of it, which caused in turn the collection of the Confederates on the lines below to defend Richmond. It is plain that if the Federals can cover Washington, and at the same time assemble a force at Monroe strong enough to march on Richmond, as they desire, the Confederates will be placed in an exceedingly hazardous position, scarcely possible to escape from; and there is no reason why the North, with their overwhelming preponderance, should not do so, unless they be carried away by the fatal spirit of brag and bluster which comes from their press to overrate their own strength and to despise their enemy's.

July 15th. I need not speak much of the events of last night, which were not unimportant, perhaps, to some of the insects which played a leading part in them. The heat was literally overpowering; for in addition to the hot night there was the full power of most irritable boilers close at hand to aggravate the natural *désagréments* of the situation. About an hour after dawn, when I turned out on deck, there was nothing visible, but a warm grey mist; but a knotty old pilot on deck told me we were only going six knots an hour against tide and wind, and that we were likely to make less way as the day wore on. In fact, instead of being near Baltimore, we were much nearer Fortress Monroe.

Need I repeat the horrors of this day? Stewed, boiled, baked, and grilled on board this miserable *Elizabeth,* I wished M. Montalembert could have experienced with me what such an impassive nature could inflict in misery on those around it. The captain was a shy, silent man, much given to short naps in my temporary berth, and the mate was so wild, he might have swam off with perfect propriety to the woods on either side of us, and taken to a tree as an aborigine or chimpanzee. Two men of most retiring habits, the Negro, a black boy, and a very fat Negress who officiated as cook filled up the "balance" of the crew.

I could not write, for the vibration of the deck of the little craft gave a St. Vitus' dance to pen and pencil; reading was out of the question from the heat and flies; and below stairs the fat cook banished repose by vapours from her dreadful caldrons, where, Medea-like, she was boiling some death broth. Our breakfast was of the simplest and—may I add?—the least enticing; and if the dinner could have been worse it was so; though it was rendered attractive by hunger, and by the kindness of the sailors who shared it with me. The old pilot had the most wholesome hatred of the Britishers, and not having the least idea till late in the day that I belonged to the old country, favoured me with some very remarkable views respecting their general mischievousness and inutility. As soon as he found out my secret he became more reserved, and explained to me that he had some reason for not liking us, because all he had in the world, as pretty a schooner as ever floated and a fine cargo, had been taken and burnt by the English when they sailed up the Potomac to Washington. He served against us at Bladensburg. I did not ask him how fast he ran; but he had a good rejoinder ready if I had done so, inasmuch as he was up West under Commodore Perry on the lakes when we suffered our most serious reverses. Six knots an hour! Hour after hour! And nothing to do but listen to the pilot.

By-and-by the houses of a considerable town, crowned by steeples, and a large Corinthian-looking building, came in view.

"That's the State House. That's where George Washington—first in peace, first in war, and first in the hearts of his countrymen—laid down his victorious sword without any one asking him, and retired amid the applause of the civilised world." This flight I am sure was the old man's treasured relic of school-boy days, and I'm not sure he did not give it to me three times over. Annapolis looks very well from the river side. A dismantled sloop of war lay off a sea wall, banking up a green lawn covered with trees, in front of an old-fashioned pile of buildings, which formerly, I think, and very recently indeed, was occupied by the cadets of the United States Naval School. "There was a lot of them Seceders. Lord bless you! these young ones is all took by these States Rights' doctrines—just as the ladies is caught by a new fashion."

About seven o'clock the steamer hove alongside a wooden pier which was quite deserted. Only some ten or twelve sailing boats, yachts, and schooners lay at anchor in the placid waters of the port which was once the capital of Maryland, and for which the early Republicans prophesied a great future. But Baltimore has eclipsed Annapolis into utter obscurity. I walked to the only hotel in the place, and found that the train for the junction with Washington had started, and that the next train left at some impossible hour in the morning. It is an odd Rip Van Winkle sort of a place. Quaint-looking boarders came down to the tea-table and talked Secession, and when I was detected, as must ever soon be the case, owing to the hotel book, I was treated to some ill-favoured glances, as my recent letters have been denounced in the strongest way for their supposed hostility to States' Rights and the Domestic Institution.

Chapter XLVIII

July 16th. I baffled many curious and civil citizens by breakfasting in my room where I remained writing till late in the day. In the afternoon I walked to the State House. The hall door was open, but the rooms were closed; and I remained in the hall, which is graced by two indifferent huge statues of Law and Justice holding gas lamps, and by an old rusty cannon, dug out of the river, and supposed to have belonged to the original British colonists, whilst an officer whom I met in the portico went to look for the porter and the keys. Whether he succeeded I cannot say, for after waiting some half hour I was warned by my watch that it was time to get ready for the train, which started at 4:15 P.M. At the junction with the Washington line from Baltimore there is a strong guard thrown out from the camp near at hand. The officers, who had a mess in a little wayside inn on the line, invited me to rest till the train came up, and from them I heard that an advance had been actually ordered, and that if the "rebels" stood there would soon be a tall fight close to Washington. They were very cheery, hospitable fellows, and enjoyed their new mode of life amazingly. The men of the regiment to which they belonged were Germans, almost to a man. When the train came in I found it was full of soldiers, and I learned that three more heavy trains were to follow, in addition to four which had already passed laden with troops.

On arriving at the Washington platform, the first person I saw was General McDowell alone, looking anxiously into the carriages. He asked where I came from, and when he heard from Annapolis, inquired eagerly if I had seen two batteries of artillery —Barry's and another—which he had ordered up, and was waiting for, but which had "gone astray." I was surprised to find the General engaged on such duty, and took leave to say so. "Well, it is quite true, Mr. Russell; but I am obliged to look after them myself, as I have so small a staff, and they are all engaged out with my headquarters. You are aware I have advanced? No! Well, you have just come in time, and I shall be happy, indeed, to take you with me. I have made arrangements for the correspondents of our papers to take the field under certain regulations, and I have suggested to them they should wear a white uniform, to indicate the purity of their character." The General could hear nothing of his guns; his carriage was waiting, and I accepted his offer of a seat to my lodgings. Although he spoke confidently, he did not seem in good spirits. There was the greatest difficulty in finding out anything about the enemy. Beauregard was said to have advanced to Fairfax Court House, but he could not get any certain knowledge of the fact. "Can you not order a reconnaissance?" "Wait till you see the country. But even if it were as flat as Flanders, I have not an officer on whom I could depend for the work. They would fall into some trap, or bring on a general engagement when I did not seek it or desire it. I have no cavalry such as you work with in Europe." I think he was not so much disposed to undervalue the Confederates as before, for he said they had selected a very strong position, and had made a regular *levée en masse* of the people of Virginia, as a proof of the energy and determination with which they were entering the campaign.

July 17th. I went up to General Scott's quarters, and saw some of his staff—young men, some of whom knew nothing of soldiers, not even the enforcing of drill—and found them reflecting, doubtless, the shades which cross the mind of the old chief, who was now seeking repose. McDowell is to advance tomorrow from Fairfax Court House, and will march some eight or ten miles to Centreville, directly in front of which, at a place called Manassas, stands the army of the Southern enemy. I look around me for a staff, and look in vain. There are a few plodding old pedants, with map and rules and compasses, who sit in small rooms and write memoranda; and there are some ignorant and not very active young men, who loiter about the headquarters' halls, and strut up the street with brass spurs on their heels and kepis raked over their eyes as though they were soldiers, but I see no system, no order, no knowledge, no dash!

The worst-served English general has always a young fellow or two about him who can fly across country, draw a rough sketch map, ride like a foxhunter, and find something out about the enemy and their position, understand and convey orders, and obey them. I look about for the types of these in vain. McDowell can find out nothing about the enemy; he has not a trustworthy map of the country; no knowledge of their position, force, or numbers. All the people, he says, are against the Government. Fairfax Courthouse was abandoned as he approached, the enemy in their retreat being followed by the inhabitants. "Where were the Confederate entrenchments?" "Only in the imagination of those New York newspapers; when they want to fill up a column they write a full account of the enemy's fortifications. No one can contradict them at the time, and it's a good joke when it's found out to be a lie." Colonel Cullum went over the maps with me at General Scott's, and spoke with some greater confidence of McDowell's prospects of success. There is a considerable force of Confederates at a place called Winchester, which is connected with Manassas by rail, and this force could be thrown on the right of the Federals as they advanced, but that other corps, under Patterson, is in observation, with orders to engage them if they attempt to move eastwards.

The batteries for which General McDowell was looking last night have arrived, and were sent on this morning. One is under

Barry, of the United States regular artillery, whom I met at Fort Pickens. The other is a volunteer battery. The onward movement of the army has been productive of a great improvement in the streets of Washington, which are no longer crowded with turbulent and disorderly volunteers, or by soldiers disgracing the name, who accost you in the byways for money. There are comparatively few today; small shoals which have escaped the meshes of the net are endeavouring to make the most of their time before they cross the river to face the enemy.

In the evening I received a message to say that the advance of the army would take place tomorrow as soon as General McDowell had satisfied himself by a reconnaissance that he could carry out his plan of turning the right of the enemy by passing Occagunga Creek. Along Pennsylvania Avenue, along the various shops, hotels, and drinking bars, groups of people were collected, listening to the most exaggerated accounts of desperate fighting and of the utter demoralisation of the rebels. I was rather amused by hearing the florid accounts which were given in the hall of Willard's by various inebriated officers, who were drawing upon their imagination for their facts, knowing, as I did, that the entrenchments at Fairfax had been abandoned without a shot on the advance of the Federal troops. The New York papers came in with glowing descriptions of the magnificent march of the Grand Army of the Potomac, which was stated to consist of upwards of seventy thousand men; whereas I knew not half that number were actually on the field. Multitudes of people believe General Winfield Scott, who was now fast asleep in his modest bed in Pennsylvania Avenue, is about to take the field in person. The horse dealers are still utterly impracticable. A citizen who owned a dark bay, spavined and ringboned, asked me $1,000 for the right of possession. I ventured to suggest that it was not worth the money. "Well," said he, "take it or leave it. If you want to see this fight $1,000 is cheap. I guess there were chaps paid more than that to see Jenny Lind on her first night; and this battle is not going to be repeated, I can tell you. The price of horses will rise when the chaps out there have had themselves pretty well used up with bowie-knives and six-shooters."

July 18th. After breakfast. Leaving headquarters, I went across to General Mansfield's and was going upstairs, when the General * himself, a white-headed, grey-bearded, and rather soldierly-looking man, dashed out of his room in some excitement, and exclaimed, "Mr. Russell, I fear there is bad news from the front." "Are they fighting, General?" "Yes, sir. That fellow Tyler has been engaged, and we are whipped." Again I went off to the horse dealer; but this time the price of the steed had been raised to £220; "for," says he, "I don't want my animals to be ripped up by them cannon and them musketry, and those who wish to be guilty of such cruelty must pay for it." At the War Office, at the Department of State, at the Senate, and at the White House, messengers and orderlies running in and out, military aides, and civilians with anxious faces, betokened the activity and perturbation which reigned within. I met Senator Sumner radiant with joy. "We have obtained a great success; the rebels are falling back in all directions. General Scott says we ought to be in Richmond by Saturday night." Soon afterwards a United States officer, who had visited me in company with General Meigs, riding rapidly past, called out, "You have heard we are whipped; these confounded volunteers have run away." I drove to the Capitol, where people said one could actually see the smoke of the cannon; but on arriving there it was evident that the fire from some burning houses, and from wood cut down for cooking purposes, had been mistaken for tokens of the fight.

I entered one shop, where the proprietor and his wife ran forward to meet me. "Have you heard the news? Beauregard has knocked them into a cocked hat." "Believe me," said the good lady, "it is the finger of the Almighty is in it. Didn't he curse the niggers, and why should he take their part now with

* Since killed in action.

[211]

these Yankee Abolitionists, against true white men?" "But how do you know this?" said I. "Why, it's all true enough, depend upon it, no matter how we know it. We've got our underground railway as well as the Abolitionists."

On my way to dinner at the Legation I met the President crossing Pennsylvania Avenue, striding like a crane in a bullrush swamp among the great blocks of marble, dressed in an oddly cut suit of grey, with a felt hat on the back of his head, wiping his face with a red pocket handkerchief. He was evidently in a hurry, on his way to the White House, where I believe a telegraph has been established in communication with McDowell's headquarters.

On my return to Captain Johnson's lodgings I received a note from the headquarters of the Federals, stating that the serious action between the two armies would probably be postponed for some days. McDowell's original idea was to avoid forcing the enemy's position directly in front, which was defended by movable batteries commanding the fords over a stream called "Bull's Run." He therefore proposed to make a demonstration on some point near the centre of their line, and at the same time throw the mass of his force below their extreme right, so as to turn it and get possession of the Manassas Railway in their rear; a movement which would separate him, by-the-by, from his own communications, and enable any general worth his salt to make a magnificent counter by marching on Washington, only 27 miles away, which he could take with the greatest ease, and leave the enemy in the rear to march 120 miles to Richmond, if they dared, or to make a hasty retreat upon the higher Potomac, and to cross into the hostile country of Maryland.

McDowell, however, has found the country on his left densely wooded and difficult. It is as new to him as it was to Braddock, when he cut his weary way through forest and swamp in this very district to reach, hundreds of miles away, the scene of his fatal repulse at Fort De Quesne (sic). And so, having moved his whole army, McDowell finds himself obliged to form a new plan of attack, and, prudently fearful of pushing his under-done and over-praised levies into a river in face of an enemy, is endeavouring to ascertain with what chance of success he can attack and turn their left.

Whilst he was engaged in a reconnaissance today, General Tyler did one of those things which must be expected from ambitious officers, without any fear of punishment, in countries where military discipline is scarcely known. Ordered to reconnoitre the position of the enemy on the left front, when the army moved from Fairfax to Centreville this morning, General Tyler thrust forward some 3000 or 4000 men of his division down to the very banks of "Bull's Run," which was said to be thickly wooded, and there brought up his men under a heavy fire of artillery and musketry, from which they retired in confusion.

July 19th. I rose early this morning in order to prepare for contingencies and to see off Captain Johnson, who was about to start with dispatches for New York, containing, no doubt, the intelligence that the Federal troops had advanced against the enemy. Yesterday was so hot that officers and men on the field suffered from something like sun-stroke. To unaccustomed frames today the heat felt unsupportable. A troop of regular cavalry, riding through the street at an early hour, were so exhausted, horse and man, that a runaway cab could have bowled them over like ninepins.

I hastened to General Scott's quarters, which were besieged by civilians outside and full of orderlies and officers within.

After dinner I walked over with Lieutenant H. Wise, inspected a model of Stevens' ram, which appears to me an utter impossibility in face of the iron-clad embrasured fleet now coming up to view, though it is spoken of highly by some naval officers and by many politicians.

Chapter XLIX

July 20th. The great battle which is to arrest rebellion, or to make it a power in the land, is no longer distant or doubtful. McDowell has completed his reconnaissance of the country in front of the enemy, and General Scott anticipates that he will be in possession of Manassas tomorrow night. All the statements of officers concur in describing the Confederates as strongly entrenched along the line of Bull's Run covering the railroad.

I was desirous of seeing what impression was produced upon the Congress of the United States by the crisis which was approaching, and drove down to the Senate at noon. There was no appearance of popular enthusiasm, excitement, or emotion, among the people in the passages. They drank their iced water, ate cakes or lozenges, chewed and chatted, or dashed at their acquaintances amongst the members, as though nothing more important than a railway bill or a postal concession was being debated inside. I entered the Senate, and found the House engaged in not listening to Mr. Latham, the Senator for California, who was delivering an elaborate lecture on the aspect of political affairs from a Republican point of view. The Senators were, as usual, engaged in reading newspapers, writing letters, or in whispered conversation, whilst the Senator received his applause from the people in the galleries, who were scarcely restrained from stamping their feet at the most highly-flown passages. Whilst I was listening to what is by courtesy called the debate, a messenger from Centreville sent in a letter to me, stating that

General McDowell would advance early in the morning, and expected to engage the enemy before noon. At the same moment a Senator who had received a despatch left his seat and read it to a brother legislator, and the news it contained was speedily diffused from one seat to another, and groups formed on the edge of the floor eagerly discussing the welcome intelligence.

The President's hammer again and again called them to order; and from out of this knot, Senator Sumner, his face lighted with pleasure, came to tell me the good news. "McDowell has carried Bull's Run without firing a shot. Seven regiments attacked it at the point of the bayonet, and the enemy immediately fled. General Scott only gives McDowell till midday tomorrow to be in possession of Manassas." Soon afterwards, Mr. Hay, the President's secretary, appeared on the floor to communicate a message to the Senate. I asked him if the news was true. "All I can tell you," said he, "is that the President has heard nothing at all about it, and that General Scott, from whom we have just received a communication, is equally ignorant of the reported success."

Every carriage, gig, wagon, and hack has been engaged by people going out to see the fight. The price is enhanced by mysterious communications respecting the horrible slaughter in the skirmishes at Bull's Run. The French cooks and hotel-keepers, by some occult process of reasoning, have arrived at the conclusion that they must treble the prices of their wines and of the hampers of provisions which the Washington people are ordering to comfort themselves at their bloody Derby. "There was not less than eighteen thousand men, sir, killed and destroyed. I don't care what General Scott says to the contrary, he was not there. I saw a reliable gentleman, ten minutes ago, as come straight from the place, and he swore there was a string of wagons three miles long with the wounded. While these Yankees lie so, I should not be surprised to hear they did not lose one thousand men in that big fight the day before yesterday."

General Johnston, who has been for some days with a considerable force in an entrenched position at Winchester, in the Valley of the Shenandoah, had occupied General Scott's attention, in consequence of the facility which he possessed to move into Maryland by Harper's Ferry, or to fall on the Federals by the Manassas Gap Railway, which was available by a long march from the town he occupied. General Patterson, with a Federal corps of equal strength, had accordingly been despatched to attack him, or, at all events, to prevent his leaving Winchester without an action; but the news tonight is that Patterson, who was an officer of some reputation, has allowed Johnston to evacuate Winchester, and has not pursued him; so that it is impossible to predict where the latter will appear.

Having failed utterly in my attempts to get a horse, I was obliged to negotiate with a livery-stable keeper, who had a hooded gig, or tilbury, left on his hands, to which he proposed to add a splinter-bar and pole, so as to make it available for two horses, on condition that I paid him the assessed value of the vehicle and horses, in case they were destroyed by the enemy. Of what particular value my executors might have regarded the guarantee in question the worthy man did not inquire, nor did he stipulate for any value to be put upon the driver; but it struck me that, if these were in any way seriously damaged, the occupants of the vehicle were not likely to escape. The driver, indeed, seemed by no means willing to undertake the job; and again and again it was proposed to me that I should drive, but I persistently refused.

Chapter L

———⊷⊷◆⊷⊷———

July 21st. The calmness and silence of the streets of Washington this lovely morning suggested thoughts of the very different scenes which, in all probability, were taking place at a few miles' distance.

Punctual to time our carriage appeared at the door, with a spare horse, followed by the black quadruped on which the Negro boy sat with difficulty, in consequence of its high spirits and excessively hard mouth. I swallowed a cup of tea and a morsel of bread, put the remainder of the tea into a bottle, got a flask of light Bordeaux, a bottle of water, a paper of sandwiches, and having replenished my small flask with brandy, stowed them all away in the bottom of the gig; but my friend, who is not accustomed to rise very early in the morning, did not make his appearance, and I was obliged to send several times to the legation to quicken his movements. Each time I was assured he would be over presently; but it was not till two hours had elapsed, and when I had just resolved to leave him behind, that he appeared in person, quite unprovided with *viaticum,* so that my slender store had now to meet the demands of two instead of one. We are off at last. The amicus and self find contracted space behind the driver. The Negro boy, grinning half with pain and "the balance" with pleasure, as the Americans say, held on his rampant charger, which made continual efforts to leap into the gig, and thus through the deserted city we proceeded towards the Long Bridge, where a sentry examined our papers, and said with a grin, "You'll find plenty of Congressmen on before you." And then our driver whipped his horses through the embankment of Fort Runyon, and dashed off along a country road, much cut up with gun and cart wheels, towards the main turnpike.

The promise of a lovely day, given by the early dawn, was likely to be realised to the fullest, and the placid beauty of the scenery as we drove through the woods below Arlington, and beheld the white buildings shining in the early sunlight, and the Potomac, like a broad silver riband dividing the picture, breathed of peace.

The road was so cut up by gun-wheels, ammunition and commissariat wagons that our horses made but slow way against the continual draft upon the collar; but at last the driver, who had known the country in happier times, announced that we had entered the high road for Fairfax Courthouse. Unfortunately my watch had gone down, but I guessed it was then a little before nine o'clock. In a few minutes afterwards I thought I heard, through the eternal clatter and jingle of the old gig, a sound which made me call the driver to stop. He pulled up, and we listened. In a minute or so, the well-known boom of a gun, followed by two or three in rapid succession, but at a considerable distance, reached my ear. "Did you hear that?" The driver heard nothing, nor did my companion, but the black boy on the lead horse, with eyes starting out of his head, cried, "I hear them, Massa; I hear them, sure enough, like de gun in de Navy Yard"; and as he spoke the thudding noise, like taps with a gentle hand upon a muffled drum, were repeated. "They are at it! We shall be late! Drive on as fast as you can!" We rattled on still faster, and presently came up to a farmhouse, where a man and woman, with some Negroes beside them, were standing out by the hedgerow above us, looking up the road in the direction of a cloud of dust, which we could see rising above the tops of the trees. We halted for a moment. "How long have the guns been going, sir?" "Well, ever since early this morning," said he; "They've been

[218]

having a fight. And I do really believe some of our poor Union chaps have had enough of it already. For here's some of them darned Secessionists marching down to go to Alexandry." The driver did not seem altogether content with this explanation of the dust in front of us, and presently, when a turn of the road brought to view a body of armed men, stretching to an interminable distance, with bayonets glittering in the sunlight through the clouds of dust, seemed inclined to halt or turn back again. A nearer approach satisfied me they were friends, and as soon as we came up with the head of the column I saw that they could not be engaged in the performance of any military duty. The men were marching without any resemblance of order, in twos and threes or larger troops. Some without arms, carrying great bundles on their backs; others with their coats hung from their firelocks; many foot-sore. They were all talking and in haste; many plodding along laughing, so I concluded that they could not belong to a defeated army, and imagined McDowell was effecting some flank movement. "Where are you going to, may I ask?"

"If this is the road to Alexandria, we are going there."

"There is an action going on in front, is there or not?"

"Well, so we believe, but we have not been fighting."

Although they were in such good spirits, they were not communicative, and we resumed our journey, impeded by the straggling troops and by the country cars containing their baggage and chairs, and tables and domestic furniture, which had never belonged to a regiment in the field. Still they came pouring on. I ordered the driver to stop at a rivulet, where a number of men were seated in the shade, drinking the water and bathing their hands and feet. On getting out I asked an officer, "May I beg to know, sir, where your regiment is going to?" "Well, I reckon, sir, we are going home to Pennsylvania." "This is the 4th Pennsylvania Regiment, is it not, sir?" "It is so, sir; that's the fact." "I should think there is severe fighting going on behind you, judging

[219]

from the firing [for every moment the sound of the cannon had been growing more distinct and more heavy]?" "Well, I reckon, sir, there is." I paused for a moment, not knowing what to say, and yet anxious for an explanation; and the epauletted gentleman, after a few seconds' awkward hesitation, added, "We are going home because, as you see, the men's time's up, sir. We have had three months of this sort of work, and that's quite enough of it."

It must have been about eleven o'clock when we came to the first traces of the Confederate camp, in front of Fairfax Courthouse, where they had cut a few trenches and levelled the trees across the road, so as to form a rude abattis; but the works were of a most superficial character, and would scarcely have given cover either to the guns, for which embrasures were left at the flanks to sweep the road, or to the infantry intended to defend them.

Some time before noon the driver, urged continually by adjurations to get on, whipped his horses into Fairfax Courthouse, a village which derives its name from a large brick building, in which the sessions of the county are held. Some thirty or forty houses, for the most part detached, with gardens or small strips of land about them, form the main street. The inhabitants who remained had by no means an agreeable expression of countenance, and did not seem on very good terms with the Federal soldiers, who were lounging up and down the streets, or standing in the shade of the trees and doorways. I asked the sergeant of a picket in the street how long the firing had been going on. He replied that it had commenced at half past seven or eight, and had been increasing ever since. "Some of them will lose their eyes and back teeth," he said, "before it is over." The driver, pulling up at a roadside inn in the town, here made the startling announcement that both he and his horses must have something to eat, and although we would have been happy to join him, seeing that we had no breakfast, we could not afford the time, and were not displeased when a thin-faced, shrewish woman, in black, came out into the verandah, and said she could not let us have anything unless we liked to wait till the regular dinner hour of the house, which was at one o'clock. The horses got a bucket of water, which they needed in that broiling sun; and the cannonade, which by this time had increased into a respectable tumult that gave evidence of a well-sustained action, added vigour to the driver's arm, and in a mile or two more we dashed into a village of burnt houses, the charred brick chimney stacks standing amidst the blackened embers being all that remained of what was once German Town.

The driver, passing through the town, drove straight on, but after some time I fancied the sound of the guns seemed dying away towards our left.

In an hour more we had gained the high road to Centreville, on which were many buggies, commissariat carts, and wagons full of civilians, and a brisk canter brought us in sight of a rising ground, over which the road led directly through a few houses on each side, and dipped out of sight, the slopes of the hill being covered with men, carts, and horses, and the summit crested with spectators, with their backs turned towards us, and gazing on the valley beyond. "There's Centreville," says the driver, and on our poor panting horses were forced, passing directly through the Confederate bivouacs, commissariat parks, folds of oxen, and two German regiments, with a battery of artillery, halting on the rising ground by the roadside. The heat was intense. Our driver complained of hunger and thirst, to which neither I nor my companion were insensible; and so pulling up on the top of the hill, I sent the boy down to the village which we had passed, to see if he could find shelter for the horses, and a morsel for our breakfastless selves.

It was a strange scene before us. From the hill a densely wooded country, dotted at intervals with green fields and cleared lands, spread five or six miles in front, bounded by a line of blue and purple ridges, terminating abruptly in escarpments towards the left front, and swelling gradually towards the right into the lower spines of an offshoot from the Blue Ridge Mountains. On our left the view was circumscribed by a forest which clothed the side of the ridge on which we stood, and covered its shoulder far down into the plain. A gap in the nearest chain of the hills in our front was pointed out by the bystanders as the Pass of Manassas, by which the railway from the West is carried into the plain, and still nearer at hand, before us, is the junction of that rail with the line from Alexandria, and with the railway leading southwards to Richmond. The intervening space was not a dead level; undulating lines of forest marked the course of the streams which intersected it, and gave, by their variety of colour and shading, an additional charm to the landscape which, enclosed in a framework of blue and purple hills, softened into violet in the extreme distance, presented one of the most agreeable displays of simple pastoral woodland scenery that could be conceived.

But the sounds which came upon the breeze, and the sights which met our eyes, were in terrible variance with the tranquil character of the landscape. The woods far and near echoed to the roar of cannon, and thin frayed lines of blue smoke marked the spots whence came the muttering sound of rolling musketry; the white puffs of smoke burst high above the treetops, and the gunners' rings from shell and howitzer marked the fire of the artillery.

Clouds of dust shifted and moved through the forest; and through the wavering mists of light blue smoke, and the thicker masses which rose commingling from the feet of men and the mouths of cannon, I could see the gleam of arms and the twinkling of bayonets.

From the line of the smoke it appeared to me that the action was in an oblique line from our left, extending farther outwards towards the right, bisected by a road from Centreville, which descended the hill close at hand and ran right across the undulating plain, its course being marked by the white covers of the baggage and commissariat wagons as far as a turn of the road, where the trees closed in upon them. Beyond the right of the curling smoke, clouds of dust appeared from time to time in the distance, as if bodies of cavalry were moving over a sandy plain.

The clouds of dust on the right were quite inexplicable. As we were looking, my philosophic companion asked me in perfect seriousness, "Are we really seeing a battle now? Are they supposed to be fighting where all that smoke is going on? This is rather interesting, you know."

Loud cheers suddenly burst from the spectators as a man dressed in the uniform of an officer, whom I had seen riding violently across the plain in an open space below, galloped along the front, waving his cap and shouting at the top of his voice. He was brought up by the press of people round his horse close to where I stood. "We've whipped them on all points," he cried. "We have taken all their batteries. They are retreating as fast as they can and we are after them." Such cheers as rent the welkin! The Congressmen shook hands with each other, and cried out, "Bully for us! Bravo! Didn't I tell you so?"

By the time I reached the lane, already mentioned, which was in a few minutes, the string of commissariat wagons was moving onwards pretty briskly, and I was detained until my friends appeared at the roadside. Then getting into the fields, I pressed my horse, which was quite recovered from his twenty-seven miles' ride and full of spirit and mettle, as fast as I could, making detours here and there to get through the ox fences, and by the small streams which cut up the country. The firing did not increase, but rather diminished in volume, though it now sounded close at hand.

I had ridden between three and a half and four miles, as well as I could judge, when I was obliged to turn for the third and fourth time into the road by a considerable stream, which was spanned by a bridge, towards which I was threading my way, when my attention was attracted by loud shouts in advance, and I perceived several wagons coming from the direction of the battlefield, the drivers of which were endeavouring to force their horses past the ammunition carts going in the contrary direction near the bridge; a thick cloud of dust rose behind them, and running by the side of the wagons were a number of men in uniform, whom I supposed to be the guard. My first impression was that the wagons were returning for fresh supplies of ammunition. But every moment the crowd increased; drivers and men cried out with the most vehement gestures, "Turn back! Turn back! We are whipped." They seized the heads of the horses and swore at the opposing drivers. Emerging from the crowd, a breathless man, in the uniform of an officer, with an empty scabbard dangling by his side, was cut off by getting between my horse and a cart for a moment. "What is the matter, sir? What is all this about?" "Why it means we are pretty badly whipped, that's the truth," he gasped, and continued.

By this time the confusion had been communicating itself through the line of wagons towards the rear, and the drivers endeavoured to turn round their vehicles in the narrow road, which caused the usual amount of imprecations from the men and plunging and kicking from the horses.

The crowd from the front continually increased, the heat, the uproar, and the dust were beyond description, and these were augmented when some cavalry soldiers, flourishing their sabres and preceded by an officer, who cried out, "Make way there—make way there for the General," attempted to force a covered wagon, in which was seated a man with a bloody handkerchief round his head, through the press.

I had succeeded in getting across the bridge with great difficulty before the wagon came up, and I saw the crowd on the road was still gathering thicker and thicker. Again I asked an officer, who was on foot, with his sword under his arm, "What is all this for?" "We are whipped, sir. We are all in retreat. You are all to go back." "Can you tell me where I can find General McDowell?" "No! nor can any one else."

A few shells could be heard bursting not very far off, but there was nothing to account for such an extraordinary scene. A third officer, however, confirmed the report that the whole army was in retreat, and that the Federals were beaten on all points, but there was nothing in this disorder to indicate a general rout. All these things took place in a few seconds. I got up out of the road into a cornfield, through which men were hastily walking or running, their faces streaming with perspiration, and generally without arms, and worked my way for about half a mile or so, as well as I could judge, against an increasing stream of fugitives, the ground being strewed with coats, blankets, firelocks, cooking tins, caps, belt, bayonets—asking in vain where General McDowell was.

Again I was compelled by the condition of the fields to come into the road; and having passed a piece of wood and a regiment which seemed to be moving back in column of march in tolerably good order, I turned once more into an opening close to a white house, not far from the lane, beyond which there was a belt of forest. Two fieldpieces unlimbered near the house, with panting horses in the rear, were pointed towards the front, and along the road beside them there swept a tolerably steady column of men mingled with field ambulances and light baggage cars, back to Centreville. I had just stretched out my hand to get a cigar-light from a German gunner, when the dropping shots which had been sounding through the woods in front of us suddenly swelled into an animated fire. In a few seconds a crowd of men rushed out of the wood down towards the guns, and the artillerymen near me seized the trail of a piece, and were wheeling it round to fire, when an officer or sergeant called out, "Stop! Stop! They are our own men;" and in two or three minutes the whole battalion came sweeping past the guns at the double, and in the utmost disorder.

Some of the artillerymen dragged the horses out of the tumbrils; and for a moment the confusion was so great I could not understand what had taken place; but a soldier whom I stopped, said, "We are pursued by their cavalry; they have cut us all to pieces."

There was nothing left for it but to go with the current one could not stem. I turned round my horse from the deserted guns, and endeavoured to find out what had occurred as I rode quietly back on the skirts of the crowd. I talked with those on all sides of me. Some uttered prodigious nonsense, describing batteries tier over tier, and ambuscades, and blood running knee deep. Others described how their boys carried whole lines of intrenchments, but were beaten back for want of reinforcements. The names of many regiments were mentioned as being utterly destroyed. Cavalry and bayonet charges and masked batteries played prominent parts in all the narrations. Some of the officers seemed to feel the disgrace of defeat; but the strangest thing was the general indifference with which the event seemed to be regarded by those who collected their senses as soon as they got out of fire, and who said they were just going as far as Centreville, and would have a big fight tomorrow.

By this time I was unwillingly approaching Centreville in the midst of heat, dust, confusion, inprecations inconceivable. On arriving at the place where a small rivulet crossed the road, the throng increased still more. The ground over which I had passed going out was now covered with arms, clothing of all kinds, accoutrements thrown off and left to be trampled in the dust under the hoofs of men and horses. The runaways ran alongside the wagons, striving to force themselves in among the occupants, who resisted tooth and nail. The drivers spurred, and whipped, and urged the horses to the utmost of their bent. I felt an inclination to laugh, which was overcome by disgust, and by that vague sense of something extraordinary taking place which is experienced when a man sees a number of people acting as if driven by some unknown terror. As I rode in the crowd, with men clinging to the stirrup-leathers, or holding on by anything they could lay hands on, so that I had some apprehension of being pulled off, I spoke to the men, and asked them over and over again not to be in such a hurry. "There's no enemy to pursue you. All the cavalry in the world could not get at you." But I might as well have talked to the stones.

It never occurred to me that this was a grand debacle. All along I believed the mass of the army was not broken, and that all I saw around was the result of confusion created in a crude organisation by a forced retreat; and knowing the reserves were at Centreville and beyond, I said to myself, "Let us see how this will be when we get to the hill." Trotting along briskly through the fields, I arrived at the foot of the slope on which Centreville stands, and met a German regiment just deploying into line very well and steadily—the men in the rear companies laughing, smoking, singing, and jesting with the fugitives, who were filing past; but no thought of stopping the wagons, as the orders repeated from mouth to mouth were that they were to fall back beyond Centreville.

The air of the men was good. The officers were cheerful, and one big German with a great pipe in his bearded mouth, with spectacles on nose, amused himself by pricking the horses with his sabre point, as he passed, to the sore discomfiture of the riders. Behind the regiment came a battery of brass fieldpieces, and another regiment in column of march was following the guns. They were going to form line at the end of the slope, and no fairer position could well be offered for a defensive attitude, although it might be turned. But it was getting too late for the enemy, wherever they were, to attempt such an extensive operation. Several times I had been asked by officers and men, "Where do you think we will halt? Where are the rest of the army?" I always replied, "Centreville," and I had heard hundreds of the fugitives say they were going to Centreville.

I rode up the road, turned into the little street which carries the road on the right-hand side to Fairfax Courthouse and the hill, and went straight to the place where I had left the buggy in a lane on the left of the road beside a small house and shed, expecting to find Mr. Warre ready for a start, as I had faithfully promised Lord Lyons he should be back that night in Washington. The buggy was not there. I pulled open the door of the shed in which the horses had been sheltered out of the sun. They were gone. "Oh," said I, to myself, "of course! What a stupid fellow I am! Warre has had the horses put in, and taken the gig to the top of the hill, in order to see the last of it before we go." And so I rode over to the ridge; but arriving there, could see no sign of our vehicle far or near. There were two carriages of some kind or other still remaining on the hill, and a few spectators, civilians and military, gazing on the scene below, which was softened in the golden rays of the declining sun. The smoke wreaths had ceased to curl over the green sheets of billowy forest as sea foam crisping in a gentle breeze breaks the lines of the ocean. But far and near yellow and dun-coloured piles of dust seamed the landscape, leaving behind them long trailing clouds of lighter vapours which were dotted now and then by white puff-balls from the bursting of shell. On the right these clouds were very heavy and seemed to approach rapidly, and it occurred to me they might be caused by an advance of the much-spoken-of and little-seen cavalry; and remembering the crossroad from German Town, it seemed a very fine and very feasible operation for the Confederates to cut right in on the line of retreat and communication, in which case the fate of the army and of Washington could not be dubious. There were now few civilians on the hill, and these were thinning away.

I put up my glass, and turning from the hill, with difficulty forced my way through the crowd of vehicles which were making their way towards the main road in the direction of the lane, hoping that by some lucky accident I might find the gig in waiting for me.

[228]

Nothing was left for it but to brace up the girths for a ride to the Capitol, for which, hungry and fagged as I was, I felt very little inclination. I was trotting quietly down the hill road beyond Centreville, when suddenly the guns on the other side, or from a battery very near, opened fire, and a fresh outburst of artillery sounded through the woods. In an instant the mass of vehicles and retreating soldiers, teamsters, and civilians, as if agonised by an electric shock, quivered throughout the tortuous line. With dreadful shouts and cursings, the drivers lashed their maddened horses, and leaping from the carts, left them to their fate, and ran on foot. Artillerymen and foot soldiers, and Negroes mounted on gun horses, with the chain traces and loose trappings trailing in the dust, spurred and flogged their steeds down the road or by the side paths. The firing continued and seemed to approach the hill, and at every report the agitated body of horsemen and wagons was seized, as it were, with a fresh convulsion.

Once more the dreaded cry, "The cavalry! cavalry are coming!" rang through the crowd, and looking back to Centreville, I perceived coming down the hill, between me and the sky a number of mounted men, who might, at a hasty glance, be taken for horsemen in the act of sabreing the fugitives. In reality, they were soldiers and civilians, with, I regret to say, some officers among them who were whipping and striking their horses with sticks or whatever else they could lay hands on. I called out to the men who were frantic with terror beside me, "They are not cavalry at all; they're your own men"—but they did not heed me. A fellow who was shouting out, "Run! run!" as loud as he could, beside me, seemed to take delight in creating alarm; and as he was perfectly collected as far as I could judge, I said, "What on earth are you running for? What are you afraid of?" He was in the roadside below me, and at once turning on me, and exclaiming, "I'm not afraid of you," presented his piece and pulled the trigger so instantaneously, that, had it gone off, I could not have swerved from the ball. As the scoundrel de-

[229]

liberately drew up to examine the nipple, I judged it best not to give him another chance, and spurred on through the crowd, where any man could have shot as many as he pleased without interruption. The only conclusion I came to was that he was mad or drunken.

I galloped on for a short distance to head the ruck, for I could not tell whether this body of infantry intended moving back towards Centreville or were coming down the road; but the mounted men galloping furiously past me, with a cry of "Cavalry! cavalry!" on their lips, swept on faster than I did, augmenting the alarm and excitement. I came up with two officers who were riding more leisurely; and touching my hat, said, "I venture to suggest that these men should be stopped, sir. If not, they will alarm the whole of the post and pickets on to Washington. They will fly next, and the consequences will be most disastrous." One of the two, looking at me for a moment, nodded his head without saying a word, spurred his horse to full speed, and dashed on in front along the road. Following more leisurely, I observed the fugitives in front were suddenly checked in their speed; and as I turned my horse into the wood by the roadside to get on so as to prevent the chance of another blockup, I passed several private vehicles, in one of which Mr. Raymond, of the *New York Times,* was seated with some friends, looking by no means happy.

Having received full directions from the people at the inn for the road to the Long Bridge, which I was most anxious to reach instead of going to Alexandria or to Georgetown, I galloped on for a mile, until I got into the cover of a wood, where I dismounted to examine the horse's hoofs and shift the saddle for a moment, wipe the sweat off his back, and make him and myself as comfortable as could be for our ride into Washington, which was still seventeen or eighteen miles before me.

The sun had set, but the rising moon was adding every moment to the lightness of the road as I mounted once more and set out at a long trot for the capital.

All by the sides of the old camps the men were standing, lining the road, and I was obliged to evade many a grasp at my bridle by shouting out, "Don't stop me; I've important news; it's all well!" and still the good horse, refreshed by the cool night air, went clattering on, till from the top of the road beyond Arlington I caught a sight of the lights of Washington and the white buildings of the Capitol, and of the Executive Mansion, glittering like snow in the moonlight. At the entrance to the Long Bridge the sentry challenged, and asked for the countersign. "I have not got it, but I've a pass from General Scott." An officer advanced from the guard, and on reading the pass permitted me to go on without difficulty. He said, "I have been obliged to let a good many go over tonight before you, Congressmen and others. I suppose you did not expect to be coming back so soon. I fear it's a bad business. "Oh, not so bad, after all; I expected to have been back tonight before nine o'clock, and crossed over this morning without the countersign." "Well, I guess," said he, "we don't do such quick fighting as that in this country."

As I crossed the Long Bridge there was scarce a sound to dispute the possession of its echoes with my horse's hoofs. The poor beast had carried me nobly and well, and I made up my mind to buy him, as I had no doubt he would answer perfectly to carry me back in a day or two to McDowell's army by the time he had organised it for a new attack upon the enemy's position.

The letter that I was to write occupied my mind whilst I was crossing the Long Bridge, gazing at the lights reflected in the Potomac from the city. The night had become overcast, and heavy clouds rising up rapidly obscured the moon, forming a most fantastic mass of shapes in the sky.

At the Washington end of the bridge I was challenged again by the men of a whole regiment, who, with piled arms, were halted on the *chausée,* smoking, laughing, and singing. "Stranger, have you been to the fight?" "I have been only a little beyond Centreville."

As I passed Willard's hotel a little further on, a clock—I think the only public clock which strikes the hours in Washington—tolled out the hour; and I suppósed, from what the sentry told me, though I did not count the strokes, that it was eleven o'clock. All the rooms in the hotel were a blaze of light. The pavement before the door was crowded, and some mounted men and the clattering of sabres on the pavement led me to infer that the escort of the wounded officer had arrived before me. I passed on to the livery-stables, where every one was alive and stirring.

Chapter LI

————▸◂◆▸◂————

July 22nd. I awoke from a deep sleep this morning, about six o'clock. The rain was falling in torrents, and beat with a dull, thudding sound on the leads outside my windows; but, louder than all, came a strange sound, as if of the tread of men, a confused tramp and splashing, and a murmuring of voices. I got up and ran to the front room, the windows of which looked on the street, and there, to my intense surprise, I saw a steady stream of men covered with mud, soaked through with rain, who were pouring irregularly, without any semblance of order, up Pennsylvania Avenue towards the Capitol. A dense stream of vapour rose from the multitude; but looking closely at the men, I perceived they belonged to different regiments, New Yorkers, Michiganders, Rhode Islanders, Massachusetters, Minnesotians, mingled pellmell together. Many of them were without knapsacks, crossbelts, and firelocks. Some had neither greatcoats nor shoes, others were covered with blankets. Hastily putting on my clothes, I ran downstairs and asked an "officer," who was passing by, a pale young man, who looked exhausted to death, and who had lost his sword, for the empty sheath dangled at his side, where the men were coming from. "Where from? Well, sir, I guess we're all coming out of Verginny as far as we can, and pretty well whipped too." "What! the whole army, sir?" "That's more than I know. They may stay like that. I know I'm going home. I've had enough of fighting to last my lifetime."

Whilst the rain fell, the tramp of feet went steadily on. As I lifted my eyes now and then from the paper, I saw the beaten, footsore spongy-looking soldiers, officers, and all the debris of the army filing through mud and rain, and forming in crowds in front of the spirit-stores. Underneath my room is the magazine of Jost, *negociant en vins,* and he drives a roaring trade this morning, interrupted occasionally by loud disputes as to the score. When the lad came in with my breakfast he seemed a degree or two lighter in colour than usual. "What's the matter with you?" "I 'spects, massa, the Seceshers soon be in here. I'm a free nigger; I must go, sar, afore de come cotch me."

General Scott is quite overwhelmed by the affair, and is unable to stir. General McDowell has not yet arrived. The Secretary of War knows not what to do, Mr. Lincoln is equally helpless, and Mr. Seward, who retains some calmness, is, notwithstanding his military rank and militia experience, without resource or expedient. There are a good many troops hanging on about the camps and forts on the other side of the river, it is said; but they are thoroughly disorganised, and will run away if the enemy comes in sight without a shot, and then the capital must fall at once. Why Beauregard does not come I know not, nor can I well guess.

Towards dark the rain moderated and the noise in the streets waxed louder; all kinds of rumours respecting the advance of the enemy, the annihilation of Federal regiments, the tremendous losses on both sides, charges of cavalry, stormings of great intrenchments and stupendous masked batteries, and elaborate reports of unparalleled feats of personal valour, were circulated under the genial influence of excitement, and by the quantities of alcohol necessary to keep out the influence of the external moisture. I did not hear one expression of confidence, or see one cheerful face in all that vast crowd which but a few days before constituted an army, and was now nothing better than a semi-armed mob. I could see no cannon returning, and to my inquiries after them, I got generally the answer, "I suppose the Seceshers have got hold of them."

Whilst I was at table, several gentlemen who have *entrée* called on me, who confirmed my impressions respecting the magnitude of the disaster that is so rapidly developing its proportions. They agree in describing the army as disorganised. Washington is rendered almost untenable, in consequence of the conduct of the army, which was not only to have defended it, but to have captured the rival capital. Some of my visitors declared it was dangerous to move abroad in the streets. Many think the contest is now over; but the gentlemen of Washington have Southern sympathies, and I, on the contrary, am persuaded this prick in the great Northern balloon will let out a quantity of poisonous gas, and rouse the people to a sense of the nature of the conflict on which they have entered. The inmates of the White House are in a state of the utmost trepidation, and Mr. Lincoln, who sat in the telegraph operator's room with General Scott and Mr. Seward, listening to the dispatches as they arrived from the scene of action, left it in their despair when the fatal words tripped from the needle, and the defeat was clearly revealed to him.

July 23rd. The morning was far advanced when I awoke, and hearing the roll of wagons in the street, I at first imagined the Federals were actually about to abandon Washington itself; but on going to the window, I perceived it arose from an irregular train of commissariat carts, country wagons, ambulances, and sutlers' vans, in the centre of the street, the paths being crowded as before with soldiers, or rather with men in uniform, many of whom seemed as if they had been rolling in the mud. Poor General Mansfield was running back and forwards between his quarters and the War Department, and in the afternoon some efforts were made to restore order, by appointing rendezvous to which the fragment of regiments should repair, and by organising mounted patrols to clear the streets. In the middle of the day I went out through the streets, and walked down to the long bridge with the intention of crossing, but it was literally blocked up from end to end with a mass of wagons and ambulances full of wounded men, whose cries of pain echoed above the shouts of the drivers, so that I abandoned the attempt to get across, which, indeed, would not have been easy with any comfort, owing to the depth of mud in the roads.

As I returned towards my lodgings a scene of greater disorder and violence than usual attracted my attention. A body of Confederate prisoners, marching two and two, were with difficulty saved by their guard from the murderous assaults of a hooting rabble, composed of civilians and men dressed like soldiers, who hurled all kinds of missiles they could lay their hands upon over the heads of the guard at their victims, spattering them with mud and filthy language.

Poor McDowell has been swiftly punished for his defeat, or rather for the unhappy termination of his advance. As soon as the disaster was ascertained beyond doubt, the President telegraphed to General McClellan to come and take command of his army. It is a commentary full of instruction on the military system of the Americans that they have not a soldier who has ever handled a brigade in the field fit for service in the North.

The new commander-in-chief is a brevet-major who has been in civil employ on a railway for several years. He went once, with two other West Point officers, commissioned by Mr. Jefferson Davis, then Secretary of War, to examine and report on the operations in the Crimea, who were judiciously despatched when the war was over, and I used to see him and his companions poking about the ruins of the deserted trenches and batteries, mounted on horses furnished by the courtesy of British officers, just as they lived in English quarters, when they were snubbed and refused an audience by the Duke of Malakhoff in the French camp. Major McClellan forgot the affront, did not even mention it, and showed his Christian spirit by praising the allies, and damning John Bull with very faint applause, seasoned with lofty censure. He was very young, however, at the time, and is so well spoken of that his appointment will be popular; but all that he has done to gain such reputation, and to earn the confidence of the government, is to have had some skirmishes with bands of Confederates in western Virginia. That success, however, at such a time, is quite enough to elevate any man to the highest command. McClellan is about thirty-six years of age, was educated at West Point, where he was junior to McDowell, and a classfellow of Beauregard.

It had been rumoured that the Confederates were advancing, and the President and the Foreign Minister set out in a carriage to see with their own eyes the state of the troops. The plateau was covered with the men of different regiments, driven by the patrols out of the city, or arrested in their flight at the bridges. In Fort Corcoran the men were in utter disorder, threatening to murder the officer of regulars who was essaying to get them into some state of efficiency to meet the advancing enemy. He had menaced one of the officers of the 69th with death for flat disobedience to orders; the men had taken the part of their captain; and the President drove into the work just in time to witness the confusion. The soldiers with loud cries demanded that the officer should be punished, and the President asked him why he had used such violent language towards his subordinate. "I told him,

Mr. President, that if he refused to obey my orders I would shoot him on the spot; and I here repeat it, sir, that if I remain in command here, and he or any other man refuses to obey my orders, I'll shoot him on the spot."

The firmness of Sherman's language and demeanour in presence of the chief of the State overawed the mutineers, and they proceeded to put the work in some kind of order to resist the enemy.

July 24th. I rode out before breakfast in company with Mr. Monson across the Long Bridge over to Arlington House. General McDowell was seated at a table under a tree in front of his tent, and got out his plans and maps to explain the scheme of the battle.

Cast down from his high estate, placed as a subordinate to his junior, covered with obloquy and abuse, the American General displayed a calm self-possession and perfect amiability which could only proceed from a philosophic temperament and a consciousness that he would outlive the calumnies of his countrymen. He accused nobody; but it was not difficult to perceive he had been sacrificed to the vanity, self-seeking, and disobedience of some of his officers, and to radical vices in the composition of his army.

When McDowell found he could not turn the enemy's right as he intended, because the country by the Occoquan was unfit for the movements of artillery, or even infantry, he reconnoitred the ground towards their left, and formed the project of turning it by a movement which would bring the weight of his columns on their extreme left, and at the same time overlap it, whilst a strong demonstration was made on the ford at Bull's Run, where General Tyler brought on the serious skirmish of the 18th. In order to carry out this plan, he had to debouch his columns from a narrow point at Centreville, and march them round by various roads to points on the upper part of the Run, where it was fordable in all directions, intending to turn the enemy's batteries on the lower roads and bridges. But although he started them at an early hour, the troops moved so slowly the Confederates became aware of their design, and were enabled to concentrate considerable masses of troops on their left.

The Federals were not only slow, but disorderly. The regiments in advance stopped at streams to drink and fill their canteens, delaying the regiments in the rear. They wasted their provisions, so that many of them were without food at noon, when they were exhausted by the heat of the sun and by the stifling vapours of their own dense columns. When they at last came into action, some divisions were not in their places, so that the line of battle was broken; and those which were in their proper position were exposed, without support, to the enemy's fire. A delusion of masked batteries pressed on their brain. To this was soon added a hallucination about cavalry, which might have been cured had the Federals possessed a few steady squadrons to manoeuvre on their flanks and in the intervals of their line. Nevertheless, they advanced and encountered the enemy's fire with some spirit; but the Confederates were enabled to move up fresh battalions, and to a certain extent to establish an equality between the numbers of their own troops and the assailants, whilst they had the advantages of better cover and ground. An apparition of a disorderly crowd of horsemen in front of the much-boasting Fire Zouaves of New York threw them into confusion and flight, and a battery which they ought to have protected was taken. Another battery was captured by the mistake of an officer, who allowed a Confederate regiment to approach the guns, thinking they were Federal troops, till their first volley destroyed both horses and gunners. At the critical moment, General Johnston, who had escaped from the feeble observation and untenacious grip of General Patterson and his time-expired volunteers, and had been hurrying down his troops from Winchester by train, threw his fresh battalions on the flank and rear of the Federal right. When the General ordered a retreat, rendered necessary by the failure

[238]

of the attack—disorder spread, which increased—the retreat became a flight, which degenerated—if a flight can degenerate—into a panic, and the Confederates pressed them with a few cavalry and horse artillery. The efforts of the Generals to restore order and confidence were futile. Fortunately a weak reserve was posted at Centreville, and these were formed in line on the slope of the hill, whilst McDowell and his officers exerted themselves with indifferent success to arrest the mass of the army, and make them draw up behind the reserve, telling the men a bold front was their sole chance of safety. At midnight it became evident the *morale* of the army was destroyed, and nothing was left but a speedy retrograde movement, with the few regiments and guns which were in a condition approaching to efficiency, upon the defensive works of Washington.

Chapter LII

July 27th. So ill today from heat, bad smells in the house, and fatigue that I sent for Dr. Miller, a great, fine Virginian practitioner, who ordered me powders to be taken in "mint juleps." Now mint juleps are made of whiskey, sugar, ice, very little water, and sprigs of fresh mint, to be sucked up after the manner of sherry cobblers, if so it be pleased, with a straw.

"A powder every two hours, with a mint julep. Why, that's six a day, Doctor. Won't that be—eh?—won't that be rather intoxicating?"

"Well, sir, that depends on the constitution. You'll find they will do you no harm, even if the worst takes place."

Day after day, till the month was over and August had come, I passed in a state of powder and julep, which the Virginian doctor declared saved my life. The first time I stirred out the change which had taken place in the streets was at once apparent: no drunken rabblement of armed men, no begging soldiers; instead of these were patrols in the streets, guards at the corners, and a rigid system of passes. Round the corner, with a kind of staff at his heels and an escort, comes Major General George B. McClellan, the young Napoleon (of western Virginia), the conqueror of Garnett, the captor of Peagram, the Commander-in-Chief, under the President, of the Army of the United States. He is a very squarely-built, thick-throated, broad-chested man, under the middle height, with slightly-bowed legs, a tendency to *embonpoint*. His head, covered with a closely-cut crop of dark auburn hair, is well set on his shoulders. His features are regular and prepossessing—the brow small, contracted, and furrowed; the eyes deep and anxious-looking. A short, thick reddish moustache conceals his mouth; the rest of his face is clean shaven. He has made his father-in-law, Major Marcy, chief of his staff, and is a good deal influenced by his opinions, which are entitled to some weight as Major Marcy is a soldier, and has seen frontier wars, and is a great traveller. The task of licking this army into shape is of Herculean magnitude. Every one, however, is willing to do as he bids: the President confides in him, and "Georges" him; the press fawn upon him, the people trust him; he is "the little corporal" of unfought fields—*omnis ignotus pro mirifico,* here. He looks like a stout little captain of dragoons, but for his American seat and saddle. The latter is adapted to a man who cannot ride: if a squadron so mounted were to attempt a fence or ditch, half of them would be ruptured or spilled. The seat is a marvel to any European. But McClellan is nevertheless "the man on horseback" just now, and the Americans must ride in his saddle, or in anything he likes.

In the evening of my first day's release from juleps the President held a reception or levée, and I went to the White House about nine o'clock, when the rooms were at their fullest. The company were arriving on foot, or crammed in hackney coaches, and did not affect any neatness of attire or evening dress. The doors were open: any one could walk in who chose.

The President, in a suit of black, stood near the door of one of the rooms near the hall, and shook hands with every one of the crowd, who was then "passed" on by his secretary, if the President didn't wish to speak to him. Mr. Lincoln has recovered his spirits, and seemed in good humour. Mrs. Lincoln,who did the honours in another room surrounded by a few ladies, did not appear to be quite so contented. All the ministers are present except Mr. Seward, who has gone to his own state to ascertain the frame of mind of the people, and to judge for himself of the sentiments they entertain respecting the war. After walking up and down the hot and crowded rooms for an hour, and seeing and speaking to all the celebrities, I withdrew. Colonel Richardson, in his official report, states Colonel Miles lost the battle of Bull Run by being drunk and disorderly at a critical moment. Colonel Miles, who commanded a division of three brigades, writes to say he was not in any such state, and has demanded a court of inquiry. In a Philadelphia paper it is stated McDowell was helplessly drunk during the action, and sat up all the night before drinking, smoking, and playing cards. McDowell never drinks, and never has drunk, wine, spirits, malt, tea, or coffee, or smoked or used tobacco in any form, nor does he play cards; and that remark does not apply to many other Federal officers.

August 3rd. McClellan orders regular parades and drills in every regiment, and insists on all orders being given by bugle note. I had a long ride through the camps, and saw some improvement in the look of the men. Coming home by Georgetown, met the Prince driving with M. Mercier, to pay a visit to the President. I am sure that the politicians are not quite well pleased with this arrival, because they do not understand it, and cannot imagine a man would come so far without a purpose. The drunken soldiers now resort to quiet lanes and courts in the suburbs. Georgetown was full of them. It is a much more respectable and old-world looking place than its vulgar, empty, overgrown, mushroom neighbour, Washington. An officer who had fallen in his men to go on duty was walking down the line this evening, when his eye rested on the neck of a bottle sticking out of a man's coat. "Thunder," quoth he, "James, what have you got there?" "Well, I guess, captain, it's a drop of real good Bourbon." "Then let us have a drink," said the captain; and thereupon proceeded to take a long pull and a strong pull, till the man cried out, "That is not fair, Captain. You won't leave me a drop"—a remonstrance which had a proper effect, and the captain marched down his company to the bridge.

August 5th. The roads from the station are crowded with troops, coming from the North as fast as the railway can carry them. It is evident, as the war fever spreads, that such politicians as Mr. Crittenden, who resist the extreme violence of the Republican party, will be stricken down. The Confiscation Bill, for the emancipation of slaves and the absorption of property belonging to rebels, has, indeed, been boldly resisted in the House of Representatives; but it passed with some trifling amendments. The journals are still busy with the affair of Bull Run, and each seems anxious to eclipse the other in the absurdity of its statements.

August 7th. In the evening I went to Mr. Seward's, who gave a reception in honour of Prince Napoleon. The Minister's rooms were crowded and intensely hot. Lord Lyons and most of the diplomatic circle were present. The Prince wore his Order of the Bath, and bore the onslaughts of politicians, male and female, with much good humour. The contrast between the uniforms of the officers of the United States Army and Navy and those of the French in the Prince's suit by no means redounded to the credit of the military tailoring of the Americans. The Prince, to whom

I was presented by Mr. Seward, asked me particularly about the roads from Alexandria to Fairfax Courthouse, and from there to Centreville and Manassas. I told him I had not got quite so far as the latter place, at which he laughed. He inquired with much interest about General Beauregard, whether he spoke good French, if he seemed a man of capacity, or was the creation of an accident and of circumstances. He has been to Mount Vernon, and is struck with the air of neglect around the place. Two of his horses dropped dead from the heat of the journey, and the Prince, who was perspiring profusely in the crowded room, asked me whether the climate was not as bad as midsummer in India. His manner was perfectly easy, but he gave no encouragement to bores, nor did he court popularity by unusual affability, and he moved off long before the guests were tired of looking at him.

Chapter LIII

On the 17th August I returned to Baltimore on my way to Drohoregan Manor, the seat of Colonel Carroll, in Maryland, where I had been invited to spend a few days by his son-in-law, an English gentleman of my acquaintance. Leaving Baltimore at 5:40 P.M., in company with Mr. Tucker Carroll, I proceeded by train to Ellicott's Mills, a station fourteen miles on the Ohio and Baltimore railroad, from which our host's residence is distant more than an hour's drive. The country through which the line passes is picturesque and undulating, with hills and valleys and brawling streams, spreading in woodland and glade, ravine and high uplands on either side, haunted by cotton factories, poisoning air and water; but it has been a formidable district for the engineers to get through, and the line abounds in those triumphs of engineering which are generally the ruin of shareholders.

All these lines are now in the hands of the military. At the Washington terminus there is a guard placed to see that no unauthorised person or unwilling volunteer is going north; the line is watched by patrols and sentries; troops are encamped along its course. The factory chimneys are smokeless; half the pleasant villas which cover the hills or dot the openings in the forest have a deserted look and closed windows. And so these great works, the Carrollton Viaduct, the Thomas Viaduct, and the high embankments and great cuttings in the ravine by the river side, over which the line passes, have almost a depressing effect, as if the people for whose use they were intended had all become extinct. At Ellicott's Mills, which is a considerable manufacturing town, more soldiers and Union flags. The people are Unionists, but the neighbouring gentry and country people are Seceshers.

This is the case wherever there is a manufacturing population in Maryland, because the workmen are generally foreigners, or have come from the Northern States, and feel little sympathy with States Rights' doctrines, and the tendencies of the landed gentry to a conservative action on the slave question. There was no good will in the eyes of the mechanicals as they stared at our vehicles; for the political bias of Colonel Carroll was well known, as well as the general sentiments of his family. It was dark when we reached the manor, which is approached by an avenue of fine trees. The house is old-fashioned, and has received additions from time to time. But for the black faces of the domestics, one might easily fancy he was in some old country house in Ireland. The family have adhered to their ancient faith. The founder of the Carrolls in Maryland came over with the Catholic colonists led by Lord Baltimore, or by his brother, Leonard Calvert, and the colonel possesses some interesting deeds of grant and conveyance of the vast estates, which have been diminshed by large sales year

[244]

after year, but still spread over a considerable part of several counties in the State.

Colonel Carroll is an immediate descendant of one of the leaders in the revolution of 1776, and he pointed out to me the room in which Carroll, of Carrollton, and George Washington, were wont to meet when they were concocting their splendid treason.

August 21st. The echoes of Bull Run are coming back with a vengeance. This day month the miserable fragments of a beaten, washed out, demoralised army were flooding in disorder and dismay the streets of the capital from which they had issued forth to repel the tide of invasion. This day month, and all the editors and journalists in the States, weeping, wailing, and gnashing their teeth, infused extra gall into their ink, and poured out invective, abuse, and obloquy on their defeated general and their broken hosts. The President and his ministers, stunned by the tremendous calamity, sat listening in fear and trembling for the sound of the enemy's cannon. The veteran soldier, on whom the boasted hopes of the nation rested, heartsick and beaten down, had neither counsel to give nor action to offer. At any moment the Confederate columns might be expected in Pennsylvania Avenue to receive the welcome of their friends and the submission of their helpless and disheartened enemies.

August 22nd. A general officer said to me, "Of course you will never remain when once all the press are down upon you. I would not take a million dollars and be in your place." "But is what I've written untrue?" "God bless you! Do you know, in this country, if you can get enough of people to start a lie about any man, he would be ruined, if the Evangelists came forward to swear the story was false. There are thousands of people who this moment believe that McDowell, who never tasted anything stronger than a watermelon in all his life, was helplessly drunk at Bull's Run. Mind what I say; they'll run you into a mudhole as sure as you live." I was not much impressed with the danger of my position further than that I knew there would be a certain amount of risk from the rowdyism and vanity of what even the Americans admit to be the lower orders, for which I had been prepared from the moment I had despatched my letter; but I confess I was not by any means disposed to think that the leaders of public opinion would seek the small gratification of revenge, and the petty popularity of pandering to the passions of the mob, by creating a popular cry against me. I am not aware that any foreigner ever visited the United States who was injudicious enough to write one single word derogatory to their claims to be the first of created beings, who was not assailed with the most viperous malignity and rancour.

August 24th. Before dinner I walked down to the Washington Navy Yard. Captain Dahlgren was sorely perplexed with an intoxicated Senator, whose name it is not necessary to mention, and who seemed to think he paid me a great compliment by expressing his repeated desire "to have a good look at" me. "I guess you're quite notorious now. You'll excuse me because I've dined, now—and so you are the Mr. &c., &c., &c." The Senator informed me that he was "none of your d——d blackfaced Republicans. He didn't care a d—— about niggers—his business was to do good to his fellow white men, to hold our glorious Union together, and let the niggers take care of themselves."

I was glad when a diversion was effected by the arrival of Mr. Fox, Assistant-Secretary of the Navy, and Mr. Blair, Postmaster-General, to consult with the Captain, who is greatly looked up to by all the members of the Cabinet—in fact he is rather inconvenienced by the perpetual visits of the President, who is animated by a most extraordinary curiosity about naval matters and machinery, and is attracted by the novelty of the whole department, so that he is continually running down "to have a talk with Dahlgren" when he is not engaged in "a chat with George."

Chapter LIV

━━━━━◦◦◦━━━━━

August 26th. General Van Vliet called from General McClellan to say that the Commander-in-Chief would be happy to go round the camps with me when he next made an inspection, and would send round an orderly and charger in time to get ready before he started. These little excursions are not the most agreeable affairs in the world; for McClellan delights in working down staff and escort, dashing from the Chain Bridge to Alexandria, and visiting all the posts, riding as hard as he can, and not returning till past midnight, so that if one has a regard for his cuticle, or his mail-days, he will not rashly venture on such excursions. Today he is to inspect McDowell's division.

General McDowell seems on most excellent terms with the present Commander-in-Chief, as he is with the President. Immediately after Bull's Run, when the President first saw McDowell, he said to him, "I have not lost a particle of confidence in you," to which the General replied, "I don't see why you should, Mr. President." But there was a curious commentary, either on the sincerity of Mr. Lincoln, or in his utter subserviency to mob opinion, in the fact that he who can overrule Congress and act pretty much as he pleases in time of war had, without opportunity for explanation or demand for it, at once displaced the man in whom he still retained the fullest confidence, degraded him to command of a division of the army of which he had been General-in-Chief, and placed a junior officer over his head.

After some ordinary movements, the march past took place,

which satisfied me that the new levies were very superior to the three months' men, though far, indeed, from being soldiers. Finer material could not be found in physique. With the exception of an assemblage of miserable scarecrows in rags and tatters, swept up in New York and commanded by a Mr. Kerrigan, no division of the ordinary line, in any army, could show a greater number of tall, robust men in the prime of life.

General Sherman, whom I met for the first time, said, "Mr. Russell, I can endorse every word that you wrote; your statements about the battle, which you say you did not witness, are equally correct. All the stories about charging batteries and attacks with the bayonet are simply falsehoods, so far as my command is concerned, though some of the troops did fight well. As to cavalry charges, I wish we had had a few cavalry to have tried one; those Black Horse fellows seemed as if their horses ran away with them."

August 29th. In the afternoon I drove to the waste grounds beyond the Capitol, in company with Mr. Olmsted and Captain Haworth, to see the 18th Massachusetts Regiment, who had just marched in, and were pitching their tents very probably for the first time. They arrived from their state with camp equipments, wagons, horses, harness, commissariat stores complete, and were clad in the blue uniform of the United States; for the volunteer fancies in greys and greens are dying out. The men were uncommonly stout young fellows, with an odd, slouching, lounging air about some of them, however, which I could not quite understand till I heard one sing out, "Hallo, sergeant, where am I to sling my hammock in this tent?" Many of them, in fact, are fishermen and sailors from Cape Cod, New Haven, and similar maritime places.

Chapter LV

———❯◆❮———

August 31st. I dined with Lieutenant Wise, and met Captain Dahlgren, Captain Davis, U.S.N., Captain Foote, U.S.N., and Colonel Fletcher Webster,* son of the great American statesman, now commanding a regiment of volunteers. Foote, who is designated to the command of the flotilla which is to clear the Mississippi downwards, will, I am certain, do good service—a calm, energetic, skillful officer. Dahlgren, who, like all men with a system, very properly watches everything which bears upon it, took occasion to call for Captain Foote's testimony to the fact that he battered down a six-foot granite wall in China with Dahlgren shells. It will run hard against the Confederates when they get such men at work on the rivers and coasts, for they seem to understand their business thoroughly, and all they are not quite sure of is the readiness of the land forces to cooperate with their expeditionary movements.

September 1st. Took a ride early this morning over the Long Bridge. As I was passing out of the earthwork called a fort on the hill, a dirty German soldier called out from the parapet, "Pull-Run Russell! you shall never write Pull's Runs again," and at the same time cocked his piece, and levelled it at me. I immediately rode round into the fort, the fellow still presenting his firelock, and asked him what he meant, at the same time calling for the sergeant of the guard, who came at once, and, at my request, arrested the man, who recovered arms, and said, "It was a

* Since killed in action.

[249]

choake—I vant to freeken Pull-Run Russell." However, as his rifle was capped and loaded, and on full cock, with his finger on the trigger, I did not quite see the fun of it, and I accordingly had the man marched to the tent of the officer, who promised to investigate the case and make a formal report of it to the brigadier, on my return to lay the circumstances before him. On reflection I resolved that it was best to let the matter drop; the joke might spread, and it was quite unpleasant enough as it was to bear the insolent looks and scowling faces of the guards at the posts, to whom I was obliged to exhibit my pass whenever I went out to ride.

On my return I heard of the complete success of the Hatteras expedition, which shelled out and destroyed some sand batteries guarding the entrance to the great inland sea and navigation called Pamlico Sound, in North Carolina, furnishing access to coasters for many miles into the Confederate States, and most useful to them in forwarding supplies and keeping up communications throughout. The force was commanded by General Butler, who has come to Washington with the news, and has already made his speech to the mob outside Willard's. I called down to see him, but he had gone over to call on the President.

September 2nd. Going out for my usual ride today, I saw General Scott, between two aides-de-camp, slowing pacing homewards from the War Office. He is still Commander-in-Chief of the Army, and affects to direct movements and to control the disposition of the troops, but a power greater than his increases steadily at General McClellan's headquarters. For my own part, I confess that General McClellan does not appear to me a man of action, or, at least, a man who intends to act as speedily as the crisis demands. He should be out with his army across the Potomac, living among his generals, studying the composition of his army, investigating its defects, and, above all, showing himself to the men as soon afterwards as possible, if he cannot be with them at the time, in the small affairs which constantly occur

[250]

along the front, and never permitting them to receive a blow without taking care that they give at least two in return. General Scott, *jam fracta membra labore,* would do all the work of departments and superintendence admirably well; but, as Montesquieu taught long ago, faction and intrigue are the cancers which peculiarly eat into the body politic of republics, and McClellan fears, no doubt, that his absence from the capital, even though he went but across the river, would animate his enemies to undermine and supplant him.

Sept. 6th. A new Major-General—Halleck—has been picked up in California, and is highly praised by General Scott and by Colonel Cullum, with whom I had a long talk about the officers on both sides. Halleck is a West Point officer, and has published some works on military science which are highly esteemed in the States. Before California became a State, he was secretary to the governor or officer commanding the territory, and eventually left the service and became a lawyer in the district, where he has amassed a large fortune. He is a man of great ability, very calm, practical, earnest, and cold, devoted to the Union—a soldier, and something more. Lee is considered the ablest man on the Federal * side, but he is slow and timid. "Joe" Johnson is their best strategist. Beauregard is nobody and nothing—so think they at headquarters. All of them together are not equal to Halleck, who is to be employed in the West.

I dined at the Legation, where were the Russian Minister, the Secretary of the French Legation, the representative of New Granada, and others. As I was anxious to explain to General McClellan the reason of my inability to go out with him, I called at his quarters about eleven o'clock, and found he had just returned from his ride. He received me in his shirt, in his bedroom at the top of the house; introduced me to General Burnside—a soldierly, intelligent-looking man, with a very lofty forehead, and uncommonly bright dark eyes; and we had some conversation

* Clearly a typographical error for "Confederate."

about matters of ordinary interest for some time, till General Mc-
Clellan called me into an antechamber, where an officer was
writing a dispatch, which he handed to the General.

Sept. 8th. Going home, I met Mr. and Mrs. Lincoln in their
new open carriage. The President was not so good-humoured,
nor Mrs. Lincoln so affable, in their return to my salutation as
usual. My unpopularity is certainly spreading upwards and
downwards at the same time, and all because I could not turn
the battle of Bull's Run into a Federal victory, because I would
not pander to the vanity of the people, and, least of all, because
I will not bow my knee to the degraded creatures who have made
the very name of a free press odious to honourable men.

Chapter LVI

September 11th. It is now quite plain McClellan has no intention of making a general offensive movement against Richmond.
He is aware his army is not equal to the task—commissariat deficient, artillery wanting, no cavalry; above all, ill-officered, in-
coherent battalions. He hopes, no doubt, by constant reviewing
and inspection, and by weeding out the preposterous fellows who
render epaulettes ridiculous, to create an infantry which shall be
able for a short campaign in the fine autumn weather; but I am
quite satisfied he does not intend to move now, and possibly will
not do so until next year. I have arranged therefore to pay a short
visit to the West, penetrating as far as I can, without leaving telegraphs and railways behind, so that if an advance takes place I
shall be back in time at Washington to assist at the earliest battle.

These Federal armies do not move like the corps of the French republic, or Crawford's Light Division.

In truth, Washington life is becoming exceedingly monotonous and uninteresting. The pleasant little evening parties or tertulias which once relieved the dulness of this dullest of capitals, take place no longer.

September 16th. On the 18th of September, I left Baltimore in company with Major-General Bell, C. B., and Mr. Lamy, who was well acquainted with the Western States: stopping one night at Altoona, in order that we might cross by daylight the fine passes of the Alleghenies, which are traversed by bold gradients, and remarkable cuttings, second only in difficulty and extent to those of the railroad across the Sommering.

So far as my observation extends, no route in the United States can give a stranger a better notion of the variety of scenery and resources, the vast extent of territory, the difference in races, the prosperity of the present, and the probable greatness of the future, than the line from Baltimore by Harrisburg and Pittsburgh to Chicago, traversing the great States of Pennsylvania, Ohio, and Indiana.

Pittsburgh, where we halted next night, on the Ohio, is certainly, with the exception of Birmingham, the most intensely sooty, busy, squalid, foul-housed, and vile-suburbed city I have ever seen. Under its perpetual canopy of smoke, pierced by a forest of blackened chimneys, the ill-paved streets, swarm with a streaky population whose white faces are smudged with soot-streaks—the noise of vans and drays which shake the houses as they pass, the turbulent life in the thoroughfares, the wretched brick tenements—built in waste places on squalid mounds, surrounded by heaps of slag and broken brick—all these give the stranger the idea of some vast manufacturing city of the Inferno; and yet a few miles beyond, the country is studded with beautiful villas, and the great river, bearing innumerable barges and

[253]

steamers on its broad bosom, rolls its turbid waters beween banks rich with cultivated crops.

From Chicago, where we descended at a hotel which fairly deserves to be styled magnificent, for comfort and completeness, Mr. Lamy and myself proceeded to Racine, on the shores of Lake Michigan, and thence took the rail for Freeport, where I remained for some days, going out in the surrounding prairie to shoot in the morning, and returning at nightfall. The prairie chickens were rather wild. The delight of these days, notwithstanding bad sport, cannot be described, nor was it the least ingredient in it to mix with the fresh and vigorous race who are raising up cities on these fertile wastes. Fortunately for the patience of my readers, perhaps, I did not fill my diary with the records of each day's events, or of the contents of our bags; and the notebook in which I jotted down some little matters which struck me to be of interest has been mislaid; but in my letters to England I gave a description of the general aspect of the country, and of the feelings of the people, and arrived at the conclusion that the tax-gatherer will have little chance of returning with full notebooks from his tour in these districts. The dogs which were lent to us were generally abominable; but every evening we returned in company with great leather-greaved and jerkined men, hung round with belts and hooks, from which were suspended strings of defunct prairie chickens. The farmers were hospitable, but were suffering from a morbid longing for a failure of crops in Europe, in order to give some value to their corn and wheat, which literally cumbered the earth.

October 3rd. In Washington once more—all the world laughing at the pump and the wooden guns at Munson's Hill, but angry withal because McClellan should be so befooled as they considered it, by the Confederates. The fact is, McClellan was not prepared to move, and therefore not disposed to hazard a general engagement, which he might have brought on had the enemy been in force; perhaps he knew they were not, but found it convenient nevertheless to act as though he believed they had established themselves strongly in his front, as half the world will give him credit for knowing more than the civilian strategists who have already got into disgrace for urging McDowell on to Richmond. The Federal armies are not handled easily. They are luxurious in the matter of baggage, and canteens, and private stores; and this is just the sort of war in which the general who moves lightly and rapidly, striking blows unexpectedly and deranging communications, will obtain great results.

October 4th. The new expedition, of which I have been hearing for some time past, is about to sail to Port Royal, under the command of General Burnside, in order to reduce the works erected at the entrance of the South, to secure a base of operations against Charleston, and to cut in upon the communication between that place and Savannah. Alas, for poor Trescot! His plantations, his secluded home! What will the good lady think of the Yankee invasion, which surely must succeed, as the naval force will be overwhelming?

Chapter LVII

October 8th. A review of the artillery at this side of the river took place today, which has been described in very inflated language by the American papers, the writers on which pronounce the sight to have been of unequalled splendour; whereas the appearance of horses and men was very far from respectable in all matters relating to grooming, cleanliness and neatness. General Barry has done wonders in simplifying the force and reducing the number of calibres, which varied according to the fancy of each State, or men of each officer who raised a battery; but there are still field-guns of three inches and of three inches and a half, Napoleon guns, rifled ten pound Parrots, ordinary nine-pounders, a variety of howitzers, twenty pound Parrot rifled guns, and a variety of different projectiles in the caissons. As the men rode past, the eye was distressed by discrepancies in dress. Many wore red or white worsted comforters round their necks, few had straps to their trousers; some had new coats, others old; some wore boots, others shoes; not one had clean spurs, bits, curb-chains, or buttons. The officers cannot get the men to do what the latter regard as works of supererogation.

There were seventy-two guns in all; and if the horses were not so light, there would be quite enough to do for the Confederates to reduce their fire, as the pieces are easily handled, and the men like artillery and take to it naturally.

Calling on the General the other night at his usual time of return, I was told by the orderly, who was closing the door, "The General's gone to bed tired, and can see no one. He sent the same message to the President, who came inquiring after him ten minutes ago."

This poor President! He is to be pitied; surrounded by such scenes, and trying with all his might to understand strategy, naval warfare, big guns, the movements of troops, military maps, reconnaissances, occupations, interior and exterior lines, and all the technical details of the art of slaying. He runs from one house to another, armed with plans, papers, reports, recommendations, sometimes good-humoured, never angry, occasionally dejected, and always a little fussy. The other night, as I was sitting in the parlour at headquarters, with an English friend who had come to see his acquaintance, the General, walked in a tall man with a navvy's cap, and an ill-made shooting suit, from the pockets of which protruded paper and bundles. "Well," said he to Brigadier Van Vliet, who rose to receive him, "is George in?"

"Yes, sir. He's come back, but is lying down, very much fatigued. I'll send up, sir, and inform him you wish to see him."

"Oh, no; I can wait. I think I'll take supper with him. Well, and what are you now—I forget your name—are you a major, or a colonel, or a general?"

"Whatever you like to make me, sir."

Seeing that General McClellan would be occupied, I walked out with my friend, who asked me when I got into the street why I stood up when that tall fellow came into the room. "Because it was the President." "The President of what?" "Of the United States." "Oh! come, now you're humbugging me. Let me have another look at him." He came back more incredulous than ever, but when I assured him I was quite serious, he exclaimed, "I give up the United States after this."

But for all that, there have been many more courtly Presidents who, in a similar crisis, would have displayed less capacity, honesty, and plain dealing than Abraham Lincoln.

October 16th. Day follows day and resembles its predecessor. McClellan is still reviewing, and the North are still waiting for victories and paying money, and the orators are still wrangling over the best way of cooking the hares which they have not yet caught. I visited General McDowell today in his tent at Arlington, and found him in a state of divine calm with his wife and *parvus Iulus*. A public man in the United States is very much like a great firework—he commences with some small scintillations which attract the eye of the public, and then he blazes up and flares out in blue, purple, and orange fires, to the intense admiration of the multitude, and dying out suddenly is thought of no more, his place being taken by a fresh Roman candle or catherine wheel which is thought to be far finer than those which have just dazzled the eyes of the fickle spectators.

October 22nd. Rain falling in torrents. As I write, in come reports of a battle last night, some forty miles up the river, which by signs and tokens I am led to believe was unfavourable to the

[257]

Federals. They crossed the river intending to move upon Leesburg—were attacked by overwhelming forces and repulsed, but maintained themselves on the right bank till General Banks reinforced them and enabled them to hold their own. McClellan has gone or is going at once to the scene of action. Late at night the White House was placed in deep grief by the intelligence that in addition to other losses, Brigadier and Senator Baker of California was killed. The President was inconsolable, and walked up and down his room for hours lamenting the loss of his friend. Mrs. Lincoln's grief was equally poignant.

Chapter LVIII

November 1st. Again stagnation; not the smallest intention of moving; General Scott's resignation, of which I was aware long ago, is publicly known, and he is about to go to Europe, and end his days probably in France. McClellan takes his place, minus the large salary.

November 11th. The United States have now, according to the returns, 600,000 infantry, 600 pieces of artillery, 61,000 cavalry in the field, and yet they are not only unable to crush the Confederates, but they cannot conquer the Secession ladies in their capital. The Southern people here trust in a break-down in the North before the screw can be turned to the utmost; and assert that the South does not want corn, wheat, leather, or food. Georgia makes cloth enough for all—the only deficiency will be in metal and *materiel* of war. When the North comes to discuss the question whether the war is to be against slavery or for the

Union, leaving slavery to take care of itself, they think a split will be inevitable. Then the pressure of taxes will force on a solution, for the State taxes already amount to two to three per cent, and the people will not bear the addition. The North has set out with the principle of paying for everything, the South with the principle of paying for nothing; but this will be reversed in time. All the diplomatists, with one exception, are of opinion the Union is broken for ever, and the independence of the South virtually established.

November 12th. An eruption of dirty little boys in the streets shouting out, "Glorious Union victory! Charleston taken!" The story is that Burnside has landed and reduced the forts defending Port Royal. I met Mr. Fox, Assistant-Secretary to the Navy, and Mr. Hay, Secretary to Mr. Lincoln, in the Avenue. The former showed me Burnside's dispatches from Beaufort, announcing reduction of the Confederate batteries by the ships and the establishment of the Federals on the skirts of Port Royal. I had a long conversation with Mr. Chase, who is still sanguine that the war must speedily terminate. The success at Beaufort has made him radiant, and he told me that the Federal General Nelson—who is no other than the enormous blustering, boasting lieutenant in the Navy whom I met at Washington on my first arrival—has gained an immense victory in Kentucky, killing and capturing a whole army and its generals.

November 14th. I dined with Mr. Seward—Mr. Raymond, of New York, and two or three gentlemen, being the only guests. Mr. Lincoln came in whilst we were playing a rubber, and told some excellent West-country stories. "Here, Mr. President, we have got the two *Times*—of New York and of London—if they would only do what is right and what we want, all will go well." "Yes," said Mr. Lincoln, "if the bad Times would go where we want them, good Times would be sure to follow." Talking over Bull's Run, Mr. Seward remarked "that civilians sometimes displayed more courage than soldiers, but perhaps the courage was

[259]

unprofessional. When we were cut off from Baltimore, and the United States troops at Annapolis were separated by a country swarming with malcontents, not a soldier could be found to undertake the journey and communicate with them. At last a civilian"—(I think he mentioned the name of Mr. Cassius Clay) —"volunteered, and executed the business. So, after Bull's Run, there was only one officer, General Sherman, who was doing anything to get the troops into order when the President and myself drove over to see what we could do on that terrible Tuesday evening."

November 16th. A cold, raw day. As I was writing, a small friend of mine, who appears like a stormy petrel in moments of great storm, fluttered into my room, and having chirped out something about a "Jolly row"—"Seizure of Mason and Slidell" —"British flag insulted," and the like, vanished. Somewhat later, going down 17th Street, I met the French Minister, M. Mercier, wrapped in his cloak, coming from the British Legation. "Vous avez entendu quelqu' chose de nouveau?" "Maise non, excellence." And then, indeed, I learned there was no doubt about the fact that Captain Wilkes, of the U.S. steamer *San Jacinto,* had forcibly boarded the *Trent,* British mail steamer, off the Bahamas, and had taken Messrs. Mason, Slidell, Eustis, and McClernand from on board by armed force, in defiance of the protests of the captain and naval officer in charge of the mails. This was indeed grave intelligence, and the French Minister considered the act a flagrant outrage, which could not for a moment be justified.

I went to the Legation, and found the young diplomatists in the "Chancellerie" as demure and innocent as if nothing had happened, though perhaps they were a trifle more lively than usual. An hour later, and the whole affair was published in full in the evening papers. Extraordinary exultation prevailed in the hotels and bar-rooms. The State Department has made of course no communication respecting the matter. All the English are

satisfied that Mason and his friends must be put on board an
English mail packet from the *San Jacinto* under a salute.

November 18th. There is a storm of exultation sweeping over
the land. Wilkes is the hero of the hour. I saw Mr. F. Seward at
the State Department at ten o'clock; but as at the British Legation the orders are not to speak of the transaction, so at the State
Department a judicious reticence is equally observed.

Chapter LIX

December 3rd. I dined with Mr. Cameron, Secretary-of-War,
where I met Mr. Forney, Secretary of the Senate; Mr. House,
Mr. Wilkeson, and others, and was exceedingly interested by the
shrewd conversation and candid manner of our host. He told me
he once worked as a printer in the city of Washington, at ten
dollars a week, and twenty cents an hour for extra work at the
case on Sundays. Since that time he has worked onwards and
upwards, and amassed a large fortune by contracts for railways
and similar great undertakings. He says the press rules America,
and that no one can face it and live; which is about the worst
account of the chances of an honest longevity I can well con-
ceive. His memory is exact, and his anecdotes, albeit he has
never seen any but Americans, or stirred out of the States, very
agreeable. Once there lived at Washington a publican's daughter,
named Mary O'Neil, beautiful, bold, and witty. She captivated a
Member of Congress, who failed to make her less than his wife;
and by degrees Mrs. Eaton—who may now be seen in the streets
of Washington, an old woman, still bright-eyed and alas! bright

cheeked, retaining traces of her great beauty—became a leading personage in the State, and ruled the imperious, rugged, old Andrew Jackson so completely that he broke up his Cabinet and dismissed his ministers on her account. In the days of her power she had done some trifling service to Mr. Cameron, and he has just repaid it by conferring some military appointment on her grandchild.

December 16th. I met Mr. Seward at the ball and cotillion party, given by M. de Lisboa; and as he was in very good humour, and was inclined to talk, he pointed out to the Prince de Joinville, and all who were inclined to listen, and myself, how terrible the effects of a war would be if Great Britain forced it on the United States. "We will wrap the whole world in flames!" he exclaimed. "No power so remote that she will not feel the fire of our battle and be burned by our conflagration." It is inferred that Mr. Seward means to show fight. One of the guests, however, said to me, "That's all bugaboo talk. When Seward talks that way, he means to break down. He is most dangerous and obstinate when he pretends to agree a good deal with you."

December 20th. Mr. Seward will, however, control the situation, as the Cabinet will very probably support his views; and Americans will comfort themselves, in case the captives are surrendered, with a promise of future revenge, and with the reflection that they have avoided a very disagreeable intervention between their march of conquest and the Southern Confederacy. The general belief of the diplomatists is, that the prisoners will not be given up, and in that case Lord Lyons and the Legation will retire from Washington for the time, probably to Halifax, leaving Mr. Monson to wind up affairs and clear out the archives. But it is understood that there is no ultimatum, and that Lord Lyons is not to indicate any course of action, should Mr. Seward inform him the United States Government refuses to comply with the demands of Great Britain.

Chapter LX

———✦———

December 27th. This morning Mr. Seward sent in his reply to Lord Russell's dispatch—*"grandis et verbosa epistola."* The result destroys my prophecies, for, after all, the Southern Commissioners or Ambassadors are to be given up. Yesterday, indeed, in an under-current of whispers among the desponding friends of the South, there went a rumour that the Government had resolved to yield.

December 28th. The rage of the friends of compromise, and of the South, who saw in a war with Great Britain the complete success of the Confederacy, is deep and burning, if not loud; but they all say they never expected anything better from the cowardly and braggart statesmen who now rule in Washington.

The illness which had prostrated some of the strongest men in Washington, including General McClellan himself, developed itself as soon as I ceased to be sustained by the excitement, such as it was, of daily events at the capital, and by expectations of a move; and for some time an attack of typhoid fever confined me to my room, and left me so weak that I was advised not to return to Washington till I had tried change of air. I remained in New York till the end of January, when I proceeded to make a tour in Canada, as it was quite impossible for any operation to take place on the Potomac, where deep mud, alternating with snow and frost, bound the contending armies in winter quarters.

On my return to New York, at the end of February, the North was cheered by some signal successes achieved in the West, principally by gun-boats, operating on the lines of the great rivers. The greatest results have been obtained in the capture of Fort Donaldson and Fort Henry, by Commodore Foote's flotilla co-operating with the land forces. The possession of an absolute naval supremacy, of course, gives the North United States powerful means of annoyance and inflicting injury and destruction on the enemy; it also secures for them the means of seizing upon bases of operations wherever they please, of breaking up the enemy's lines, and maintaining communications; but the example of Great Britain in the Revolutionary War should prove to the United States that such advantages do not, by any means, enable a belligerent to subjugate a determined people resolved on resistance to the last.

On the 1st March, I arrived in Washington once more, and found things very much as I had left them: the army recovering the effect of the winter's sickness and losses, animated by the victories of their comrades in Western fields, and by the hope that the ever-coming tomorrow would see them in the field at last. In place of Mr. Cameron, an Ohio lawyer named Stanton has been appointed Secretary of War. He came to Washington, a few years ago, to conduct some legal proceedings for Mr. Daniel Sickles, and by his energy, activitiy, and a rapid conversion from Democratic to Republican principles, as well as by his Union sentiments, recommended himself to the President and his Cabinet.

The month of March passed over without any remarkable event in the field. When the army started at last to attack the enemy—a movement which was precipitated by hearing that they were moving away—they went out only to find the Confederates had fallen back by interior lines towards Richmond, and General McClellan was obliged to transport his army from Alexandria to the peninsula of York Town, where his reverses, his sufferings, and his disastrous retreat are so well known and so recent, that I need only mention them as among the most remarkable events which have yet occurred in this war.

I had looked forward for many weary months to participating in the movement and describing its results. Immediately on my arrival in Washington, I was introduced to Mr. Stanton by Mr. Ashman, formerly member of Congress and Secretary to Mr. Daniel Webster, and the Secretary, without making any positive pledge, used words, in Mr. Ashman's presence, which led me to believe he would give me permission to draw rations, and undoubtedly promised to afford me every facility in his power. Subsequently he sent me a private pass to the War Department to enable me to get through the crowd of contractors and jobbers; but on going there to keep my appointment, the Assistant-Secretary of War told me Mr. Stanton had been summoned to a Cabinet Council by the President.

We had some conversation respecting the subject matter of my application, which the Assistant-Secretary seemed to think would be attended with many difficulties, in consequence of the number of correspondents to the American papers who might demand the same privileges, and he intimated to me that Mr. Stanton was little disposed to encourage them in any way whatever. Now this is undoubtedly honest on Mr. Stanton's part, for he knows he might render himself popular by granting what they ask; but he is excessively vain, and aspires to be considered a rude, rough, vigorous Oliver Cromwell sort of man, mistaking some of the disagreeable attributes and the accidents of the external husk of the Great Protector for the brain and head of a statesman and a soldier.

On the evening of the private theatricals by which Lord Lyons enlivened the ineffable dulness of Washington, I saw Mr. Stanton at the Legation, and he conversed with me for some time. I mentioned the difficulty connected with passes. He asked me what I wanted. I said, "An order to go with the army to Manassas." At his request I procured a sheet of paper, and he

[265]

wrote me a pass, took a copy of it, which he put in his pocket, and then handed the other to me. On looking at it, I perceived that it was a permission for me to go to Manassas and back, and that all officers, soldiers, and others, in the United States service, were to give me every assistance and show me every courtesy; but the hasty return of the army to Alexandria rendered it useless.

The *Merrimac* and *Monitor* encounter produced the profoundest impression in Washington, and unusual strictness was observed respecting passes to Fortress Monroe.

March 19th. All my arrangements were made that day with General Van Vliet, the Quartermaster-General of headquarters. I was quite satisfied, from Mr. Stanton's promise and General Marcy's conversation, that I should have no further difficulty. Our party was made up, consisting of Colonel Neville; Lieutenant-Colonel Fletcher, Scotch Fusilier Guards; Mr. Lamy, and myself; and our passage was to be provided in the Quartermaster-General's boat. On the 26th of March, I went to Baltimore in company with Colonel Rowan, of the Royal Artillery, who had come down for a few days to visit Washington, intending to go on by the steamer to Fortress Monroe, as he was desirous of seeing his friends on board the *Rinaldo,* and I wished to describe the great flotilla assembled there and to see Captain Hewett once more.

On arriving at Baltimore, we learned it would be necessary to get a special pass from General Dix, and on going to the General's headquarters his aide-de-camp informed us that he had received special instructions recently from the War Department to grant no passes to Fortress Monroe, unless to officers and soldiers going on duty, or to persons in the service of the United States. The aide-de-camp advised me to telegraph to Mr. Stanton for permission, which I did, but no answer was received, and Colonel Rowan and I returned to Washington, thinking there would be a better chance of securing the necessary order there.

Next day we went to the Department of War, and were shown into Mr. Stanton's room—his secretary informing us that he was engaged in the next room with the President and other Ministers in a council of war, but that he would no doubt receive a letter from me and send me out a reply. I accordingly addresesd a note to Mr. Stanton, requesting he would be good enough to give an order to Colonel Rowan, of the British army, and myself, to go by the mail boat from Baltimore to Monroe. In a short time Mr. Stanton sent out a note in the following words:—"Mr. Stanton informs Mr. Russell no passes to Fortress Monroe can be given at present, unless to officers in the United States service." We tried the Navy Department, but no vessels were going down, they said; and one of the officers suggested that we should ask for passes and go down and visit H.M.S. *Rinaldo* exclusively, which could not well be refused, he thought, to British subjects, and promised to take charge of the letter for Mr. Stanton and to telegraph the permission down to Baltimore. Then we returned by the afternoon train and waited, but neither reply nor pass came for us.

Next day we were disappointed also, and an officer of the *Rinaldo,* who had come up on duty from the ship, was refused permission to take us down on his return.

So far as I know, Mr. Stanton sent no reply to my last letter, and calling with General Van Vliet at his house on his reception night, the door was opened by his brother-in-law, who said, "The Secretary was attending a sick child and could not see any person that evening," so I never met Mr. Stanton again.

The rest of the story may be told in a few words. It was perfectly well known in Washington that I was going with the army, and I presume Mr. Stanton, if he had any curiosity about such a trifling matter, must have heard it also. I am told he was informed of it at the last moment, and then flew out into a coarse passion against General McClellan because he had dared to invite or to take anyone without his permission.

It was plain I had now but one course left. My mission in the United States was to describe military events and operations, or, in defect of them, to deal with such subjects as might be interesting to people at home. In the discharge of my duty, I had visited the South, remaining there until the approach of the actual operations and the establishment of the blockade, which cut off all communication from the Southern States except by routes which would deprive my correspondence of any value, compelled me to return to the North, where I could keep up regular communication with Europe. Soon after my return, as unfortunately for myself as for the United States, the Federal troops were repulsed in an attempt to march upon Richmond, and terminated a disorderly retreat by a disgraceful panic.

I went to America to witness and describe the operations of the great army before Washington in the field, and when I was forbidden by the proper authorities to do so, my mission terminated at once.

On the evening of April 4th, as soon as I was in receipt of the President's last communication, I telegraphed to New York to engage a passage by the steamer which left on the following Wednesday. I arrived in New York late on Tuesday evening, and next day I saw the shores receding into a dim grey fog, and ere the night fell was tossing about once more on the stormy Atlantic, with the head of our good ship pointing, thank Heaven, towards Europe.